Hans Mol

English for
TOURISM AND HOSPITALITY

in Higher Education Studies
Teacher's Book

Series editor: Terry Phillips

English for Specific Academic Purposes

Garnet
EDUCATION

Published by
Garnet Publishing Ltd.
8 Southern Court
South Street
Reading RG1 4QS, UK

First published 2008

ISBN 978 1 85964 950 3

British Cataloguing-in-Publication Data
A catalogue record for this book is available from
the British Library.

Production
Series editor: Terry Phillips
Lead authors: Carolyn Walker, Marian Dunn
Project management: Louise Elkins, Martin Moore
Editorial team: Jane Gregory, Rebecca Snelling
Academic review: Frances Devine
Design: Henry Design Associates and Mike Hinks
Photography: Sally Henry and Trevor Cook; Alamy (Mike
Goldwater); Clipart.com; Corbis (Bobby Yip); Getty Images
(Eightfish, Yellow Dog Productions)

Audio recorded at Motivation Sound Studios produced by
EFS Television Production Ltd.

The author and publisher would like to thank the following
for permission to reproduce from copyright material:
Times online for page 31 article adapted from *Time to go
backpacking in style* by Stephen Bleach and Brian Schofield
The Guardian for page 36 article adapted from *Is it as green
as it's painted?* by Esther Addley
Google for results listings on page 66

Every effort has been made to trace copyright holders and
we apologize in advance for any unintentional omission. We
will be happy to insert the appropriate acknowledgements
in any subsequent editions.

Printed and bound in Lebanon by International Press

Contents

Book map

Vocabulary focus	Skills focus		Unit
• words from general English with a special meaning in tourism • prefixes and suffixes	**Listening**	• preparing for a lecture • predicting lecture content from the introduction • understanding lecture organization • choosing an appropriate form of notes • making lecture notes	**1**
	Speaking	• speaking from notes	
• English–English dictionaries: headwords · definitions · parts of speech · phonemes · stress markers · countable/uncountable · transitive/intransitive	**Reading**	• using research questions to focus on relevant information in a text • using topic sentences to get an overview of the text	**2**
	Writing	• writing topic sentences • summarizing a text	
• stress patterns in multi-syllable words • hospitality outlets	**Listening**	• preparing for a lecture • predicting lecture content • making lecture notes • using different information sources	**3**
	Speaking	• reporting research findings • formulating questions	
• computer jargon • abbreviations and acronyms • job titles • discourse and stance markers • verb and noun suffixes	**Reading**	• identifying topic development within a paragraph • using the Internet effectively • evaluating Internet search results	**4**
	Writing	• reporting research findings	
• word sets: synonyms, antonyms, etc. • the language of trends • common lecture language	**Listening**	• understanding 'signpost language' in lectures • using symbols and abbreviations in note-taking	**5**
	Speaking	• making effective contributions to a seminar	
• synonyms, replacement subjects, etc. for sentence-level paraphrasing	**Reading**	• locating key information in complex sentences	**6**
	Writing	• writing complex sentences • reporting findings from other sources: paraphrasing	
• compound nouns • fixed phrases from tourism • fixed phrases from academic English • common lecture language	**Listening**	• understanding speaker emphasis	**7**
	Speaking	• asking for clarification • responding to queries and requests for clarification	
• synonyms • nouns from verbs • definitions • common 'direction' verbs in essay titles (*discuss, analyse, evaluate,* etc.)	**Reading**	• understanding dependent clauses with passives	**8**
	Writing	• paraphrasing • expanding notes into complex sentences • recognizing different essay types/structures: descriptive · analytical · comparison/evaluation · argument • writing essay plans • writing essays	
• fixed phrases from tourism • fixed phrases from academic English	**Listening**	• using the Cornell note-taking system • recognizing digressions in lectures	**9**
	Speaking	• making effective contributions to a seminar • referring to other people's ideas in a seminar	
• 'neutral' and 'marked' words • job titles (management/supervisory) • fixed phrases from management • fixed phrases from academic English	**Reading**	• recognizing the writer's stance and level of confidence or tentativeness • inferring implicit ideas	**10**
	Writing	• writing situation–problem–solution–evaluation essays • using direct quotations • compiling a bibliography/reference list	
• words/phrases used to link ideas (*moreover, as a result,* etc.) • stress patterns in noun phrases and compounds • fixed phrases from academic English • words/phrases related to environmental issues	**Listening**	• recognizing the speaker's stance • writing up notes in full	**11**
	Speaking	• building an argument in a seminar • agreeing/disagreeing	
• verbs used to introduce ideas from other sources (*X contends/accepts/asserts that …*) • linking words/phrases conveying contrast (*whereas*), result (*consequently*), reasons (*due to*), etc. • words for quantities (*a significant minority*)	**Reading**	• understanding how ideas in a text are linked	**12**
	Writing	• deciding whether to use direct quotation or paraphrase • incorporating quotations • writing research reports • writing effective introductions/conclusions	

Introduction

The ESAP series

The aim of the titles in the ESAP series is to prepare students for academic study in a particular discipline. In this respect, the series is somewhat different from many ESP (English for Specific Purposes) series, which are aimed at people already working in the field, or about to enter the field. This focus on *study* in the discipline rather than *work* in the field has enabled the authors to focus much more specifically on the skills which a student of tourism and hospitality needs.

It is assumed that prior to using titles in this series students will already have completed a general EAP (English for Academic Purposes) course such as *Skills in English* (Garnet Publishing, up to the end of at least Level 3), and will have achieved an IELTS level of at least 5.

English for Tourism and Hospitality

English for Tourism and Hospitality is designed for students who plan to take a course in the area of tourism and/or hospitality entirely or partly in English. The principal aim of *English for Tourism and Hospitality* is to teach students to cope with input texts, i.e., listening and reading, in the discipline. However, students will also be expected to produce output texts in speech and writing throughout the course.

The syllabus concentrates on key vocabulary for the discipline and on words and phrases commonly used in academic and technical English. It covers key facts and concepts from the discipline, thereby giving students a flying start for when they meet the same points again in their faculty work. It also focuses on the skills that will enable students to get the most out of lectures and written texts. Finally, it presents the skills required to take part in seminars and tutorials and to produce essay assignments. For a summary of the course content, see the book map on pages 4–5.

Components of the course

The course comprises:
- the student Course Book
- this Teacher's Book, which provides detailed guidance on each lesson, full answer keys, audio transcripts and extra photocopiable resources
- audio CDs with lecture and seminar excerpts

Organization of the course

English for Tourism and Hospitality has 12 units, each of which is based on a different aspect of tourism or hospitality. Odd-numbered units are based on listening (lecture/seminar extracts). Even-numbered units are based on reading.

Each unit is divided into four lessons:

Lesson 1: vocabulary for the discipline; vocabulary skills such as word-building, use of affixes, use of synonyms for paraphrasing

Lesson 2: reading or listening text and skills development

Lesson 3: reading or listening skills extension. In addition, in later reading units, students are introduced to a writing assignment which is further developed in Lesson 4; in later listening units, students are introduced to a spoken language point (e.g., making an oral presentation at a seminar) which is further developed in Lesson 4

Lesson 4: a parallel listening or reading text to that presented in Lesson 2, which students have to use their new skills (Lesson 3) to decode; in addition, written or spoken work is further practised

The last two pages of each unit, *Vocabulary bank* and *Skills bank*, are a useful summary of the unit content.

Each unit provides between four and six hours of classroom activity with the possibility of a further two to four hours on the suggested extra activities. The course will be suitable, therefore, as the core component of a faculty-specific pre-sessional or foundation course of between 50 and 80 hours.

Vocabulary development

English for Tourism and Hospitality attaches great importance to vocabulary. This is why one lesson out of four is devoted to vocabulary and why, in addition, the first exercise at least in many of the other three lessons is a vocabulary exercise. The vocabulary presented can be grouped into two main areas:
- key vocabulary for tourism and hospitality studies
- key vocabulary for academic English

In addition to presenting specific items of vocabulary, the course concentrates on the vocabulary skills and strategies that will help students to make sense of lectures and texts. Examples include:
- understanding prefixes and suffixes and how these affect the meaning of the base word
- guessing words in context
- using an English–English dictionary effectively
- understanding how certain words/phrases link ideas
- understanding how certain words/phrases show the writer/speaker's point of view

Skills development

Listening and reading in the real world involve extracting communicative value in real time – i.e., as the spoken text is being produced or as you are reading written text. Good listeners and readers do not need to go back to listen or read again most of the time. Indeed, with listening to formal speech such as a lecture, there is no possibility of going back. In many ELT materials second, third, even fourth listenings are common. The approach taken in the ESAP series is very different. We set out to teach and practise 'text-attack' skills – i.e., listening and reading strategies that will enable students to extract communicative value at a single listening or reading.

Students also need to become familiar with the way academic 'outputs' such as reports, essays and oral presentations are structured in English. Conventions may be different in their own language – for example, paragraphing conventions, or introduction–main body–conclusion structure. All students, whatever their background, will benefit from an awareness of the skills and strategies that will help them produce written work of a high standard.

Examples of specific skills practised in the course include:

Listening

- predicting lecture content and organization from the introduction
- following signposts to lecture organization
- choosing an appropriate form of lecture notes
- recognizing the lecturer's stance and level of confidence/tentativeness

Reading

- using research questions to focus on relevant information
- using topic sentences to get an overview of the text
- recognizing the writer's stance and level of confidence/tentativeness
- using the Internet effectively

Speaking

- making effective contributions to a seminar
- asking for clarification – formulating questions
- speaking from notes
- summarizing

Writing

- writing notes
- paraphrasing
- reporting findings from other sources – avoiding plagiarism

- recognizing different essay types and structures
- writing essay plans and essays
- compiling a bibliography/reference list

Specific activities

Certain types of activity are repeated on several occasions throughout the course. This is because these activities are particularly valuable in language learning.

Tasks to activate schemata

It has been known for many years, since the research of Bartlett in the 1930s, that we can only understand incoming information, written or spoken, if we can fit it into a schemata. It is essential that we build these schemata in students before exposing them to new information, so all lessons with listening or reading texts begin with one or more relevant activities.

Prediction activities

Before students are allowed to listen to a section of a lecture or read a text, they are encouraged to make predictions about the contents, in general or even specific terms, based on the context, the introduction to the text or, in the case of reading, the topic sentences in the text. This is based on the theory that active listening and reading involve the receiver in being ahead of the producer.

Working with illustrations, diagrams, figures

Many tasks require students to explain or interpret visual material. This is clearly a key task in a field which makes great use of such material to support written text. Students can be taken back to these visuals later on in the course to ensure that they have not forgotten how to describe and interpret them.

Vocabulary tasks

Many tasks ask students to group key words, to categorize them in some way or to find synonyms or antonyms. These tasks help students to build relationships between words which, research has shown, is a key element in remembering words. In these exercises, the target words are separated into blue boxes so you can quickly return to one of these activities for revision work later.

Gap-fill

Filling in missing words or phrases in a sentence or a text, or labelling a diagram, indicates comprehension both of the missing items and of the context in which they correctly fit. You can vary the activity by, for example, going through the gap-fill text with the whole class first orally, pens down, then setting the same task for individual completion. Gap-fill activities can be photocopied and set as revision at the end of the unit or later, with or without the missing items.

Breaking long sentences into key components

One feature of academic English is the average length of sentences. Traditionally, EFL classes teach students to cope with the complexity of the verb phrase, equating level with more and more arcane verb structures, such as the present perfect modal passive. However, research into academic language, including the corpus research which underlies the *Longman Grammar of Spoken and Written English,* suggests that complexity in academic language does not lie with the verb phrase but rather with the noun phrase and clause joining and embedding. For this reason, students are shown in many exercises later in the course how to break down long sentences into kernel elements, and find the subject, verb and object of each element. This receptive skill is then turned into a productive skill, by encouraging students to think in terms of kernel elements first before building them into complex sentences.

Activities with stance marking

Another key element of academic text is the attitude (or stance) of the writer or speaker to the information which is being imparted. This could be dogmatic, tentative, incredulous, sceptical, and so on. Students must learn the key skill of recognizing words and phrases marked for stance.

Crosswords and other word puzzles

One of the keys to vocabulary learning is repetition. However, the repetition must be active. It is no good if students are simply going through the motions. The course uses crosswords and other kinds of puzzles to bring words back into the students' consciousness through an engaging activity. However, it is understood by the writers that such playful activities are not always seen as serious and academic. The crosswords and other activities are therefore made available as photocopiable resources at the back of the Teacher's Book and can be used at the teacher's discretion, after explaining to the students why they are valuable.

Methodology points

Setting up tasks

The teaching notes for many of the exercises begin with the word *Set …* . This single word covers a number of vital functions for the teacher, as follows:

- Refer students to the rubric (instructions).
- Check that they understand **what** to do – get one or two students to explain the task in their own words.
- Tell students **how** they are to do the task, if this is not clear in the Course Book instructions – as individual work, pairwork or in groups.
- Go through the example, if there is one. If not, make it clear what the target output is – full sentences, short answers, notes, etc.
- Go through one or two of the items, working with a good student to elicit the required output.

Use of visuals

There is a considerable amount of visual material in the book. This should be exploited in a number of ways:

- before an exercise, to orientate students, to get them thinking about the situation or the task, and to provide an opportunity for a small amount of pre-teaching of vocabulary (be careful not to pre-empt any exercises, though)
- during the exercise, to remind students of important language
- after the activity, to help with related work or to revise the target language

Comparing answers in pairs

This is frequently suggested when students have completed a task individually. It provides all students with a chance to give and explain their answers, which is not possible if the teacher immediately goes through the answers with the whole class.

Self-checking

Learning only takes place after a person has noticed that there is something to learn. This noticing of an individual learning point does not happen at the same time for all students. In many cases, it does not even happen in a useful sense when a teacher has focused on it. So learning occurs to the individual timetable of each student in a group. For this reason, it is important to give students time to notice mistakes in their own work and try to correct them individually. Take every opportunity to get students to self-check to try to force the noticing stage.

Confirmation and correction

Many activities benefit from a learning tension, i.e., a period of time when students are not sure whether something is right or wrong. The advantages of this tension are:

- a chance for all students to become involved in an activity before the correct answers are given

- a higher level of concentration from the students (tension is quite enjoyable!)
- a greater focus on the item as students wait for the correct answer
- a greater involvement in the process – students become committed to their answers and want to know if they are right and, if not, why not

In cases where learning tension of this type is desirable, the teacher's notes say, *Do not confirm or correct (at this point).*

Feedback

At the end of each task, there should be a feedback stage. During this stage, the correct answers (or a model answer in the case of freer exercises) are given, alternative answers (if any) are accepted, and wrong answers are discussed. Unless students' own answers are required (in the case of very free exercises), answers or model answers are provided in the teacher's notes.

Highlighting grammar

This course is not organized on a grammatical syllabus and does not focus on grammar specifically. It is assumed that students will have covered English grammar to at least upper intermediate level in their general English course. However, at times it will be necessary to focus on the grammar, and indeed occasionally the grammar is a main focus (for example, changing active to passive or vice versa when paraphrasing).

To highlight the grammar:

- focus students' attention on the grammar point, e.g., *Look at the word order in the first sentence.*
- write an example of the grammar point on the board
- ask a student to read out the sentence/phrase
- demonstrate the grammar point in an appropriate way (e.g., numbering to indicate word order; paradigms for verbs; time lines for tenses)
- refer to the board throughout the activity if students are making mistakes

Pronunciation

By itself, the mispronunciation of a single phoneme or a wrong word stress is unlikely to cause a breakdown in communication. However, most L2 users make multiple errors in a single utterance, including errors of word order, tense choice and vocabulary choice. We must therefore try to remove as many sources of error as possible. When you are working with a group of words, make sure that students can pronounce each word with reasonable accuracy in phonemic terms, and with the correct stress for multiple syllable words. Many researchers have found that getting the stress of a word wrong is a bigger cause of miscommunication than getting individual phonemes wrong.

Pair and group activities

Pairwork and group activities are, of course, an opportunity for students to produce spoken language. As mentioned above, this is not the main focus of this course. But the second benefit of these interactional patterns is that they provide an opportunity for the teacher to check three points:

- Are students performing the correct task, in the correct way?
- Do students understand the language of the task they are performing?
- Which elements need to be covered again for the benefit of the class, and which points need to be dealt with on an individual basis with particular students?

Vocabulary and Skills banks

Each unit has clear targets in terms of vocabulary extension and skills development. These are detailed in the checks at the end of the unit (*Vocabulary bank* and *Skills bank*). However, you may wish to refer students to one or both of these pages at the start of work on the unit, so they have a clear idea of the targets. You may also wish to refer to them from time to time during lessons.

1 WHAT IS TOURISM?

This introductory unit explores what we understand by the term 'tourism'. Students listen to an extract from a lecture which puts forward a definition of tourism, and discuss what makes up the tourist experience. They also listen to a series of mini-lectures which introduce different aspects of tourism, from the development of mass travel in the 19th century to the scale of the industry today. The content of the mini-lectures will be explored in more detail in subsequent units.

Skills focus

🎧 Listening

- preparing for a lecture
- predicting lecture content from the introduction
- understanding lecture organization
- choosing an appropriate form of notes
- making lecture notes

Speaking

- speaking from notes

Vocabulary focus

- words from general English with a special meaning in tourism
- prefixes and suffixes

Key vocabulary

accommodation	impact (n)	recreation
advertisement	information	region
beverage	international	relaxation
book (v)	leisure	reservation
check in (v)	mass travel	satisfaction
check-in (n)	overbook	stay (n and v)
customer	overnight	ticket
destination	package (holiday)	transit route
dissatisfaction	promotion	transport (n)
environment	promotional	travel agency
hospitality	reconfirm	travel agent

1.1 Vocabulary

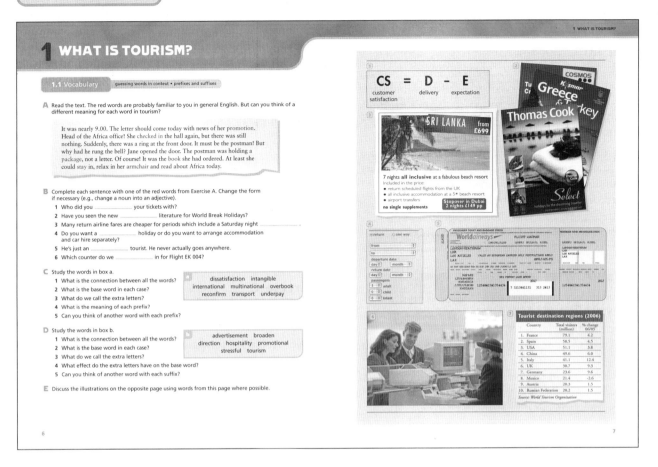

1 WHAT IS TOURISM?

1.1 Vocabulary guessing words in context • prefixes and suffixes

A Read the text. The red words are probably familiar to you in general English. But can you think of a different meaning for each word in tourism?

It was nearly 9.00. The letter should come today with news of her promotion. Head of the Africa office! She checked in the hall again, but there was still nothing. Suddenly, there was a ring at the front door. It must be the postman! But why had he rung the bell? Jane opened the door. The postman was holding a package, not a letter. Of course! It was the book she had ordered. At least she could stay in, relax in her armchair and read about Africa today.

B Complete each sentence with one of the red words from Exercise A. Change the form if necessary (e.g., change a noun into an adjective).
1 Who did you _____ your tickets with?
2 Have you seen the new _____ literature for World Break Holidays?
3 Many return airline fares are cheaper for periods which include a Saturday night _____ .
4 Do you want a _____ holiday or do you want to arrange accommodation and car hire separately?
5 He's just an _____ tourist. He never actually goes anywhere.
6 Which counter do we _____ in for Flight EK 004?

C Study the words in box a.
1 What is the connection between all the words?
2 What is the base word in each case?
3 What do we call the extra letters?
4 What is the meaning of each prefix?
5 Can you think of another word with each prefix?

> dissatisfaction intangible
> international multinational overbook
> reconfirm transport underpay

D Study the words in box b.
1 What is the connection between all the words?
2 What is the base word in each case?
3 What do we call the extra letters?
4 What effect do the extra letters have on the base word?
5 Can you think of another word with each suffix?

> advertisement broaden
> direction hospitality promotional
> stressful tourism

E Discuss the illustrations on the opposite page using words from this page where possible.

6 / 7

General note

Read the *Vocabulary bank* at the end of the Course Book unit. Decide when, if at all, to refer students to it. The best time is probably at the very end of the lesson or the beginning of the next lesson, as a summary/revision.

Lesson aims

- identify words for the discipline in context, including words which contain affixes
- gain fluency in the target vocabulary

Introduction

Write the phrase *tourism* on the board. Ask students about the origin of the word. Elicit the base word *tour* and possible collocations students may know with the word *tourism* or *tourist*.

Ask students where the word *hospitality* comes from. They might forge a link with the word *hospital*, which is not so strange as there is a common meaning there, but a closer relative of the word is *hospice* (see *Language note*). Finally, ask students where they think the word *leisure* comes from.

Make sure students can say the words correctly:

tourism /ˈtʊərɪzəm/
hospitality /ˌhɒspɪˈtæləti/
leisure /ˈleʒə/ (BrE) /ˈliːʒər/ (AmE)

Allow students to describe experiences with tourism, hospitality and/or leisure.

Language note

Here are entries for key words from the discipline from the *Online Etymology Dictionary*, www.etymonline.com.

tour (n.) c.1320, "a turn, a shift on duty," from O.Fr. *tour*, *tourn* "a turn, trick, round, circuit, circumference," from *torner*, *tourner* "to turn," from L. *tornare* "to polish, round off, fashion" (see **turn**). Sense of "a traveling around, journey" is first recorded 1643. The verb is attested from 1746. *Tourist* is first attested 1780; *tourist trap* attested from 1939 in Graham Greene; *tourism* is from 1811. *Tour de force* "feat of strength" is 1802, from Fr., from *force* "strength." *Tour de France* is recorded from 1922. *The Grand Tour*, a journey through France, Germany, Switzerland, and Italy formerly was the finishing touch in the education of a gentleman.

hospitality 1375, "act of being hospitable," from O.Fr. *hospitalité*, from L. *hospitalitem* (gen. *hospitalitas*) "friendliness to guests," from *hospes* (gen. *hospitis*) "guest" (see **host** (1)).

hospice 1818, "rest house for travelers," from Fr. *hospice*, from L. *hospitum* "guest house, hospitality," from *hospes* (gen. *hospitis*) "guest, host" (see **host** (1)). Sense of "home for the aged and terminally ill" is from 1893; *hospice movement* first attested 1979.

leisure 1303, "opportunity to do something," also "time at one's disposal," from O.Fr. *leisir* (Fr. *loisir*) "permission, leisure, spare time," noun use of infinitive *leisir* "be permitted," from L. *licere* "be permitted" (see **license**). The *-u-* appeared 16c., probably on analogy of words like *pleasure*.

Exercise A

Set for individual work and pairwork checking. Point out that this is a text which introduces some important basic vocabulary related to tourism – although it may not seem like that, at first glance. Do the first one as an example, e.g., *a promotion is a move to a better position at work; in tourism it can also mean a special offer*. Ask students if there is a relationship between the two meanings in general English and tourism. (Both have the meaning of supporting or enhancing.)

Tell students to use these structures where possible:

- *a(n) X is (a(n)) ...* to define a noun
- *to X is to Y* to define a verb

Make sure students can say the words correctly, e.g.,

- diphthong /əʊ/ in *promotion*
- /ɪ/ in *package*

Answers

Model answers:

Word	Meaning in tourism
promotion	a special offer
check(ed) in	report at the airport for a flight
package	a package tour (transport, accommodation, etc. all included)
book	as a verb: make a reservation
stay	spend time at a holiday destination; often used as a noun in this context
armchair	armchair tourist/tourism: someone who takes an interest in travel and tourism without actually visiting the destination

Exercise B

Set for individual work and pairwork checking. Make sure students understand that they should change the form if necessary, e.g., noun to adjective, or verb to noun. Feed back.

Answers

1 Who did you <u>book</u> your tickets with?
2 Have you seen the new <u>promotional</u> literature for World Break Holidays?
3 Many return airline fares are cheaper for periods which include a Saturday night <u>stay</u>.
4 Do you want a <u>package</u> holiday or do you want to arrange accommodation and car hire separately?
5 He's just an <u>armchair</u> tourist. He never actually goes anywhere.
6 Which counter do we <u>check</u> in for Flight EK 004?

Exercise C

Set the first question for pairwork. See which pair can work out the answer first.

Set the remainder for pairwork. Feed back, building up the table in the Answers section below on the board.

Answers

Model answers:

1 They all have a base word + extra letters at the beginning/prefixes.
2 See table.
3 Prefix.
4 See table.
5 See table.

Prefix	Base word	Meaning of prefix	Another word
dis	satisfaction	not	disinterest
in	tangible	not	incorrect
inter	national	between	intercultural
multi	national	many	multicultural
over	book	more; sometimes = too much	overspend
re	confirm	again	redevelop
trans	port*	between	translate
under	pay	below; sometimes = not enough	underspend

*in fact, here *port* comes from *portare* = carry, not from *port* = place for ships

Language note

English is a lexemic language. In other words, the whole meaning of a word is usually contained within the word itself, rather than coming from a root meaning plus prefixes or suffixes (affixes). In most texts, written or spoken, there will only be a tiny number of words with affixes. However, these often add to a base meaning in a predictable way and it is important that students learn to detach affixes from a new word and see if they can find a recognizable base word.

Some words beginning with letters from prefixes are NOT in fact base + prefix, e.g., *research, adventure, impact*. In other cases, the base word does not exist anymore in English and therefore may not help students, e.g., *transfer, transit, translate*, although even in these cases the root meaning of the prefix may be a guide to the meaning of the whole word.

Exercise D

Repeat the procedure from Exercise C.

Answers

Model answers:

1 They all have a base word + extra letters at the end/suffixes.
2 See table.
3 Suffix.
4/5 See table.

Base word	Suffix	Effect/meaning of suffix	Another word
advertise	ment	the action described by a verb, or the result	improvement
broad	en	make more – adjective → verb	strengthen
direct	ion	the action described by a verb, or the result	inspection
hospita(ble)	ity	indicates that the word is a noun; usually something abstract, a quality	originality
promotion	al	related to; noun → adjective	original
stress	ful	having a particular quality; noun → adjective	powerful
tour	ism	indicates a noun; often a set of beliefs or attitudes	racism

Language note

Note that with prefixes we rarely change the form of the base word. However, with suffixes, there are often changes to the base word, so students must:

- take off the suffix
- try to reconstruct the base word

Exercise E

Set for pairwork. Try to elicit more than just the words from this lesson. Tell students to use adjectives as well as nouns. Establish common collocations, e.g., *customer satisfaction, an airline ticket, tourist destinations*.

Subject note

$CS = D–E$ is one of the formulas used in hospitality research that attempts to measure customer satisfaction. The idea is to measure how satisfied customers are while they are enjoying the tourism or hospitality service. Researchers do this by quantifying both the services delivered and customers' expectations. Researchers collect data on both, translate the results into a value (a number) and then, literally, subtract one from the other to get another value which can be used for further analysis. This is one of many methods of researching customer satisfaction.

Answers

Students may use the following words in their discussion of each picture:

1 a formula for customer **satisfaction**
2 **promotional** literature – brochures
3 an advertisement for a **package holiday**
4 a website for **booking tickets** (e.g., plane, train, bus)
5 an airline **ticket** (may need to be **reconfirmed**)
6 an airline **check-in** (can be **stressful** for travellers)
7 a table showing top ten destinations for **international tourism** worldwide

Closure

If you have not done so already, refer students to the *Vocabulary bank* at the end of Unit 1. Tell students to explain how this lesson can help them deal with new words in context. If you wish, make three groups. Group A looks at the first section, *Using related words*. Group B looks at the second section, *Removing prefixes*. Group C looks at the third section, *Removing suffixes*. Then make new groups of three with an ABC in each to explain to each other.

1.2 Listening preparing for a lecture • predicting lecture content • making notes

A You are a student in the School of Tourism and Hospitality Management of Hadford University.

1 The title of your first lecture is *What is tourism?* Write a definition of tourism.

2 What other ideas will be in this lecture? Make some notes.

See *Skills bank*

B 🎧 Listen to Part 1 of the lecture.

1 What is the lecturer going to talk about? Make a list.

2 The lecturer mentions some reasons for studying tourism. Make a list.

C In Part 2, the lecturer talks about the impacts of tourism.

1 What are the main impacts of tourism? Make a list.

2 🎧 Listen to Part 2 of the lecture. Tick any points on your list. Add any extra points.

D In Part 3, the lecturer talks about some aspects of tourism.

1 Copy Table 1 into your notebook. You will need space for 12 aspects.

2 🎧 Listen to Part 3 of the lecture. Take notes and complete Table 1 with five aspects of tourism.

3 Add examples of each aspect from your own experience.

E In Part 4 of the talk, the lecturer describes two more aspects of tourism.

1 🎧 Listen to Part 4 and add these aspects to your table. Add examples.

2 What three branches of tourism are mentioned? (Clue: look at the pictures!)

F In the final part of the talk, the lecturer discusses five more aspects of tourism.

🎧 Listen to Part 5 and add these aspects to your table. Add examples.

G Rewrite your definition of tourism from Exercise A. Use words and ideas from Table 1.

H Look back at your notes from Exercise A. Did you predict:
• the main ideas?
• most of the special vocabulary?

Table 1:
Aspects of tourism (according to Leiper)

	Aspect	Example
1		
2		
3		
4		
5		

8

General note

The recording should only be played once, since this reflects what happens in a real lecture. Students should be encouraged to listen for the important points, since this is what a native speaker would take from the text. However, students can be referred to the transcript at the end of the lesson to check their detailed understanding and word recognition, or to try to discover reasons for failing to comprehend.

Read the *Skills bank* at the end of the Course Book unit. Decide when, if at all, to refer students to it. The best time is probably at the very end of the lesson or the beginning of the next lesson, as a summary/revision.

Lesson aims

● prepare for a lecture
● predict lecture content
● make notes

Introduction

1 Show students flashcards of some or all of the words from Lesson 1. Tell students to say the words correctly and quickly as you flash them. Give out each word to one of the students. Say the words again. The student with the word must hold it up. Repeat the process saying the words in context.

2 Refer students to the photos. Briefly elicit ideas of what they depict.

Exercise A

Introduce the fictional Hadford University.

1 Refer students to the lecture title. Set for pair or group work. Feed back, but do not confirm or correct at this time.

2 Set for pairwork. Elicit some ideas but do not confirm or correct.

Methodology note

You may prefer to refer students to the *Skills bank – Making the most of lectures* at this point. Set the following for individual work and pairwork checking. Tell students to cover the points and try to remember what was under each of the Ps – Plan, Prepare, Predict, Produce. Then tell students to work through the points to make sure they are prepared for the lecture they are about to hear.

🎧 Exercise B

Set the questions for individual work and pairwork checking. Point out that they are only going to hear the introduction once, as in an authentic lecture situation. Then play Part 1. Feed back. If students' answers differ, discuss which is the best answer and why. Ask students which of the reasons for studying tourism applies to them.

Answers

Model answers:

1 ● why study tourism?
   ● the theory of tourism
   ● links between tourism and other fields of study (if time)

2 ● required for a degree
   ● useful for career
   ● personal interest
   ● large impact on the world

Transcript 🎧 1.1

Part 1

Today we're going to talk about tourism. We'll look at why you study tourism. We'll also study the core theory of tourism, the basic theory, developed by researchers such as Leiper and Tribe. If we have time, we'll go into interdisciplinary studies that link tourism to other fields of study.

First of all, why do you study tourism? Probably, most of you will be studying tourism because you realize it's required to get a degree. Possibly, you feel it may be useful for a future career, or perhaps you're simply motivated because you've decided it's an interesting area of study. Tourism is certainly having a very great impact on our world.

This is something that Professor John Tribe recognizes when he writes that tourism is the world's biggest industry and it attracts undergraduates in ever-increasing numbers. He raises the very interesting point that because tourism has a large impact on the world, tourism courses need to show students what this impact is.

🎧 Exercise C

1 Set for pairwork discussion before listening. Do not feed back at this point.

2 Set for individual work and pairwork checking. Play Part 2. Feed back, building up a list of impacts on the board.

Answers

Model answers:

1 Answers depend on the students.

2 • creates industrial landscape

　• causes changes to social relationships

　• causes changes to economic relationships = creates a 'tourism society'

Transcript 🎧 1.2

Part 2

I'll just summarize for you this one paragraph from an article by Tribe – *The Philosophic Practitioner*. He says that the purpose of a course in tourism is to enable graduates to operate in their career. However, if we just focused on that alone, this would overlook an important feature of a big industry like tourism. Yes, it generates consumer satisfaction, employment and wealth; but tourism also leaves its imprint on the world in other ways. It creates an industrial landscape and causes changes to the social and economic relationships between people. When we develop tourism we

create what you could call a *tourism society*. This society is made up not just of tourism-associated businesses, but of all individuals, communities, governments and the physical environments affected by tourism. So a special responsibility is placed on education to make people aware of the important role tourism plays.

Methodology note

In many course books with listening activities, students are allowed to listen to material again and again. This does not mirror real-life exposure to spoken text. In this course, students are taught to expect only one hearing during the lesson and are encouraged to develop coping strategies to enable them to extract the key points during this one hearing. Listening texts may be repeated for further analysis but not for initial comprehension.

🎧 Exercise D

Write the two abbreviations TGR and TDR on the board. Ask if students know what they stand for. Elicit ideas but do not confirm or correct. Explain that they will hear definitions in the next part of the lecture.

1 Give students time to copy the table. Tell them to allow enough space for 12 aspects/examples, with cells large enough to write a sentence or so.

2 Set for individual work and pairwork checking. Play Part 3. Feed back, building up the table on the board. Check meanings of TGR and TDR as you go.

3 Set for pairwork. Feed back, adding good examples to the table on the board.

Answers

Model answers:

TGR = tourism generating region = where tourists come from

TDR = tourism destination region = where they go to

2/3 Examples will depend on students' knowledge and personal experiences.

Aspect	Example
1 travel away from home	
2 at least one night away	
3 there is a TGR	
4 there is a TDR	
5 there is a transit route	

Transcript 🎧 1.3

Part 3

Let's move on. What does 'tourism' mean? In a theory of tourism put forward by Professor Leiper in his book *Tourism Management*, it is defined as 'travelling away temporarily on overnight trips and visiting places for leisure-related purposes'. Leiper explains that there are a number of essential aspects to this definition, which I'll run through very briefly today.

To begin with, tourism involves travelling away from home and expecting to return to your usual residence. The second point is that you must spend at least one night away: it is, after all, a time when you're away from home. Thirdly, tourism involves a TGR, and fourthly a TDR. In other words, there is a place which the tourist comes from – the TGR or tourism generating region, and a destination – a place which the tourist goes to – the TDR, or tourism destination region. So if you live in London, then London is your TGR; if you live in Tokyo, then that is your TGR. That is where you would normally buy the resources that you require: you will buy your ticket there, you will buy your rucksack there; you will buy extra clothes; you will possibly even book hotels through an accommodation booking agency which, of course, gets paid for that service.

All right, the fourth point is that you would be visiting at least one, and possibly many more, tourist destinations. You might be taking just a single trip to one particular place; you might decide to go to Dubai and spend a week there; you might be doing a world tour, visiting many different places over a longer period of time. These are the destination regions, the TDRs.

A fifth and very crucial aspect of tourism is that, along the way, you will be travelling via a transit route – by plane, boat, train or any other mode of transport. This transit route may be the same for the way over as for the way back, or it may be different. And, as a tourist, you have an impact on the transit route – planes pollute the environment of countries they fly over, for instance; cars make noise; trains draw energy from valuable resources, etc.

So, in summary, you travel from home, for at least one night, prepare for your trip in your home area, travel to the tourist destination and use a route to get there, before you return home.

🎧 Exercise E

1 Set for pairwork. Play Part 4. Feed back, adding good examples to the table on the board.

2 Set for pairwork. Feed back, eliciting examples of each branch of tourism.

Answers

Model answers:

1 Examples will depend on students' knowledge and personal experiences.

Aspect	Example
6 engage in leisure-related experiences	
7 engage with a different culture	

2 Travel, leisure, hospitality.

Transcript 🎧 1.4

Part 4

Travel is one aspect of tourism, but you don't go somewhere just to come back. Another important point, and this is the sixth aspect of Leiper's theory, is that you will engage in leisure-related experiences. These are non-obligatory – you don't have to do them. They are personally pleasurable, recreational or creative. You may, for instance, decide to go snorkelling, lounge on the beach, or have a massage. To a certain degree, tourism has to do with leisure, which is why we often see leisure incorporated into tourism courses, as well as hospitality.

Whether we're talking about travel, leisure or hospitality, all tourism shows the culture of the generating regions, and most tourism involves a cultural exchange in the destination region. This is aspect number seven. As a tourist, you engage with a different culture; you're away from your own culture for a while. This gives rise to a lot of interesting theories about cultural exchange, learning more about yourself, and learning more about the culture you go to. People often say that travel broadens the mind.

Methodology note

Up to this point, you haven't mentioned how students should record information. Have a look around to see what students are doing. If some are using good methods, make a note and mention that later in the unit.

🎧 Exercise F

Ask students to predict which other aspects they think will be discussed in the last part of the lecture. Write on the board or OHP. Play Part 5. Feed back, adding good examples to the table on the board.

Answers

Model answers:

Examples will depend on students' knowledge and personal experiences.

Aspect	Example
8 information	
9 change of routine	
10 security	
11 finances	
12 tourism industries	

Transcript 🎧 1.5

Part 5

What other aspects of tourism and hospitality are there? Well, why do you go anywhere? You're motivated to travel somewhere based on information that you've received, one way or another, about the destination. You've received this information either prior to your trip in the generating region (for instance, by reading a book or looking on the Internet), or possibly on the transit route (at airports, for instance) or in the destination region, maybe at a tourist information office. So information is Leiper's eighth point.

The next point is that tourism involves change to your daily routine and activities. For a while, you experience a different way of life, a kind of time out, and you will be doing things that you may not normally do.

Leiper's tenth point is that, as a tourist, you expect that there will be a reasonable degree of security. You want the places you travel to to tolerate tourist visitors and, ideally, be hospitable. This is where the link with hospitality comes in. Hospitality is extremely important in tourism, because people need a sense of hospitality in order to feel comfortable in a place. Travelling can be quite stressful: you're in an unusual place, you don't know the people, and you may not know the language. There must be the sense that there is going to be a reasonable degree of personal security, otherwise people won't travel.

The next point concerns finances. As a tourist you will expect that your visit is going to be economically feasible, and that the activity will be worth the money spent – otherwise you wouldn't have embarked on the journey in the first place.

The final aspect is that tourists depend on the tourism industries, like hotels, accommodation providers, and the food and beverage industry. This is a bit of a grey area. Supermarkets, for instance, are not specifically aiming to foster or support tourism, but still many tourists rely on them.

So this is the end of your journey. You've travelled from home – your TGR – and you've spent at least one night away – your TDR. You've travelled to your destination via a transit route. You've participated in leisure activities, experienced a different culture and a different daily routine. You've received information about your destination, either at home or on arrival. You've felt safe, secure and welcome. You feel that your money was well spent. You've used tourist facilities and hospitality businesses, before finally returning home.

Exercise G

Set for individual work and pairwork checking. Feed back, building up a model definition on the board.

Answers

Possible answer (accept other appropriate definitions):

Tourism is travel for the purpose of recreation, and the provision of hospitality and leisure services for this.

Exercise H

Refer students back to their notes from Exercise A.

Closure

1 Ask students to relate Leiper's twelve aspects of tourism to a trip they have themselves taken.

2 Refer students to the *Skills bank* if you have not done so already and work through the section *Making the most of lectures*.

1.3 Extending skills

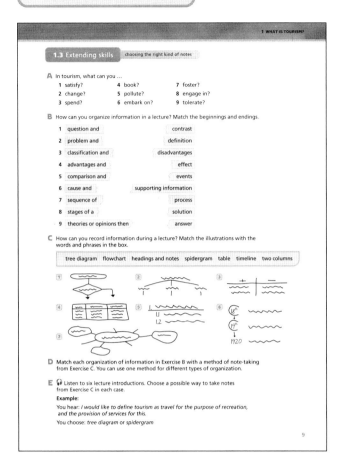

1.3 Extending skills choosing the right kind of notes

A In tourism, what can you ...
1 satisfy? 4 book? 7 foster?
2 change? 5 pollute? 8 engage in?
3 spend? 6 embark on? 9 tolerate?

B How can you organize information in a lecture? Match the beginnings and endings.

1 question and — contrast
2 problem and — definition
3 classification and — disadvantages
4 advantages and — effect
5 comparison and — events
6 cause and — supporting information
7 sequence of — process
8 stages of a — solution
9 theories or opinions then — answer

C How can you record information during a lecture? Match the illustrations with the words and phrases in the box.

tree diagram flowchart headings and notes spidergram table timeline two columns

D Match each organization of information in Exercise B with a method of note-taking from Exercise C. You can use one method for different types of organization.

E Listen to six lecture introductions. Choose a possible way to take notes from Exercise C in each case.
Example:
You hear: *I would like to define tourism as travel for the purpose of recreation, and the provision of services for this.*
You choose: *tree diagram or spidergram*

9

Lesson aims

- identify different types of lecture organization
- use the introduction to a lecture to decide the best form of notes to use

Introduction

Tell students to build up the four Ps of preparing for and attending a lecture: Plan, Prepare, Predict, Produce. You could put students into four groups, each group working on one of the stages, then feeding back to the rest of the class.

Exercise A

Set for pairwork. Tell students they must add something to each verb to make a phrase in the context of tourism or tourism research. There may be more than one possibility.

Feed back orally. The more students can say about these words, the better. Accept anything correct but let students explain their choice if they choose a combination not given below.

Answers
Possible answers:

1	satisfy	a customer, a demand
2	change	a booking, a reservation, your daily routine
3	spend	money, time
4	book	accommodation, flights, tickets
5	pollute	rivers, the air, the environment
6	embark on	a journey
7	foster	tourism, understanding
8	engage in	leisure-related experiences/activities
9	tolerate	tourist visitors

Exercise B

Point out that you can understand a lecture better if you can predict the order of information. Point out also that there are many pairs and patterns in presenting information, e.g., question and answer, or a sequence of events in chronological order.

Set for pairwork. Feed back orally. Check pronunciation. Point out that lecturers may not actually use these words, but if you recognize that what a lecturer is saying is the first of a pair, or the beginning of a sequence, you are ready for the second or next stage later in the lecture.

Answers

1	question and	answer
2	problem and	solution
3	classification and	definition
4	advantages and	disadvantages
5	comparison and	contrast
6	cause and	effect
7	sequence of	events
8	stages of a	process
9	theories or opinions then	supporting information

Exercise C

Identify the first form of notes – a flowchart. Set the rest for individual work and pairwork checking. Feed back, using an OHT or other visual medium if possible.

Answers

1 flowchart
2 tree diagram
3 two columns
4 table
5 headings and notes
6 timeline
7 spidergram

Methodology note

You might like to make larger versions of the illustrations of different note types and pin them up in the classroom for future reference.

Exercise D

Work through the first one as an example. Set for pairwork. Feed back orally.

Demonstrate how each type of notes in Exercise C can be matched with an organizational structure. Point out that:

- a tree diagram is useful for hierarchically arranged information, such as when the information moves from general to specific/examples
- a spidergram is more fluid and flexible, and can be used to show connections between things, such as interactions or causes and effects

Answers

Possible answers:

1 question and answer = headings and notes
2 problem and solution = headings and notes or two-column table
3 classification and definition = tree diagram or spidergram
4 advantages and disadvantages = two-column table
5 comparison and contrast = table
6 cause and effect = spidergram
7 sequence of events = timeline or flowchart
8 stages of a process = flowchart (or circle if it is a cycle)
9 theories or opinions then supporting information = headings and notes or two-column table

Exercise E

Explain that students are going to hear the introductions to several different lectures. They do not have to take notes, only think about the organization of information and decide what type of notes would be appropriate. Work through the example.

Play each introduction. Pause after each one and allow students to discuss then feed back. Discuss whether Lecture 5 corresponds to one of the organizational structures in Exercise B (probably not – the focus is on facts and figures, although there is a suggestion of comparison and contrast).

Feed back. Students may suggest different answers in some cases. Discuss. Establish that sometimes lecturers move from one information organization to another, e.g., cause and effect then sequence of events.

Answers

Possible answers:

1 tree diagram or spidergram (classification and definition)
2 tree diagram or spidergram (classification and definition)
3 flowchart (sequence of events or stages of a process)
4 headings and notes (question and answer)
5 table (facts and figures)
6 timeline (sequence of events)

Transcript 🎧 1.6

Introduction 1

Today I'm going to talk about tourism. Somebody once said: 'The tourism industry produces expectations, sells dreams and provides memories.' I'd like to define tourism as travel for the purpose of recreation, and the provision of services for this. So, you travel somewhere and other people make sure that you can travel and enjoy your stay in your destination.

Introduction 2

This week we're going to talk about a historical example of tourism: the Grand Tour. We're going to look at who went on a Grand Tour, why they went, and where they went. I suppose you could compare the Grand Tour to what we now call a gap year: many of you may have spent a year abroad before studying here. The difference is probably that most of you will have had to work hard and earn a living while you were away to be able to stay away that long.

Introduction 3

In today's lecture we're going to have a look at how a holiday or leisure experience actually works. Even though you may be unaware of this, you take a number of recognizable steps to prepare for your experience in the months before you actually travel. First, and this can be as long as a year before the event, you decide where you want to go and what you want to do. Then you take a few weeks, or maybe months, planning. You prepare for your trip. Then you travel, you experience, you communicate, and finally you travel home and you tell everybody about it. It's not something you can pin down to a certain time-scale, but one step follows another, so let's look at each step in turn.

Introduction 4

Let's have a closer look today at mass travel. This is something we've all experienced, right? First of all, what actually boosted the development of mass tourism? We'll look at two important factors. Secondly, what was mass travel like in the early years? We'll talk about one of the first examples. Thirdly, what are the target groups for mass travel? We'll look at how these have changed over the years.

Introduction 5

This week we're going to be talking about the UK tourist market. What kind of market is this? How successful is it? The figures are amazing. Tourism and hospitality is one of the largest industries in the UK, worth approximately £74 billion. It accounts for 4.5% of GDP and employs 2.1 million people. There are, in fact, more jobs in tourism than in, say, construction or transport. Let's have a look at some more facts and figures.

Introduction 6

When you study tourism and hospitality, space tourism is perhaps not the first thing that comes to mind. After all, this kind of tourism involves travelling into space, staying in a space hotel and taking day trips to look at stars and planets. Does this all seem a bit far-fetched to you? Don't forget that the first commercial space flights are no longer just ideas on paper. In recent years, interest in the possibilities of space tourism has grown. The international business community and the media have become very interested in space pioneers like Virgin's Richard Branson.

We're going to start off today by taking a brief look at the history of space travel, and some of the more significant steps towards space tourism. So let's travel through time … from the initial enthusiasm for space travel in the 1950s to more recent plans for a space hotel.

Closure

1 Test students on the pairs from Exercise B. Correct pronunciation again if necessary.

2 Refer students to the *Skills bank – Making perfect lecture notes*.

1.4 Extending skills

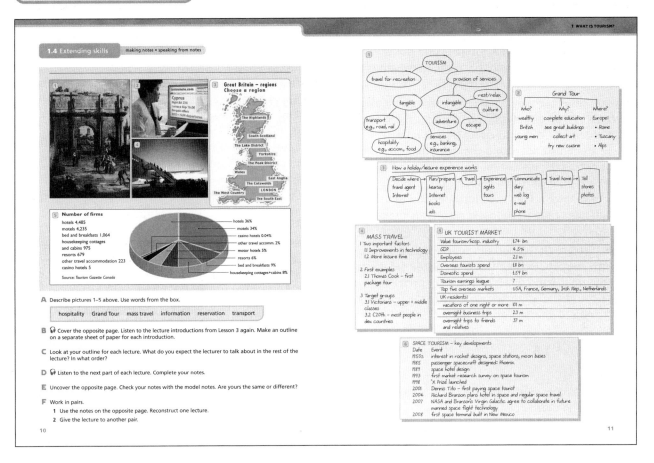

1.4 Extending skills · making notes • speaking from notes

Lesson aims

- make outline notes from lecture introductions
- make notes from a variety of lecture types
- speak from notes

Further practice in:

- predicting lecture content

Introduction

Ask students questions about the research in Lesson 2, e.g., *What does Professor Tribe say about the purpose of tourism studies?*

Exercise A

Set for individual work and pairwork checking. Feed back orally but do not confirm or correct. Point out that they are going to hear about all these things in today's lesson. You will return to these illustrations at the end.

For reference, the illustrations show:

1 the **Grand Tour** (the picture is a Canaletto painting, *The Arch of Constantine*, painted in Rome in 1742)

2 a person making a holiday **reservation**/finding out **information** about a tourist destination on the Internet

3 **information** about Great Britain, possibly from a tourist information website

4 **transport/mass travel**: tourists travelling by plane

5 a pie chart giving the availability of various types of accommodation in Canada and the number of companies that provide accommodation services. It shows that in Canada motels and hotels are by far the most popular types of accommodation followed by B&Bs and cottages/cabins. The chart represents the **hospitality** branch of tourism.

Language note

British English usage is normally *transport*.
American English usage is normally *transportation*.

Methodology note

It is best that students close the book at this stage, so they are not tempted to look at the model notes. You can give the instructions for the next few stages orally as required.

🎧 Exercise B

Make sure students understand that they are going to hear the introductions from Lesson 3 again. Ask them briefly if they can remember any of the content from the introductions. Spend a few moments on this if students are able to contribute. Elicit the suggestions for types of notes (Lesson 3, Exercise E).

Explain that this time they must create an outline using an appropriate type of notes. (You can refer them again to the *Skills bank – Making perfect lecture notes.*) Make sure students understand that they don't need to write a lot at this stage – outlines may consist of just a few words, e.g., the start of a spidergram, the first part of a table or diagram. Play each introduction in turn and give students time to choose a note-type, make the outline and check it with other students.

Feed back, getting all the outlines on the board – you may wish to copy them from the first part of the model notes on the right-hand page, or you may prefer to follow your students' suggestions. Clarify the meaning of new words and check pronunciation.

Transcript 🎧 1.6

Introduction 1

Today I'm going to talk about tourism. Somebody once said: 'The tourism industry produces expectations, sells dreams and provides memories.' I would like to define tourism as travel for the purpose of recreation, and the provision of services for this. So, you travel somewhere and other people make sure that you can travel and enjoy your stay in your destination.

Introduction 2

This week we're going to talk about a historical example of tourism: the Grand Tour. We're going to look at who went on a Grand Tour, why they went, and where they went. I suppose you could compare the Grand Tour to what we now call a gap year: many of you may have spent a year abroad before studying here. The difference is probably that most of you will have had to work hard and earn a living while you were away to be able to stay away that long.

Introduction 3

In today's lecture we're going to have a look at how a holiday or leisure experience actually works. Even though you may be unaware of this, you take a number of recognizable steps to prepare for your experience in the months before you actually travel. First, and this can be as long as a year before the event, you decide where you want to go and what you want to do. Then you take a few weeks, or maybe months, planning. You prepare for your trip. Then you travel, you experience, you communicate, and finally you travel home and you tell everybody about it. It's not something you can pin down to a certain time-scale, but one step follows another, so let's look at each step in turn.

Introduction 4

Let's have a closer look today at mass travel. This is something we've all experienced, right? First of all, what actually boosted the development of mass tourism? We'll look at two important factors. Secondly, what was mass travel like in the early years? We'll talk about one of the first examples. Thirdly, what are the target groups for mass travel? We'll look at how these have changed over the years.

Introduction 5

This week we're going to be talking about the UK tourist market. What kind of market is this? How successful is it? The figures are amazing. Tourism and hospitality is one of the largest industries in the UK, worth approximately £74 billion. It accounts for 4.5% of GDP and employs 2.1 million people. There are, in fact, more jobs in tourism than in, say, construction or transport. Let's have a look at some more facts and figures.

Introduction 6

When you study tourism and hospitality, space tourism is perhaps not the first thing that comes to mind. After all, this kind of tourism involves travelling into space, staying in a space hotel and taking day trips to look at stars and planets. Does this all seem a bit far-fetched to you? Don't forget that the first commercial space flights are no longer just ideas on paper. In recent years, interest in the possibilities of space tourism has grown. The international business community and the media have become very interested in space pioneers like Virgin's Richard Branson.

We're going to start off today by taking a brief look at the history of space travel, and some of the more significant steps towards space tourism. So let's travel through time … from the initial enthusiasm for space travel in the 1950s to more recent plans for a space hotel.

Methodology note

Spiral bound or stitched/stapled notebooks are not the best way to keep lecture notes. It is impossible to reorganize or add extra information at a later date, or make a clean copy of notes after a lecture. Encourage students to use a loose leaf file and organize it in a sensible way, with file dividers. Tell students to use a separate piece of paper for each outline in this lecture.

Exercise C

Set for pair or group work. Feed back, but do not confirm or correct. Students should be able to predict reasonably well the kind of information which will fit into their outline.

🎧 Exercise D

Before you play the next part of each lecture, refer students to their outline notes again. Tell them to orally reconstruct the introduction from their notes. They don't have to be able to say the exact words, but they should be able to give the gist.

Remind students that they are only going to hear the next part of each lecture once. Play each extract in turn, pausing if necessary to allow students to make notes but not replaying any section. Tell students to choose an appropriate type of notes for this part of the lecture – it could be a continuation of the type they chose for the introduction, or it could be a different type.

Transcripts

Lecture 1 🎧 **1.7**

A tourist, according to the World Tourism Organization, a United Nations body, is someone who travels at least 80 kilometres from home for the purpose of recreation.

A wider definition is that tourism is a service industry. It covers a number of tangible and intangible aspects. The tangible aspects are transport systems: air, rail, road, water and now, space. Other examples are hospitality services: accommodation, foods and beverages, tours, souvenirs. And then there are services such as banking, insurance and security. Examples of intangible elements are rest and relaxation, culture, escape, adventure. These are the things you experience. The intangible aspects of tourism are perhaps even more important than the tangible ones.

Lecture 2 🎧 **1.8**

The word *tour* was introduced in the 18th century, when the Grand Tour of Europe became part of the upbringing of educated and wealthy British people. Grand Tours were taken especially by young men to 'complete' their education. They travelled all over Europe to places of cultural and natural interest, such as Rome, Tuscany, and the Alps. They went to see great buildings or works of art; to learn new languages, or to try new cuisine.

The Grand Tour was very important for the British nobility. They often used it to collect art treasures. This explains why many private and public collections in Britain today are so rich.

Tourism in those days was mainly a cultural activity undertaken by the wealthy. You could say that these first tourists, through undertaking their Grand Tour, were more travellers than tourists.

Lecture 3 🎧 **1.9**

First of all, you take a decision to travel. You may go to a travel agency. Alternatively, you may book a trip through the Internet. Having done so, you can start planning and preparing for what to do and see on your trip.

The information you acquire can come from a diverse range of sources. Often people have heard about a popular destination through hearsay; but they may also have done Internet research, or read books from the library. Advertisements in the media also help because they often allow you to send for brochures.

Having reached the destination region, you visit the sights. You could possibly take organized tours. While you go about the business of travel and leisure, you may want to keep a diary and visit the local Internet café to update your web log and send e-mails. And no doubt you may wish to make the occasional phone call to friends and relatives to tell them what they are missing out on …

On return you'll relive the experience by telling others of your adventure, sharing stories and photographs, and giving people souvenirs.

Lecture 4 🎧 **1.10**

OK. So. Factors in the growth of mass travel. Well, there were two particularly important factors. Firstly, there were improvements in technology. Boats and trains enabled more and more people to travel to tourist destinations in the course of the 19th century; in the 20th century, planes made the sky the limit, literally. Secondly, there was an increase in people's spare time.

So what were some early examples of mass tourism? You may have heard the name Thomas Cook. Actually, his name is used by a well-known British travel agent. Mr Cook can be held 'responsible' for organizing the first package trip in history. In 1841 he took a group of people from Leicester to Loughborough by train. These cities were quite far apart, relatively speaking, for those days, so for most travellers this must have been a great adventure. You could say with some justification that this was the start of mass tourism as we know it today.

Who were the target groups for mass travel? The Victorians liked to travel, even though in the second half of the 19th century travel was only within the reach of the upper classes, of course, and the developing middle classes – people like merchants, traders and shopkeepers. In the 20th century more and more people earned higher incomes, planes were introduced, and travel became cheaper – within reach of most people in developed countries by the end of the century. In our 21st century society, where most people have more spare time than they know what to do with, mass travel has taken on incredible proportions. It may be difficult now to appreciate that less than 150 years ago not that many people could actually take time off work to travel, and only a few people could afford transport, accommodation and time spent away from work.

Lecture 5 🎧 1.11

UK tourism has been growing over the last decade, caused by greater mobility and the Internet. Last year overseas tourists spent £11 billion in the UK when they visited. Now this looks like a lot of money until you realize that domestic tourists spent £26 billion on trips of one night or more and a further £33 billion on day trips.

The UK ranks seventh in the international tourism earnings league behind the USA, Spain, France, Italy, China and Germany. The top five overseas markets for the UK last year were the USA, France, Germany, the Irish Republic and the Netherlands.

It can sound somewhat strange when you look at numbers. For instance, did you know that last year UK residents took 101 million vacations of one night or more, 23 million overnight business trips and 37 million overnight trips to friends and relatives?

Lecture 6 🎧 1.12

After the Second World War, in the 1950s, there was a lot of interest in rocket designs, space stations and moon bases. But as Cold War tensions grew, the focus was increasingly on the 'space race' between the USA and the Soviet Union, which ended with the first moon landing.

It wasn't until 1985 that a passenger spacecraft was designed, called Phoenix. In the US, a travel company called Society Expeditions started 'Project Space Voyage'. They were offering short trips into Earth orbit in Phoenix for 'only' 50,000 US dollars. They managed to get a few hundred people interested and collected deposits in the US, Europe and Japan, but in the end there wasn't enough investment to develop Phoenix further.

As we come closer to our own time, developments start to speed up. Shimizu Corporation, a major global construction company, chose to forget about how to actually get into space, but designed a space hotel in 1989.

A few years later, in 1993, the first market research survey on space tourism was carried out.

More than 3,000 people in Japan filled in a questionnaire. If it showed one thing, it was that the concept of space travel was extremely popular in that country.

Five years later, in 1998, the 'X Prize' was announced. This was a $10,000,000 prize for the first person to launch a reusable manned spacecraft into space twice within a two-week period. At a press conference held by NASA, Mr Goldin, administrator of NASA at the time, said: 'I hope my grandson, who is two years old, will be able to go on a trip to a lunar hotel.' A few years before that, nobody could have imagined such a speech. From that time on, space tourism became accepted by 'real' space industry people. Burt Rutan and SpaceShipOne won the X Prize in October 2004.

In 2001, Dennis Tito became the first paying space tourist. He travelled on board a Russian Soyuz rocket bound for Space Station Alpha. He enjoyed a few days there and returned safely after eight days.

In 2004, Richard Branson of multinational company Virgin presented Virgin Galactic's plans to build a hotel in space and undertake regular space travel. Tickets were sold for a mere $200,000.

In 2007 NASA and Branson's Virgin Galactic announced they would collaborate in future manned spaceflight technology, and in 2008 construction of the first space terminal started in New Mexico.

Exercise E

Allow students to uncover the opposite page or open their books. Give them plenty of time to compare their answers with the model notes. Feed back on the final question.

Exercise F

1 Ask students to work in pairs. Assign pairs a set of notes. They must try to reconstruct the lecture orally – including the introduction – from the notes.

2 Put the pairs together in groups of four, with different topics. Each pair should give their lecture to another pair.

Closure

1 Work on any problems you noticed during the pairwork (Exercise F).

2 Refer back to the pictures at the top of the Course Book page. Students should now be able to name them with confidence.

Extra activities

1 Work through the *Vocabulary bank* and *Skills bank* if you have not already done so, or as a revision of previous study.

2 Use the *Activity bank* (Teacher's Book additional resources section, Resource 1A).

A Set the crossword for individual work (including homework) or pairwork.

Answers

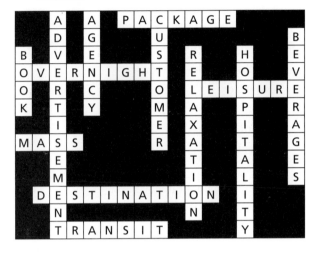

B Play noughts and crosses in pairs. There are two boards. The first contains words with affixes, the second contains names, ideas, etc.

Teach students how to play noughts and crosses if they don't know – they take it in turns to choose a word/phrase/name and try to use it in context or explain what it means. If they succeed, they can put their symbol – a nought **0** or a cross **X** – in that box. If a person gets three of their own symbols in a line, they win.

First board: Tell students to remove the affixes to find the basic word in each case. Make sure they can tell you the meaning of the basic word (e.g., *nation* for *multinational*) but don't elicit the meaning of the affixed word at this stage. Put students in pairs to play the game. Monitor and adjudicate.

Second board: Put students in different pairs to play the second game. Clearly, this time they have to actually remember the facts from the lectures. Don't let them look back at notes.

3 Each of the mini lectures from Lesson 4 can lead on to a great deal more work. Tell students to research one of the following, according to which group they ended in. Explain that they must come back and report to the rest of the class in the next lesson/next week.

Lecture	Research
1	Intangible aspects of tourism
2	Further research on the Grand Tour
3	The role of IT in bookings and reservations
4	The history of mass travel
5	Tourism in the UK
6	Space travel in the 21st century

4 Encourage students to visit a tourist office or travel agent (or browse the Internet) and collect brochures and other data. They can choose either a country or an area of a country, or a type of travel that interests them (which would cover several countries or areas). Students read the materials and prepare a short poster presentation (one or two A4s) in which they present their findings. They should highlight new tourism-related words and expressions they have picked up during their research.

5 Brainstorm note-taking techniques. For example:
- use spacing between points
- use abbreviations
- use symbols
- underline headings
- use capital letters
- use indenting
- make ordered points
- use different colours
- use key words only

2 WHAT'S YOUR KIND OF TOURISM?

Unit 2 introduces some of the many different types of tourism that exist today, such as adventure tourism, backpacking, events tourism, sports tourism and ecotourism. The first reading text looks in greater detail at a new type of tourist, the 'flashpacker'. The second reading text describes an eco-resort in Brazil and asks whether eco-tourism can ever be good for the environment.

Note that students will need dictionaries for some exercises in this unit.

Skills focus

Reading

- using research questions to focus on relevant information in a text
- using topic sentences to get an overview of the text

Writing

- writing topic sentences
- summarizing a text

Vocabulary focus

- English–English dictionaries:
  headwords
  definitions
  parts of speech
  phonemes
  stress markers
  countable/uncountable
  transitive/intransitive

Key vocabulary

accommodation	ecotourism	resort (n)
adventurous	educational tourism	rough(ing) it
adventure tourism	environment	shoestring
agritourism	events tourism	smart
backpacker	experience (n and v)	space tourism
backpacking	flashpacking	sports tourism
boom (n)	health tourism	transport (n and v)
break (n)	heritage tourism	travel (n and v)
budget (travel)	independent	traveller
cultural tourism	itinerary	trip (n)
development	lobby (n)	
disaster tourism	luxury	

2.1 Vocabulary

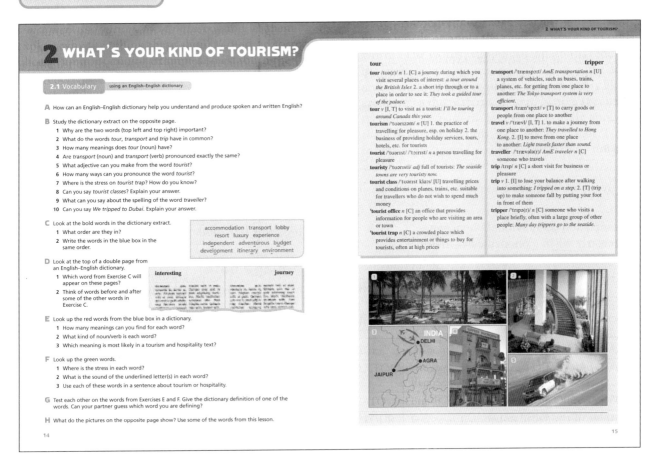

2 WHAT'S YOUR KIND OF TOURISM?

2 WHAT'S YOUR KIND OF TOURISM?

2.1 Vocabulary using an English–English dictionary

A How can an English–English dictionary help you understand and produce spoken and written English?

B Study the dictionary extract on the opposite page.
  1 Why are the two words (top left and top right) important?
  2 What do the words *tour, transport* and *trip* have in common?
  3 How many meanings does *tour* (noun) have?
  4 Are *transport* (noun) and *transport* (verb) pronounced exactly the same?
  5 What adjective can you make from the word *tourist*?
  6 How many ways can you pronounce the word *tourist*?
  7 Where is the stress on *tourist trap*? How do you know?
  8 Can you say *tourist classes*? Explain your answer.
  9 What can you say about the spelling of the word *traveller*?
  10 Can you say *We tripped to Dubai*. Explain your answer.

C Look at the bold words in the dictionary extract.
  1 What order are they in?
  2 Write the words in the blue box in the same order.

> accommodation transport lobby resort luxury experience independent adventurous budget development itinerary environment

D Look at the top of a double page of an English–English dictionary.
  1 Which word from Exercise C will appear on these pages?
  2 Think of words before and after some of the other words in Exercise C.

interesting   journey

E Look up the red words from the blue box in a dictionary.
  1 How many meanings can you find for each word?
  2 What kind of noun/verb is each word?
  3 Which meaning is most likely in a tourism and hospitality text?

F Look up the green words.
  1 Where is the stress in each word?
  2 What is the sound of the underlined letter(s) in each word?
  3 Use each of these words in a sentence about tourism or hospitality.

G Test each other on the words from Exercises E and F. Give the dictionary definition of one of the words. Can your partner guess which word you are defining?

H What do the pictures on the opposite page show? Use some of the words from this lesson.

14

tour

tour /tʊə(r)/ *n* 1. [C] a journey during which you visit several places of interest: *a tour around the British Isles* 2. a short trip through or to a place in order to see it: *They took a guided tour of the palace.*
tour *v* [I, T] to visit as a tourist: *I'll be touring around Canada this year.*
tourism /ˈtʊərɪzəm/ *n* [U] 1. the practice of travelling for pleasure, esp. on holiday 2. the business of providing holiday services, tours, hotels, etc. for tourists
tourist /ˈtʊərɪst/ /ˈtɔːrɪst/ *n* a person travelling for pleasure
touristy /ˈtʊərɪsti/ *adj* full of tourists: *The seaside towns are very touristy now.*
tourist class /ˈtʊərɪst klɑːs/ [U] travelling prices and conditions on planes, trains, etc. suitable for travellers who do not wish to spend much money
'tourist office *n* [C] an office that provides information for people who are visiting an area or town
'tourist trap *n* [C] a crowded place which provides entertainment or things to buy for tourists, often at high prices

tripper

transport /ˈtrænspɔːt/ *AmE* **transportation** *n* [U] a system of vehicles, such as buses, trains, planes, etc. for getting from one place to another: *The Tokyo transport system is very efficient.*
transport /trænˈspɔːt/ *v* [T] to carry goods or people from one place to another
travel /ˈtrævl/ [I, T] 1. to make a journey from one place to another: *They travelled to Hong Kong.* 2. [I] to move from one place to another: *Light travels faster than sound.*
traveller /ˈtrævələ(r)/ *AmE* **traveler** *n* [C] someone who travels
trip /trɪp/ *n* [C] a short visit for business or pleasure
trip *v* 1. [I] to lose your balance after walking into something: *I tripped on a step.* 2. [T] (trip up) to make someone fall by putting your foot in front of them
tripper /ˈtrɪpə(r)/ *n* [C] someone who visits a place briefly, often with a large group of other people: *Many day trippers go to the seaside.*

INDIA
DELHI
AGRA
JAIPUR

15

General note

Take in a set of English–English dictionaries.

Read the *Vocabulary bank* at the end of the Course Book unit. Decide when, if at all, to refer students to it. The best time is probably at the very end of the lesson or the beginning of the next lesson, as a summary/revision.

Lesson aims

- learn how to make full use of an English–English dictionary
- gain fluency in the target vocabulary

Introduction

1 Revise the vocabulary from the last unit. Check:
  - meaning
  - pronunciation
  - spelling

2 Ask students whether they use a translation (bilingual) dictionary or an English–English (monolingual) dictionary. Elicit the advantages and disadvantages of a translation dictionary.

Answers

Possible answers:

+	–
good when you know the word in your own language and need a translation into English	not good when there is more than one possible translation of a word – which is the correct one?
when you look up an English word, the translation into your language is easy to understand	English–English dictionaries often have more examples and precise definitions of each word

Methodology note

Recent research has shown that, despite the insistence of generations of language teachers on the use of English–English dictionaries in class, nearly 90 per cent of students use a translation dictionary when studying on their own.

Exercise A

Ask the question as a general discussion. Confirm but do not explain anything. Point out that the next exercise will make the value of this kind of dictionary clear.

Let students look at the pages that explain how a dictionary works (these pages are usually at the front) and let them talk about what kind of information they can get from the dictionary. Set for pairwork with class follow-up.

Answers

Model answers:

The following information is useful for spoken English:

- stress
- pronunciation of individual phonemes – particularly when a phoneme has multiple pronunciations

The following information is useful for written English:

- information about the type of word – C/U; T/I
- the spelling – students might make the point that if you don't know the spelling, you can't find the word in the first place, but point out that you can often guess the possible spelling – for example, *ecotourism* could be *eko* but if you don't find it there, you can try *eco* …
- examples of the word in use
- some synonyms for lexical cohesion – this is a very important point, although you may not want to elaborate on this now

Exercise B

Set for individual work and pairwork checking. Feed back, ideally using an OHT or other visual display of the dictionary extract to highlight points. You might suggest that students annotate the dictionary extract in their books, highlighting symbols, etc., and writing notes on the meaning and value.

Answers

Model answers:

1 They tell you the first and last words on the pages to help you locate the word you want.
2 All these words can both be a noun (n) and a verb (v).
3 Two.
4 No. In the noun, the stress is on the first syllable. In the verb, the stress is on the second syllable.
5 *Touristy.*
6 Two.
7 On the first syllable of the first word, indicated by ' .
8 No, *tourist class* is uncountable.

9 *Traveller* is British English spelling. *Traveler* with one *l* is American English.
10 No. *Trip* is not used as a verb in this sense. We would use *trip* as a noun: *We went on a trip to Dubai.*

Exercise C

Note: If students are from a Roman alphabet background, you may want to omit this exercise.

1 Students should quickly be able to identify alphabetical order.
2 Set for individual work and pairwork checking. Feed back, getting the words on the board in the correct order. Don't worry about stress and individual phonemes at this point – students will check this later with their dictionaries.

Language note

It may seem self-evident that words in a dictionary are in alphabetical order. But students from certain languages may not automatically recognize this. In the famous Hans Wehr dictionary of written Arabic, for example, you must first convert a given word to its root and look that up, then find the derived form. So *aflaaj* (the plural of *falaj* = irrigation channel) will not be found under A but under F since the root is *f-l-j*.

Exercise D

1 Set for pairwork. Feed back orally, explaining the principle if necessary.
2 Set for pairwork. Ask students to find words connected with tourism if they can. Feed back orally.

Answers

1 *Itinerary* will appear on the double page spread.
2 Answers depend on which words students choose.

Exercise E

Give out the dictionaries, if you have not already done so.

Remind students that dictionaries number multiple meanings of the same part of speech and multiple parts of speech. Remind them also of the countable/uncountable and transitive/intransitive markers. (Note that different dictionaries may use different methods for indicating these things. The *Oxford Advanced Learner's Dictionary*, for example, uses [V] for intransitive verbs and [Vn] for transitive verbs.)

Write the headings of the table in the Answers section on the board, and work through the first word as an example.

Set for pairwork. Feed back, building up the table in the Answers section on the board. (Students' answers will vary – accept any appropriate meanings and definitions.)

Answers

Model answers:

Word	Part of speech	Type	Meaning(s)
accommodation	n	U (BrE), C (AmE)	a place to stay
transport	n	U	a system of vehicles, such as buses, trains, planes, etc. for getting from one place to another
	v	T	carry goods and people from one place to another
lobby	n	C	a hall or passage in a hotel*
	v	T	persuade a politician to support a particular cause
resort	n	C	a holiday place, or a place considered good for your health*
	v	T	*resort to*: do something (usually unpleasant) in order to achieve something
luxury	n	U/C	1. [U] great comfort, expensive things or surroundings* 2. [C] something that is expensive but not essential
experience	n	U/C	1. [U] knowledge gained over a period of time 2. [C] events or things that happen to you*
	v	T	be affected by something

* main meaning in tourism

Exercise F

Remind students how stress and the pronunciation of individual phonemes are shown in a dictionary. Refer them to the key to symbols in the dictionary if necessary. Write the headings of the table in the Answers section on the board, and work through the first word as an example.

Set for pairwork. Feed back, building up the table in the Answers section on the board.

Answers

Model answers:

Stress	Sound	Part of speech	Type	Model sentence
inde'pendent	/ə/ or /ɪ/*	adj		He is an independent traveller, so he hates package tours.
ad'venturous	/tʃ/	adj		She has an adventurous spirit and likes to visit faraway places.
'budget	/ʌ/	n v	C I	This holiday I'm on a budget, so I can't spend too much.
de'velopment	/ə/	n	C/U	A new luxury development is opening in Cancun next month.
i'tinerary	/ə/	n	C	The travel agent e-mailed me the itinerary for my holiday.
en'vironment	/aɪ/	n	C/U (usually singular)	New developments should take the environment into account.

* depends on personal idiolect

Exercise G

Demonstrate how to do the exercise by giving a few definitions and getting students to tell you the word (without reading from the board or their books, if possible). Stick to tourism rather than general English definitions and encourage students to do the same.

Exercise H

Set for pairwork and class feedback. Let students describe the pictures and activities they see and let them ask each other questions.

For reference, the pictures show:

1 **accommodation**: a (**luxury**) **resort** hotel
2 **accommodation**: the **lobby** of an international/**luxury** hotel
3 the **itinerary** of an organized/package **tour** (to northern India)
4 **accommodation**: a **budget** hotel/hostel for backpackers
5 **adventure** holiday/**experience**: a 4-wheel drive vehicle in the desert

Closure

1 Remind students that you can identify the part of speech of an unknown word by looking at the words before or after the word, i.e.,

- nouns often come before and after verbs, so if you know that X is a verb, the next content word before or after is probably a noun
- nouns often come immediately after articles
- verbs often come after names and pronouns
- adjectives come before nouns or after the verb *be*

2 Come back to this point when you are feeding back on the reading texts in this unit.

Point out that dictionaries often use a small set of words that help to define, i.e., *place, person, device, equipment, way, kind, theory, principle*. Give definitions using these words and tell students to identify what you are defining, e.g., *It's a person who travels for pleasure (tourist, traveller); It's a place where people go to get information about an area or town they are visiting (tourist office)*, etc.

Lesson aims

● prepare for reading research

● use research questions to structure reading research

Introduction

1 Hold up an English–English dictionary and say a word from Lesson 1. Ask students where approximately they will find it in the dictionary – i.e., beginning, middle, two-thirds of the way through, etc. Follow their advice and read the word at the top left. Ask students if the target word will be before or after. Continue until you get to the right page. Repeat with several more words from Lesson 1.

2 Give definitions of some of the tourism words from Lesson 1 for students to identify.

Exercise A

Set the question for general discussion (books closed).

Exercise B

Refer students to the text from *Tourism Today* magazine. (This is a fictitious magazine.) Point out that it relates to tourism as we know it today: space tourism is the only one that looks ahead into the future. Set for individual work; feed back in pairs or to the class.

Answers

1 Answers depend on the students.

2 On the magazine cover, clockwise from top left:
    disaster tourism
    backpacking
    health tourism
    ecotourism
    (main picture) adventure tourism
Second page, clockwise from top left:
    educational tourism
    sports tourism
    heritage tourism

space tourism
agritourism
cultural tourism
events tourism

Exercise C

Set for pair or group work and encourage students to compare experiences. Class feedback.

Exercise D

Students may or may not be able to articulate preparation for reading. Elicit ideas. One thing they must identify – reading for a purpose. Point out that they should always be clear about the purpose of their reading. A series of questions to answer, or *research questions*, is one of the best purposes. To aid them in this they should also look at titles, subtitles, photos and read the first and last paragraph.

Refer students to the *Skills bank* at this stage if you wish.

Exercise E

Set for pairwork. Elicit some ideas, but do not confirm or correct.

Answers

Possible answers:

1 The article is about personal/individual tourism, specifically a variety of backpacking for people with money: 'flashpacking'.

2 *Who are the people involved in this activity?*
Why do they do it?
Where do they go?
How do they travel?

If students come up with better questions, accept these.

Exercise F

Note: *Backpacker monthly review* is a fictitious journal.

Remind students about topic sentences if they haven't mentioned them already in Exercise D. Give them time to read the topic sentences in this exercise. Make sure they have noticed the words *backpacking, flashpacking* and the names of the three countries: *Australia, Thailand* and *Argentina*. Point out that the topic sentences are in order, so they give a rough overview of the whole text. Some topic sentences clearly announce what the paragraph will be about. Others may only give a hint of how it will develop.

Remind students of the research questions they thought of in Exercise E.

Encourage students not to read ahead. Perhaps you should ask them to cover the text and only reveal each topic sentence in turn, then discuss possible contents of the paragraph. Remind them that it is not a good idea to read every part of a text unless you have to. If you have an OHP, you can tell students to close their books and just display the topic sentences from the jigsaw text in the additional resources section (Resource 2B), or you can give them as a handout (Resource 2C).

Do the first couple as examples, then set for pairwork. Feed back, eliciting and checking that they are reasonable possibilities, based on the topic sentence. You can accept multiple ideas for the same paragraph provided they are all possible.

Answers

1 Possible answers:

Topic sentence	Possible paragraph content
Many students go backpacking in their gap year, that once-in-a-lifetime period between school and college, or college and work.	where they go, what they do
Backpacking is a great way to travel, they say.	advantages of backpacking
Backpackers are proud that they 'rough it'	how they 'rough it'
Flashpacking is the latest development in personal tourism.	explanation of flashpacking
Flashpackers are looking for adventure like backpackers, but there is one important difference.	the difference between flashpacking and backpacking
Travel companies are cashing in on this development.	what travel companies are doing to exploit this trend
There are three countries where flashpacking works particularly well.	what the three countries are; why flashpacking works well there
First, there's Australia.	why flashpacking works well there
Thailand is very cheap, relatively speaking.	why flashpacking works well there
Finally, Argentina is enjoying a boom from three types of traveller.	which three types of traveller

2 Answers depend on students' research questions. Discuss.

Exercise G

Point out, if students have not already said this, that the topic sentences are normally the first sentences of each paragraph. Tell students to compare the contents of each paragraph with their predictions. Remind them of their research questions and encourage them to take notes as they read.

If necessary, the reading can be set for homework.

Discourse note

It is as well to be aware (though you may not feel it is appropriate to discuss with students at this point) that in real academic texts, the topic sentence may not be as obvious as in the texts in this unit. Sometimes there is not an explicit topic sentence, so that the overall topic of the paragraph must be inferred. Or the actual topic sentence for the paragraph can be near rather than at the beginning of the paragraph. Sometimes, also, the first sentence of a paragraph acts as a topic statement for a succession of paragraphs – as in the text on page 17, where the topic sentence *There are three countries where flashpacking works particularly well* introduces the following three paragraphs.

Closure

1 Unless you have set the reading for homework, do some extra work on oral summarizing as a comprehension check after reading (see *Skills bank – Using topic sentences to summarize*). Students work in pairs. One student says a topic sentence and the other student summarizes the paragraph from memory in his/her own words, or if necessary reads the paragraph again and then summarizes it without looking.

2 You may also want to redo the text as a jigsaw – the text is reproduced in the additional resources section at the back of this Teacher's Book (Resource 2B) to facilitate this.

3 As a further activity after reading, remind students of the note-taking skills practised in Unit 1. Discuss appropriate note-taking forms for this text. They can then write notes on the text. Tell them to keep their notes, as they will be useful for the summary exercise in Lesson 3.

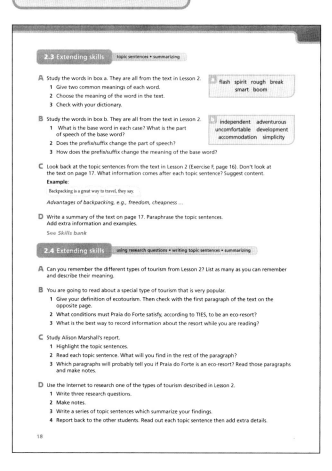

Answers

Possible answers:

Word	Sample meanings	Meaning in text
flash	1. (v) appear suddenly 2. (n) a sudden quick, bright light 3. (adj) modern and expensive-looking	3
spirit	1. a ghost 2. an attitude 3. an alcoholic drink	2
rough	1. not luxurious 2. having an uneven surface 3. not gentle	1
break	1. (n) a short holiday 2. (v) break in two/in pieces	1
smart	1. (esp. AmE) intelligent 2. operated by computers 3. (esp. BrE) well dressed and neat	3
boom	1. (n) a loud noise from an explosion 2. (n) part of a boat 3. (n) a rapid growth or increase in popularity 4. (v) grow rapidly or increase in popularity	3

Methodology note

Don't help students to find words in a text. It's a key reading skill to be able to pattern match, i.e., get a word in your mind's eye and then find it on the page.

Exercise B

Set for individual work and pairwork checking. Students can check these points in a dictionary. Feed back, taking apart the words and showing how the affixes can change the meaning.

Answers

Model answers:

Word	Base word	Affix and meaning
independent (adj)	dependent (adj) or depend (v)	*in* = not (gives an adjective its opposite meaning)
adventurous (adj)	adventure (n)	*ous* = indicates quality
uncomfortable (adj)	comfort (n)	*un* = not (gives an adjective its opposite meaning)
development (n)	develop (v)	*ment* = changes a verb into a noun
accommodation (n)	accommodate (v)	*ation* = changes a verb into a noun
simplicity (n)	simple (adj)	*city* = changes an adjective into a noun; indicates a way of doing things (a practice)

General note

Take in a set of English–English dictionaries.

Lesson aims

- produce good topic sentences and a summary text

Further practice in:

- vocabulary from Lesson 2

Introduction

Test students on the factual information in the text in Lesson 2, e.g., *What is flashpacking? How are travel companies cashing in on this development?*

If a student says, accurately, *I didn't read about that. It wasn't relevant to my research,* accept it and praise the student.

Exercise A

Set for pairwork. Refer students back to the text if necessary. Tell students to look up any cases where they didn't get two meanings. Don't let the quick ones shout them out. Feed back orally. (Students' answers will vary – accept any appropriate meanings and definitions.)

Exercise C

Ideally, display the topic sentences (or give them on a handout) so that students do not have to turn back to pages 16 and 17. The topic sentences are reproduced in the additional resources section to facilitate this (Resource 2C). Work through the example, showing that you can deduce (or in this case to some extent remember) the contents of a paragraph from the topic sentence. Do another example orally. Set for pairwork.

Feed back, eliciting possible paragraph contents and sample information. Only correct ideas which are not based on the topic sentence. Allow students to check back with the text and self-mark.

Answers

Answers depend on the students. They should be able to come up with more detail than in Lesson 2, Exercise F, as they have now read the text.

Exercise D

Refer students to the *Skills bank*. Set for individual work. If students took notes in Lesson 2, Exercise F, they should use these notes as the basis for this exercise. Encourage students to add extra information or examples to fill out the summary. Tell students to start in class, while you monitor and assist, and finish for homework.

Methodology note

There are two reasons for students to use their own words in written work (except when quoting and acknowledging sources):

1 The work involved in rewording information and ideas helps us to mentally process them and to retain them in memory.

2 Copying whole sentences from the work of other writers is plagiarism (unless the quotation is acknowledged). Universities disapprove of plagiarism and may mark down students who plagiarize. In the commercial world an accusation of plagiarism can cause legal problems, and in the academic world it can severely damage a teacher's reputation and career.

Closure

1 Give dictionary definitions of the meanings in tourism of some of the words from this lesson. Students identify the correct word. You can also play this as a class game: give two teams of students 5–10 words each and let them define these words for the other team. The team that gets most words right is the winner. Always keep a few words in reserve in case both teams are equal.

2 Ask students to do further research on the three countries mentioned as 'flashpacker' destinations (Australia, Thailand, Argentina).

2.4 Extending skills

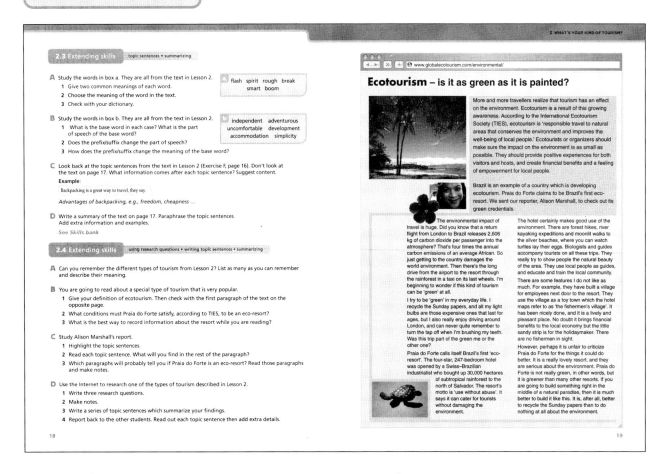

Lesson aims

- use research questions to structure reading research
- write topic sentences for a short research report/summary

Introduction

Give a word from the text in Lesson 2 which is part of a phrase. Ask students to try to complete the phrase. It's probably better if you give the first word in the phrase, but you might also try giving the second word at times or at the end of the exercise.

Possible two-word phrases:

shoe	string
tour	operator
career	break
gap	year
back	packing/packer
luxury	accommodation
round-the-world	ticket
home	comforts

Exercise A

Set for group discussion. Build up the list on the board, students' books closed.

Answers

adventure tourism
agritourism
backpacking
cultural tourism
disaster tourism
ecotourism
events tourism
educational tourism
heritage tourism
health tourism
sports tourism
space tourism

Exercise B

1 Refer students to the title of text. Set for pairwork. Feed back orally, then tell students to read the introductory paragraph of the text and compare their definition with the definition in the text.

2 Set for pairwork. Feed back, writing the criteria on the board.

3 Elicit the different kinds of notes you can use – see Unit 1 *Skills bank*. Remind students to think about the best kind of notes while they are reading.

Methodology note

It is good for students to get into the habit of thinking about the form of their notes before they read a text in detail. If they don't do this, they will tend to be drawn into narrative notes rather than notes which are specifically designed to help them answer their research questions.

Answers

Possible answers:

1 Students' own definitions. The text definition is 'responsible travel to natural areas that conserves the environment and improves the well-being of local people.'

2 According to TIES it must minimize its impact on the environment, provide positive experiences for visitors and hosts, and create financial benefits and a feeling of empowerment for local people.

3 See Unit 1 *Skills bank*.

Exercise C

1 Remind students of the importance of topic sentences. Set for individual work and pairwork checking.

2 Encourage students not to read ahead. Perhaps you should ask students to cover the text and only reveal each topic sentence in turn, then discuss possible contents of the paragraph. Remind them that it is not a good idea to read every part of a text unless you have to. If you have an OHP or other visual display, you can tell students to shut their books and just show the topic sentences from Resource 2D in the additional resources section, or you can give them as a handout.

3 Set the choice of paragraphs for pairwork. Students then read individually, make notes and compare them. Monitor and assist.

Answers

1/2 Possible answers:

Topic sentence	Possible paragraph content
The environmental impact of travel is huge.	description of impact, e.g., global warming from flying and other forms of transport
I try to be 'green' in my everyday life.	how you can be 'green' in everyday life, e.g., recycling, turn off lights, etc.
*Praia do Forte calls itself Brazil's first 'eco-resort'.	description and location of Praia do Forte; why it is an eco-resort
*The hotel certainly makes good use of the environment.	how the hotel uses the natural environment, e.g., buildings, gardens, activities
There are some features I do not like.	which features the author dislikes
*However, perhaps it is unfair to criticize Praia do Forte for the things it could do better.	positive aspects of Praia do Forte

3 Paragraphs 3, 4 and 6 of Alison Marshall's report (asterisked in the table) will probably give answers to the question.

Exercise D

Ask students to choose one of the types of tourism. Make sure that everyone has chosen.

1 Put students into groups to research the same type. Feed back, getting model research questions on the board.

2 If it is possible to research on the Internet during the lesson, send students to the computers now. They can work together. If not, set the task for homework and feed back next lesson.

3 Set for individual work and groupwork checking.

4 The idea is that students, on the basis of the topic sentences, present their information to fellow students. Make sure students realize that they only have to write the topic sentences. They can add the details in orally. Encourage them to stick to information that is relevant to their research questions.

Answers

1 Possible research questions:
What exactly is the activity?
Why do people undertake this activity?
Where do people go for this type of tourism?

2/3/4 Students' answers will depend on the type of tourism chosen and their research questions.

Closure

1 Students can use the information they gathered in Exercise D to write a full summary of their findings.

2 Ask students to talk about a type of tourism for one minute without stopping, using as many words and phrases from this unit as they can. Each student should choose a different type of tourism.

3 You may also want to redo the text as a jigsaw, as before – the text is reproduced in the additional resources section (Resource 2E) to facilitate this.

Extra activities

1 Work through the *Vocabulary bank* and *Skills bank* if you have not already done so, or as a revision of previous study.

2 Use the *Activity bank* (Teacher's Book additional resources section, Resource 2A).

   A Set the crossword for individual work (including homework) or pairwork.

   Answers

   B Students play noughts and crosses in pairs. Teach them how to play if they don't know – they take it in turns to try to use the word/ phrase in context. If they succeed, they can put their symbol – a nought 0 or a cross **X** – in that box. If a person gets three of their own symbols in a line, they win.

   You could also let them design their own board with words they have selected to challenge themselves and their 'opponent'.

3 Ask students to work in small groups to research and feed back on the other types of tourism. They should first establish their research questions. They can do their own research on the Internet, or alternatively, you can do this research before the lesson and print off some pages for them to work from. Remind students that they can't possibly read everything they find, so they must use the topic sentences to decide if a paragraph is worth reading.

4 Have a competition to practise finding words in a monolingual dictionary. Each student or pair will need an English–English dictionary. Put students in teams with their dictionaries closed. Select a word from the Unit 2 key vocabulary list (at the start of this unit of teaching notes) and instruct students to open their dictionaries and find the word. The first student to find the word is awarded a point for their team. Additional points can be awarded if the student can give the correct pronunciation and meaning.

5 Use Resource 2F in the additional resources section.

   Answers

   Model answers:

   A 1 awareness – being conscious of something
   2 impact – the influence of something or someone
   3 release – let go into the air
   4 abuse – not treating (the environment) well
   5 cater for – provide services for
   6 accompany – go along with
   7 features – attractive aspects

   B 1 The <u>environmental</u> impact of tourism on poor countries is huge.
   2 Ecotourism is the result of growing <u>awareness</u> that we have to be careful with the environment.
   3 There are many <u>financial</u> benefits for the local community.
   4 Ecotourism activities have to be <u>sustainable</u> and not damage the environment.
   5 Tourists like to enjoy <u>natural</u> beauty.
   6 I feel <u>uncomfortable</u> about flying to holiday destinations.

   C 1 economy
   This is a <u>noun</u>. The adjective is <u>economical</u>.
   2 sustain
   This is a <u>verb</u>. The adjective is <u>sustainable</u>.
   3 environment
   This is a <u>noun</u>. The adjective is <u>environmental</u>.
   4 important
   This is an <u>adjective</u>. The noun is <u>importance</u>.
   5 develop
   This is a <u>verb</u>. The noun is <u>development</u>.
   6 foreign
   This is an <u>adjective</u>. The noun is <u>foreigner</u>.
   7 education
   This is a <u>noun</u>. The adjective is <u>educational</u>.
   8 poor
   This is an <u>adjective</u>. The noun is <u>poverty</u>.
   9 aware
   This is an <u>adjective</u>. The noun is <u>awareness</u>.
   10 expense
   This is a <u>noun</u>. The adjective is <u>expensive</u>.

3 HOSPITALITY RESEARCH

In this unit, students gain a greater understanding of what hospitality is and how academics research the field.

Skills focus

🎧 Listening

- preparing for a lecture
- predicting lecture content
- making lecture notes
- using different information sources

Speaking

- reporting research findings
- formulating questions

Vocabulary focus

- stress patterns in multi-syllable words
- hospitality outlets

Key vocabulary

accommodate	guest	research (n and v)
casino	hospitality	serve
charge (n and v)	host (n)	service
consume	infrastructure	stadium/stadia
consumer	outlet	staff (n)
equipment	purchase (v)	subsidized
event	qualitative	terminal (n)
experience (n)	quantitative	theme park
facilities	real estate	venue

3.1 Vocabulary

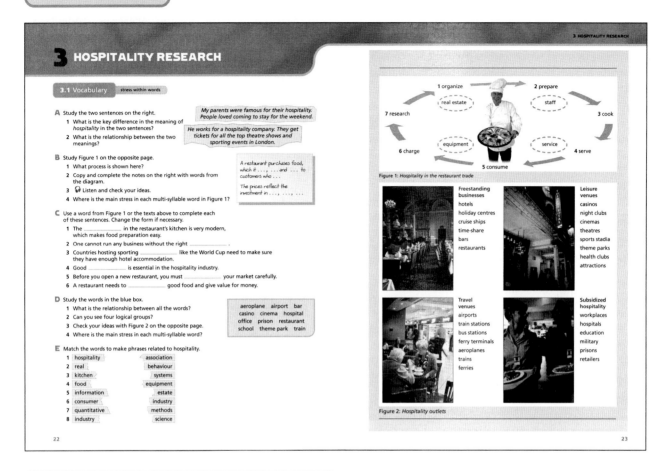

3 HOSPITALITY RESEARCH

3.1 Vocabulary   stress within words

A Study the two sentences on the right.
1 What is the key difference in the meaning of *hospitality* in the two sentences?
2 What is the relationship between the two meanings?

My parents were famous for their hospitality. People loved coming to stay for the weekend.

He works for a hospitality company. They get tickets for all the top theatre shows and sporting events in London.

B Study Figure 1 on the opposite page.
1 What process is shown here?
2 Copy and complete the notes on the right with words from the diagram.
3 Listen and check your ideas.
4 Where is the main stress in each multi-syllable word in Figure 1?

A restaurant purchases food, which it . . ., . . . and . . . to customers who . . .

The prices reflect the investment in . . ., . . ., . . .

C Use a word from Figure 1 or the texts above to complete each of these sentences. Change the form if necessary.
1 The _____ in the restaurant's kitchen is very modern, which makes food preparation easy.
2 One cannot run any business without the right _____ .
3 Countries hosting sporting _____ like the World Cup need to make sure they have enough hotel accommodation.
4 Good _____ is essential in the hospitality industry.
5 Before you open a new restaurant, you must _____ your market carefully.
6 A restaurant needs to _____ good food and give value for money.

D Study the words in the blue box.
1 What is the relationship between all the words?
2 Can you see four logical groups?
3 Check your ideas with Figure 2 on the opposite page.
4 Where is the main stress in each multi-syllable word?

aeroplane airport bar
casino cinema hospital
office prison restaurant
school theme park train

E Match the words to make phrases related to hospitality.

1	hospitality	association
2	real	behaviour
3	kitchen	systems
4	food	equipment
5	information	estate
6	consumer	industry
7	quantitative	methods
8	industry	science

22

1 organize — real estate
2 prepare — staff
7 research
3 cook
6 charge — equipment
service
4 serve
5 consume

Figure 1: Hospitality in the restaurant trade

Freestanding businesses
hotels
holiday centres
cruise ships
time-share
bars
restaurants

Leisure venues
casinos
night clubs
cinemas
theatres
sports stadia
theme parks
health clubs
attractions

Travel venues
airports
train stations
bus stations
ferry terminals
aeroplanes
trains
ferries

Subsidized hospitality
workplaces
hospitals
education
military
prisons
retailers

Figure 2: Hospitality outlets

23

General note

Read the *Vocabulary bank* at the end of the Course Book unit. Decide when, if at all, to refer your students to it. The best time is probably at the very end of the lesson or the beginning of the next lesson, as a summary/revision.

Dictionaries will be useful in this lesson.

Lesson aims

- gain fluency in the target vocabulary, including stress patterns in multi-syllable words

Introduction

1 Revise the vocabulary from the first two units. Check:
   - meaning
   - pronunciation, including stress
   - spelling

2 Write *hospi'tality* on the board. Make sure students can pronounce it with the correct word stress. Elicit from the students the three key elements of hospitality (food, drink, accommodation). Ask students to name different examples of hospitality. Do not comment or criticize. Write the names on the board. Ask students why they think these are (good) examples of hospitality. Accept any reasonable answer but force students to think about the question seriously, e.g., *Why is that a good example of hospitality? Because it shows a relationship between a host and a guest.* Check/teach the two words.

Exercise A

Set for pairwork. Feed back orally.

Answers

Possible answers:

1 The first sentence is about private hospitality. There is an idea of friendship implied in the first one. The second is about public hospitality. It is impersonal. Sometimes people go to these events even though they don't like them, just because they get free tickets.

2 In both cases there is a host and a guest.

🎧 Exercise B

1 Refer students to the diagram on the right-hand page. Set for pairwork. Feed back orally, but do not confirm or correct at this stage.

2 Set for individual work and pairwork checking. Tell students to select relevant words from the diagram. Do not feed back at this stage.

3/4 Play the recording. Feed back. Check/correct pronunciation, especially the stress in the multi-syllable words.

Answers

Possible answers:

1 Process shown – providing hospitality in a restaurant.

2/3 A restaurant purchases food, which it prepares, cooks and serves to customers who consume it on site. The prices reflect the investment in the real estate, the equipment, and the staff.

4 'organize, pre'pare, con'sume, re'search (or 'research), 'service, e'quipment, e'state (but 'real e,state)

Transcript 🎧 1.13

A restaurant purchases food, which it prepares, cooks and serves to customers who consume it on site. The prices reflect the investment in the real estate, the equipment – the kitchen equipment, tables, chairs, crockery, cutlery, and so on, and the staff – the chefs, waiters and other staff.

As a follow-up, tell students to divide the key words in Figure 1 and the texts in Exercises A and B into three categories. For example:

Verbs	Countable nouns	Uncountable nouns
organize	events	equipment
prepare	tickets	food
cook	shows	hospitality
serve	prices	investment*
consume		real estate
charge		service*
research		staff
purchase		

*can be either countable or uncountable; in this context, is uncountable

Exercise C

Set for pairwork and whole class feedback. Having used these words in the previous exercises, students should be able to complete this exercise with some ease.

Answers

Model answers:

1 The <u>equipment</u> in the restaurant's kitchen is very modern, which makes food preparation easy.

2 One cannot run any business without the right <u>staff</u>/<u>equipment</u>.

3 Countries hosting sporting <u>events</u> like the World Cup need to make sure they have enough hotel accommodation.

4 Good <u>service</u> is essential in the hospitality industry.

5 Before you open a new restaurant, you must <u>research</u> your market carefully.

6 A restaurant needs to <u>serve</u> good food and give value for money.

Exercise D

1 Set for individual work and pairwork checking.

2 Set for general discussion.

3 Refer students to Figure 2. Discuss the categories and check students understand the other examples listed. Ask students to cover Figure 2 or close their books and tell you some of the places in each category. Point out the plural *stadia*. Establish that *stadiums* is also correct usage.

Answers

Model answers:

1 Students should be able to say that there is a hospitality aspect to all these places – there is a host and a guest (even if the guest, a prisoner, is not there by choice!).

2/3 Freestanding businesses = businesses in their own right

Leisure venues = businesses which are part of other organizations

Travel venues = businesses related to the travel sector

Subsidized hospitality = hospitality that is not paid for (or not entirely paid for) by customers at the point of consumption but (for example) through taxation

Exercise E

This is further practice in using key words. Allow students to come up with different combinations, e.g., *consumer association, food industry,* and let them explain why they think these should/could be correct. Elicit definitions and/or examples to establish the meaning of the phrases. Check/correct pronunciation, and ask students to identify the stress in multi-syllable words and phrases.

Answers

Model answers:

1	ˌhospiˈtality	ˌindustry
2	ˈreal	eˌstate
3	ˈkitchen	eˌquipment
4	ˈfood	ˌscience
5	inforˈmation	ˌsystems
6	conˌsumer	beˈhaviour
7	ˈquantitative	ˌmethods
8	ˈindustry	associˈation

Closure

1 Check meanings of words using Figures 1 and 2. Ideally, use an OHT or other display method to work through the possible meanings again.

2 If you have not already done so, refer students to the *Vocabulary bank* at the end of Unit 3. Work through some or all of the stress patterns.

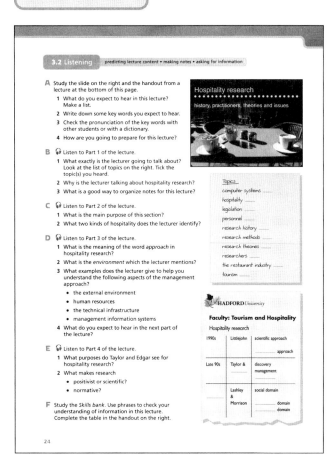

Exercise A

Refer students to the lecture slide at the top of the page and the handout at the bottom of the page. Write the title *Hospitality research* on the board.

1 Set for individual work and pairwork checking. Feed back, eliciting some ideas.

2 Brainstorm to elicit key words. Allow the class to decide whether a word should be included.

3 Set for pairwork.

4 Elicit some points – the four Ps (Plan, Prepare, Predict, Produce). If necessary, refer students to Unit 1 *Skills bank* to review preparation for a lecture. One way to help students to make provisional notes is to:

● brainstorm what they would include

● organize their topics into a logical sequence

Exercise B

1 Tell students they are only going to hear the introduction to the lecture. Ask what information they expect to get from the introduction (i.e., the outline of the lecture). Give students time to read the choices of topics. Check that they understand the meaning and relevance. Remind them they will only hear the introduction once, as in a lecture. Play Part 1. Allow them to compare answers. Feed back. Ask them to justify their choice by saying what they heard related to it. Confirm the correct answer.

2 Elicit ideas. Confirm or correct.

3 Elicit ideas.

Answers

Model answers:

1 hospitality, research history, research methods, research theories, researchers

2 It represents an important share of world economy; a lot of research has been done over the past 20 years.

3 Perhaps into a table (as in the handout at the bottom of the Course Book page), or a timeline, or headings with bullet points, e.g.,

Hospitality research

● …

● …

● …

General note

Read the *Skills bank* at the end of the Course Book unit. Decide when, if at all, to refer students to it. The best time is probably at the very end of the lesson or the beginning of the next lesson, as a summary/revision.

Lesson aims

● ask for information to complete notes

Further practice in:

● planning and preparing for a lecture

● predicting lecture content

● choosing the best form of notes

● making notes

Introduction

Review key vocabulary from Lesson 1.

Transcript 🎧 1.14

Part 1

Today, we're going to talk about hospitality research. It's a fairly new research area, but as hospitality represents a huge share of the economies of many countries in the world, it's worthwhile looking into it. Did you know that last year expenditure on travel and tourism exceeded 6 trillion US dollars globally, according to the WTTC, the World Travel and Tourism Council? You can imagine that hospitality represents a large share of that.

During this lecture, you will see that hospitality has been the subject of much academic research and debate over the past 20 years or so. First, we'll briefly look at what it actually means to be hospitable. Then we'll consider the history of hospitality research over the past 20 years. We'll look at the most important researchers of the past and present, and we'll study the most important theories and approaches or methods they've come up with. Even though, as I just indicated, tourism and hospitality are closely linked, we will not focus on tourism really this time round.

🎧 Exercise C

Before playing Part 2, refer students to the diagram in Lesson 1 again (Figure 1) and establish what it represents. Ask students what they expect to hear in Part 2, based on the introduction (Part 1). Give them time to read the questions. Tell them to write only brief notes – the main task is to absorb the meaning. Play Part 2.

Allow them to compare their answers. Give them time to answer the questions. Feed back.

When they thoroughly understand the concept of *hospitality*, ask them what they expect in the next part of the lecture. Elicit ideas but do not confirm or correct.

Answers

Model answers:

1 To define hospitality.
2 Private hospitality, and the hospitality industry (= for profit).

Transcript 🎧 1.15

Part 2

Hospitality has been defined as two very different things. In general terms, it is seen as being hospitable, as the reception and entertainment of guests, visitors, or strangers, with goodwill. Needless to say, hospitality also refers to the hospitality industry: hotels, restaurants, casinos, resorts, clubs and any place or service that deals with tourists and making them feel at home. You could simply define hospitality as 'providing accommodation, food and drink', as some researchers do, but as Paul Slattery writes in his article 'Finding the Hospitality Industry': 'Hospitality customers not only buy products, but also facilities and services.' Let's look at a restaurant, for instance, he says. 'A restaurant purchases food, which it prepares and cooks; it serves meals to customers who consume them on site. The prices reflect the investment in the real estate, the kitchen equipment, the chefs, the waiters and other staff, the tables, chairs and the atmosphere by the use of light, sound, colours, art and design and also the form of service. The task for the restaurant is to identify the specific demands of the customers at any time, and to organize the technology and processes to deliver the products, facilities and services so that customers achieve their aims in the restaurant.' I'm sure you hadn't looked at going out for a meal in this way, right?

🎧 Exercise D

1 Play the first two sentences of Part 3. Ask the first question and elicit ideas.

2 Set the second question for individual work and pairwork checking. Play the rest of the recording. Tell students to take notes. Allow students to compare their ideas. Don't, at this stage, confirm the answers.

3/4 Set for pairwork. Feed back.

Answers

Model answers:

1 An *approach* is the way in which researchers do their research. Synonyms: *method*, *philosophy*, *school* (*of thought*). Write all these words on the board.

2 The *environment* refers to the 'world' or business environment that hospitality businesses operate in; it does not refer to the 'natural' environment. (Also see 3.)

3 The examples given are included in the table on the next page. Students will probably not get all the examples from a single listening.

the external environment	what's going on in the industry, like changes in legislation, government regulation, the state of the economy, etc.
human resources	the people in the industry, such as hospitality staff, but also issues like management and training
the technical infrastructure	what you need to provide a service, such as front office integrated software packages, closed-circuit TV security systems, communication facilities, etc.
management information systems	the data you need to make decisions that allow you to improve hospitality services; how to gather and use this

4 A good prediction would be: *First the lecturer will talk about hospitality research in the past, then at more recent hospitality research theories.*

Transcript 🎧 1.16

Part 3

In the past two decades, hospitality has become the subject of much academic research. Based on research by Littlejohn in the 1990s, you could say there were two main approaches.

In the beginning, research was dominated by the natural and physical sciences, such as food science, technical equipment design or technical equipment testing. It was a very scientific type of research and, as you will see, very limited.

Another approach to research was the management approach. This took a much wider view. It looked at the balance between four areas. It studied the external environment: what's going on in the industry, what changes there are in legislation, government regulation, the state of the economy, etc. It studied human resources: the people in the industry, such as hospitality staff, but also issues like management and training. It studied the technical infrastructure: what you need to provide a service, such as front office integrated software packages, closed-circuit TV security systems, communication facilities, etc. And it studied management information systems: the software and data you need to make decisions which allow you to improve hospitality services, how to gather such data and what to do with it.

🎧 Exercise E

Tell students that this is the last part of the lecture. What do they expect to hear? Confirm that it is partly a summary. Allow them time to read the questions. Play Part 4.

1 Allow students to discuss the question in pairs or groups, then feed back as a class.
2 Elicit ideas. Get students to think of a research project of a normative or positivist nature. Write suggestions on the board: they do not necessarily have to be about hospitality if students found that too difficult.

Answers

Model answers:

1 The three purposes are:
- making sense of existing behaviour/discovery
- discovering new ways of managing within the hospitality industry
- enabling hospitality faculties at colleges and universities to educate future practitioners

2 A positivist or scientific approach focuses on facts and data that you can gather and prove (quantitative research); a normative approach is also interested in opinions and feelings (a qualitative approach).

Transcript 🎧 1.17

Part 4

Now, how has this research developed since then, and what theories have come up in recent times? In the late 1990s, Taylor and Edgar reviewed the hospitality research debate, including all the work done by Littlejohn, and they suggested that there were three purposes to hospitality research.

The first purpose is to uncover and make sense of existing behaviour. What is happening in the industry, what's out there? The focus is discovery. This is essentially a positivist or scientific approach, a method that looks at facts, data, things that can be quantified, not feelings.

The second one is to discover new ways of managing within the hospitality industry. Here the focus is on management. This is a normative approach, which is in contrast to the scientific. Normative researchers are interested in what people think and feel about hospitality.

The third purpose is to enable hospitality faculties at colleges and universities to educate future practitioners – an educational approach.

What happened after that? Well, a breakthrough really came in 2000, when Lashley and Morrison published *In Search of Hospitality – Theoretical Perspectives and Debates*. They argued that there were three domains of hospitality: there was the social domain (what happens between people on social occasions that are public), the private domain (what happens on a private level within families when they receive guests) and the commercial domain (how companies organize things). And there are various ways of looking at these domains.

OK, that'll be enough for now. We'll continue the lecture from there after the break.

Exercise F

Set for pairwork. Refer students to the *Skills bank* and encourage them to use the model questions to ask each other for information to complete the table.

Answers

Model answers:

1990s	Littlejohn	scientific approach <u>management</u> approach
Late 90s	Taylor & <u>Edgar</u>	discovery management <u>education</u>
2000	Lashley & Morrison	social domain <u>private</u> domain <u>commercial</u> domain

Closure

Ask students to explain in their own words:

- what hospitality is
- what the most important research theories are

3.3 Extending skills

3.3 Extending skills   stress within words • using information sources • reporting findings

Lesson aim

This lesson is the first in a series about writing an assignment or giving a presentation based on research. The principal objective of this lesson is to introduce students to sources of information.

Introduction

1 Tell students to ask you questions about the information in the lecture in Lesson 2 as if you were the lecturer. Refer them to the *Skills bank* again for typical language if you wish. This activity links up with the last activity of Lesson 2.

2 Put students in pairs. Student A must ask Student B about the information in the lecture in Lesson 2 to help him/her complete the notes from the lecture. Then they reverse roles. Go round, helping students to identify gaps in their notes and to think of good questions to get the missing information. Refer them to the *Skills bank* if you wish for language they can use in the pairwork.

Pairs then compare notes and decide what other information would be useful and where they could get it from. For example, technical definitions of the key words might be useful, from a specialist dictionary or an encyclopedia. In the feedback,

write a list of research sources on the board, at least including dictionaries, encyclopedias, specialist reference books and the Internet.

Point out that dictionaries are good for definitions, although you may need to go to a specialist dictionary for a technical word. Otherwise, try an encyclopedia, because technical words are often defined in articles when they are first used. You could also try Google's 'define' feature, i.e., type *define: hospitality* but remember you will get definitions from all disciplines not just your own, so you need to scan to check the relevant one.

Exercise A

Point out the importance of stressed syllables in words – see *Language note*.

In this exercise, students will hear each word with the stressed syllable emphasized, and the rest of the syllables underspoken.

Play the recording, pausing after the first few to check that students understand the task. Feed back, perhaps playing the recording again for each word before checking. Ideally, mark up an OHT of the words.

Language note

In English, speakers emphasize the stressed syllable in a multi-syllable word. Sometimes listeners may not even hear the unstressed syllables. Vowels, in any case, often change to schwa or a reduced form in unstressed syllables. Therefore it is essential that students can recognize key words from the stressed syllable alone when they hear them in context.

Answers

accommodate	5
accommodation	1
association	9
casino	7
consume	4
entertainment	6
equipment	2
facilities	8
industry	10
investment	3
purchase	12
subsidized	11

Transcript 🎧 1.18

1 accommo'dation
2 e'quipment
3 in'vestment
4 con'sume
5 a'ccommodate
6 enter'tainment
7 ca'sino
8 fa'cilities
9 associ'ation
10 'industry
11 'subsidized
12 'purchase

Exercise B

Erase the words or turn off the OHT. Ask students to guess or remember where the stressed syllable is on each word. Tell them to mark their idea with a light vertical stroke in pencil. Elicit and drill. Refer students to the *Vocabulary bank* at this stage if you wish.

Answers

See transcript for Exercise A.

Exercise C

Set for pair or group work. Go round and assist/correct.

Exercise D

Put students in groups. Encourage them to use the language from the *Skills bank* to get information from others. Feed back, building up the table in the Answers section on the board. The more meaningful sentences students come up with, the better.

Answers

Model answers:
See table below.

Exercise E

Remind students again about the four Ps. Refer students to the lecture topics and the questions. Make sure they understand that all three questions relate to before, rather than during, the lecture. Work through as a whole class if you wish.

Answers

Possible answers:

1 Look up key words in a dictionary or encyclopedia, or on the Internet. Check pronunciation so you will recognize the words in the lecture.

2 Lecture 1: definitions, examples, facts/statistics

Lecture 2: what systems theory is; researchers/practitioners

Lecture 3: principal types of hospitality education; main content; differences between countries

3 Perhaps do a spidergram so that it is easier to brainstorm with fellow students and cover all the possible areas that the lecturer might focus on.

Stress	Example sentence
aca'demic	Universities do a lot of academic research into hospitality.
a'pproach	The approach the researchers took was very technical.
'argue	The researchers argued that the systems theory was the best one.
be'haviour	Staff behaviour is a better guide to the quality of a service company than any statement of mission.
con'sider	Researchers should consider all the factors that might affect performance.
con'tribute	Many people contributed to the research report.
de'fine	Before we start, we must define exactly what we aim to do.
'journal	They published the research result in an academic journal.
'normative	Normative work is qualitative.
per'formance	We assessed the performance of the restaurant in terms of speed of service.
prac'titioner	Many practitioners from the restaurant business participated in the research project.
'qualitative	Qualitative research looks at people's opinions and feelings.
'quantitative	The research team gathered a lot of quantitative data.
re'flect	The report reflected the need of the hospitality sector for data and hard numbers.
re'view	The journal presented a review of all the research done so far.

Exercise F

Set for pairwork. If students have access in class to reference material, allow them to at least start the activity in class. Otherwise, set for homework. Before the feed back to partner stage, refer students to the *Skills bank – Reporting information to other people*. Possible websites (at the time of writing) include www.htrends.com, www.hotelschool.cornell.edu/chr/, www.icthr.bournemouth.ac.uk.

Closure

Dictate sentences with words from Exercise A in context for students to identify the words again.

3.4 Extending skills

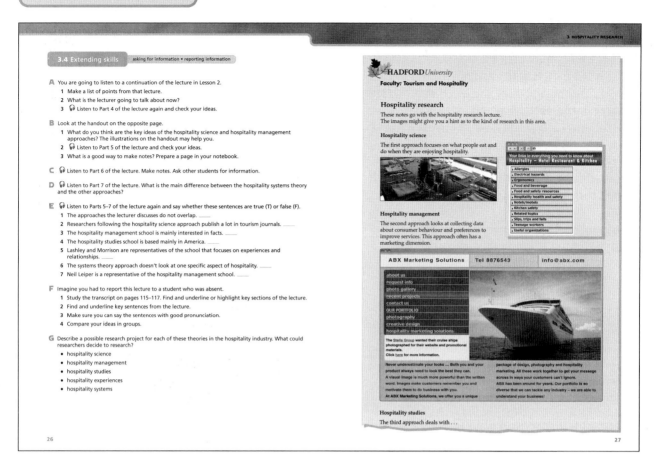

3.4 Extending skills asking for information • reporting information

A You are going to listen to a continuation of the lecture in Lesson 2.
1 Make a list of points from that lecture.
2 What is the lecturer going to talk about now?
3 🎧 Listen to Part 4 of the lecture again and check your ideas.

B Look at the handout on the opposite page.
1 What do you think are the key ideas of the hospitality science and hospitality management approaches? The illustrations on the handout may help you.
2 🎧 Listen to Part 5 of the lecture and check your ideas.
3 What is a good way to make notes? Prepare a page in your notebook.

C 🎧 Listen to Part 6 of the lecture. Make notes. Ask other students for information.

D 🎧 Listen to Part 7 of the lecture. What is the main difference between the hospitality systems theory and the other approaches?

E 🎧 Listen to Parts 5–7 of the lecture again and say whether these sentences are true (T) or false (F).
1 The approaches the lecturer discusses do not overlap. ___
2 Researchers following the hospitality science approach publish a lot in tourism journals. ___
3 The hospitality management school is mainly interested in facts. ___
4 The hospitality studies school is based mainly in America. ___
5 Lashley and Morrison are representatives of the school that focuses on experiences and relationships. ___
6 The systems theory approach doesn't look at one specific aspect of hospitality. ___
7 Neil Leiper is a representative of the hospitality management school. ___

F Imagine you had to report this lecture to a student who was absent.
1 Study the transcript on pages 115–117. Find and underline or highlight key sections of the lecture.
2 Find and underline key sentences from the lecture.
3 Make sure you can say the sentences with good pronunciation.
4 Compare your ideas in groups.

G Describe a possible research project for each of these theories in the hospitality industry. What could researchers decide to research?
• hospitality science
• hospitality management
• hospitality studies
• hospitality experiences
• hospitality systems

HADFORD *University*

Faculty: Tourism and Hospitality

Hospitality research
These notes go with the hospitality research lecture.
The images might give you a hint as to the kind of research in this area.

Hospitality science
The first approach focuses on what people eat and do when they are enjoying hospitality.

Hospitality management
The second approach looks at collecting data about consumer behaviour and preferences to improve services. This approach often has a marketing dimension.

Hospitality studies
The third approach deals with . . .

26   27

Lesson aims

Further practice in:
- choosing the best form of notes
- making notes
- asking for information from fellow students to complete notes
- reporting information

Introduction

Elicit as much information from the lecture in Lesson 2 as possible. If necessary, prompt students by reading parts of the transcript and pausing for students to complete in their own words.

🎧 Exercise A

Remind students of the language involved in asking for information from other people – see *Skills bank*. Drill some of the sentences if you wish.

1/2 Set for pairwork. Encourage students to ask each other for information.

3 Play Part 4 of the lecture from Lesson 2 again to enable students to check their answers. Feed back.

Elicit information from the students' research. Do not confirm or correct at this stage except pronunciation mistakes on key words.

Answers

Possible answers:

1 Part 2: Two kinds of hospitality: personal hospitality, and the hospitality industry.

Part 3: Early hospitality research:

1990s: focus on scientific/technical aspects; management approach.

Part 4: More recent research:

Late 1990s (Taylor and Edgar): the purposes of research: to understand existing behaviour; to establish new ways of managing within the hospitality industry; to educate future practitioners.

2000 (Lashley and Morrison): social domain, private domain, commercial domain.

2/3 Recent research/research methods.

Transcript 🎧 **1.17**

Part 4

Now, how has this research developed since then, and what theories have come up in recent times? In the late 1990s, Taylor and Edgar reviewed the hospitality research debate, including all the work done by Littlejohn, and they suggested that there were three purposes to hospitality research.

The first purpose is to uncover and make sense of existing behaviour. What is happening in the industry, what's out there? The focus is discovery. This is essentially a positivist or scientific approach, a method that looks at facts, data, things that can be quantified, not feelings.

The second one is to discover new ways of managing within the hospitality industry. Here the focus is on management. This is a normative approach, which is in contrast to the scientific. Normative researchers are interested in what people think and feel about hospitality.

The third purpose is to enable hospitality faculties at colleges and universities to educate future practitioners – an educational approach.

What happened after that? Well, a breakthrough really came in 2000, when Lashley and Morrison published *In Search of Hospitality – Theoretical Perspectives and Debates*. They argued that there were three domains of hospitality: there was the social domain (what happens between people on social occasions that are public), the private domain (what happens on a private level within families when they receive guests) and the commercial domain (how companies organize things). And there are various ways of looking at these domains.

OK, that'll be enough for now. We'll continue the lecture from there after the break.

🎧 Exercise B

Refer students to the illustrations.

1 Ask students to make the list. Do not confirm or correct.

2 Play Part 5. Feed back orally.

3 Set for pairwork discussion then individual work. Feed back.

Answers

1/2 The illustrations suggest the following, but accept other good alternatives:
Hospitality science is mainly concerned with rather technical issues such as food (diet, nutrition) and technology (equipment, ergonomics).

Hospitality management looks, among other things, at how to market your hospitality service, public relations and presentation (design).

3 The best way is probably to write 1–5, then the five key words in the left-hand column. Don't tell them the ones they can't remember. It would be quite normal in a lecture that they can't write all of them down. If they don't remember them all this time, they should at least put the key words they remember in order. They can then listen for the other key words as the text develops.

Transcript 🎧 **1.19**

Part 5

So, where does that lead us now? Having looked at the history of hospitality research, it's time to look at the present day. At the moment, there are five principal schools of thought when it comes to hospitality. When I say that, I realize that we do have to generalize a bit, of course, when talking about this. In practice, you will see that these approaches sometimes overlap. They are, after all, ways of looking at the same reality.

First, there's the hospitality science school. Studies of this type include research into people's diet, their nutrition, ergonomics – or how they sit and stand, equipment performance, and so on. There have been research journals in hospitality that report on this type of research but more and more hospitality-related studies of this type are published in specialist journals such as the *British Food Journal*. Hospitality researchers don't tend to read these, but practitioners in hospitality do.

The second principal school of thought is the hospitality management school. It's a very popular one and it's based on what we call quantitative studies, in other words, things that can be measured: how often, how much, how long, how many and things like that. And they're often related to studies of hospitality marketing, or consumer behaviour. It's based largely in North America; the *Journal of Hospitality and Tourism Management* is a good example of this approach.

🎧 Exercise C

Play Part 6 of the lecture. When students have done their best individually, put them in pairs or small groups to complete their notes by asking for information from the other student(s).

Answers

Model answers:

Research	Type/focus	Journals/books
3 hospitality studies	qualitative – what people feel about hospitality also quantitative	*International Journal of Hotel Management Tourism and Hospitality Research* (UK)
4 hospitality experiences (new/growing)	relationships and interaction between people and hospitality experiences	*In Search of Hospitality* (Lashley and Morrison – UK)

Transcript 🎧 1.20

Part 6

The third school of thought is hospitality studies, which uses qualitative, as well as quantitative, methods to look into what people feel about hospitality. Qualitative methods are those that allow people to find out not so much how often, or how much, but why, and what for, and what's the effect of it, and how do people feel about it, which, of course, is extremely important too in this industry. This school is based largely in the UK, and reflected in the *International Journal of Hotel Management* and a journal like *Tourism and Hospitality Research*.

The fourth school is the one that looks into hospitality experiences. This is a new and growing school of thought. It focuses on the relationships and interaction between people and the experiences they have when they enjoy hospitality. It emerged in the UK and, as I said, you can find out about it in Lashley and Morrison's book *In Search of Hospitality*.

🎧 Exercise D

Set for pairwork. Play Part 7 of the lecture. As before, give students time to do their own work, then set for pair or group completion.

Answer

The most important aspect of the answer should be the realization that where other approaches look at aspects of the hospitality industry, systems theory looks at everything as an integrated whole.

Transcript 🎧 1.21

Part 7

The final approach is called hospitality systems theory and there are Canadian, UK and Australian academics who have contributed to this. Like the hospitality studies school, it uses a normative approach, but it also builds on a basic philosophy. What is that philosophy? According to this approach, everything that happens in hospitality is linked. Remember that in an earlier lecture we talked about TDRs and TGRs? Systems theory looks at things like that, but also at what happens in between – transport, the environment, people, technology, finance, everything. We see systems theory reflected in the work of Professor Neil Leiper in Australia.

So, there we are. These are the five most important approaches to hospitality research – the hospitality science school, the hospitality management school, hospitality studies, the hospitality experiences model and the hospitality systems theory. Next time, when we get together, we'll look at tourism and hospitality, and how they merged together. We'll also have a look at the systems thinking of Neil Leiper.

Exercise E

Set for individual work and pairwork checking. Play Parts 5–7 of the lecture again if you have to. Feed back orally. Point out that if students do miss information on the way through a lecture, they should wait for the recap which often comes at the end. This recap may enable them to fill in some of the missing information.

Answers

Model answers:

1	false	The approaches do overlap, according to the lecturer.
2	false	They publish in specialist journals in this field.
3	true	
4	false	It is based largely in the UK.
5	true	
6	true	
7	false	Professor Leiper works in the field of hospitality systems theory.

Exercise F

Refer students to the transcript at the back of the Course Book.

1 Help students to find a key section. Set for individual work to find more.
2 Help students to find a key sentence. Set for individual work to find more.
3 Set for pairwork – students help each other. Monitor and assist.
4 Put students in groups to check whether they have all found the same sections/sentences.

At the end, play the part of the absent student. Act a little stupid – unless a student is absolutely clear in their summary and/or direct quotation, deliberately misunderstand and get another student to try to clarify.

Methodology note

End all listening lessons by referring students to the transcript at the back of the Course Book so they can read the text while the aural memory is still clear. You could set this as standard homework after a listening lesson. You can also get students to highlight key sections and underline key sentences, as in Exercise F above.

Exercise G

Set for group work. Feed back, getting students' ideas on the board. Answers will depend on students' input.

Answers

Possible answers:

Hospitality science: food quality and hygiene in seaside resorts in Italy

Hospitality management: how to train and retain staff in summer camps in America

Hospitality studies: a qualitative analysis of what visitors feel about Italian restaurants outside Italy, combined with a survey of visitor numbers

Hospitality experiences: tourist satisfaction in Disney theme parks around the world

Hospitality systems: the effect of travel on tourist routes

Closure

Elicit students' own ideas about the different schools of hospitality research. Do they think one school/approach is more valid than another?

Extra activities

1 Work through the *Vocabulary bank* and *Skills bank* if you have not already done so, or as a revision of previous study.

2 Use the *Activity bank* (Teacher's Book additional resources section, Resource 3A).

A Set the coded crossword for individual work (including homework). They can copy the words into their notebooks and check the definitions of any words they can't remember.

Answers

B This game practises pronunciation and meaning recognition. It can only be played in groups in class.

Students must think of one word for each of the categories on the bingo card. Allow them to use any of the vocabulary from this unit. They should write their words on card 1, or copy the bingo grid into their notebooks.

Each student says one of their own words at random once only, concentrating on the pronunciation. The others must identify the category and cross it out on card 2.

The winner is the first student to identify the correct category for all the words. If the teacher keeps a record of which words have been said, he/she can say when a successful card could have been completed.

3 Students can play this alphabet game by themselves or as a group/class. The aim is to think of a word related to tourism and hospitality for each letter of the alphabet. For example:

Student A: **a**ccommodation

Student B: **a**ccommodation, **b**ehaviour

Student C: **a**ccommodation, **b**ehaviour, **c**onsume

Each student adds something from the next letter of the alphabet. They should try to use words from the unit if possible. A student misses a turn if he/she can't remember the items, or add another letter.

4 Tell students to research hospitality events on the Web. They will need to search with key words/phrases such as "hospitality events". This will lead them to many sites from events companies and they will be able to research what they offer (corporate events, sports events, trade shows, etc.). Students should report back in the next lesson.

5 Choose one of the hospitality businesses from Lesson 1 (Figure 2) and describe this in the same way as in the diagram (Figure 1), in the way systems theory would do this.

4 CAREERS IN TOURISM AND HOSPITALITY

The theme of this unit is careers in tourism, hospitality and travel. However, aspects of the use of the Internet and computers for research relevant to tourism and hospitality students are also addressed.

Students will need access to a computer with an Internet connection for some exercises. Check that all students have used the Internet. If any haven't, sit them beside someone who has, to guide them.

Skills focus

Reading

- identifying topic development within a paragraph
- using the Internet effectively
- evaluating research results

Writing

- reporting research findings

Vocabulary focus

- computer jargon
- abbreviations and acronyms
- job titles
- discourse and stance markers
- verb and noun suffixes

Key vocabulary

adaptable	employee rewards	qualification
attitude	industrial and employee	recreation
attraction	relations	recruitment
benefits (n)	job training	redundancy
career development	occupation	rise (v)
catering	opportunity	satisfaction
challenge (n)	performance management	traineeship
dedicated (adj)	personality	transferable skills

Positions/jobs/careers

There is a large selection of names for positions/jobs/careers in this unit. Students will not necessarily need to learn all these, and the list is by no means exhaustive, but they are useful in terms of the ability to talk about careers.

chef	food and beverage	interior designer	sales rep
events planner	manager	marketing agent	travel agent
events manager	hiking guide	museum curator	receptionist
fitness instructor	housekeeper	overseas rep	

Abbreviations and acronyms

These are explained on page 31 of the Course Book.

Job titles: CEO, CFO, COO, DOO, GM, HRD, MD

Industry-related: AIT, APD, ARR, B&B, F&B, FIT, IT, QA, T&T, TIC, TIP, VAT

4.1 Vocabulary

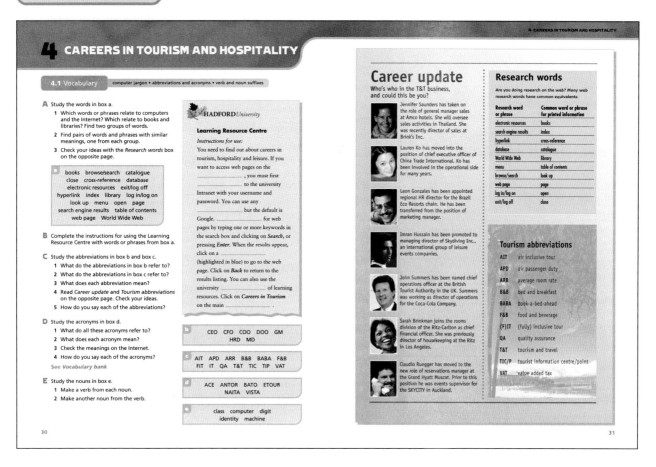

General note

If possible, hold this lesson in a room where there is a computer.

Read the *Vocabulary bank* at the end of the Course Book unit. Decide when, if at all, to refer your students to it. The best point is probably at the end of the lesson or the beginning of the next lesson, as a summary/revision.

Lesson aims

- gain fluency in the meaning, pronunciation and spelling of key acronyms and abbreviations from the field

- start thinking about careers in tourism, hospitality and leisure and become familiar with useful computer terminology that can facilitate careers research

- understand how verbs can be formed from nouns, and nouns from verbs, through the addition of suffixes

Introduction

Familiarize students with computer terminology using some or all of the following activities.

1 Using a computer or a picture of a computer as a starting point, elicit some or all of the following vocabulary.

PC	*laptop*	*database*
monitor	*screen*	*the Web*
icon	*keyboard*	*desktop*
mouse	*program*	*keys*
floppy disk	*DVD*	*hard disk*
CD	*printer*	*slot*
accessory	*Internet*	*USB port*
CD burner	*e-mail*	*scanner*

2 Ask students to suggest verbs used in computing. Elicit some or all of the following. A good way to do this is to open a program such as Word (in English) and look at the words and symbols on the toolbars.

switch on	*start up*	*shut down*
log on/log off	*click*	*double-click*
hold	*press*	*open*
close	*exit*	*save*
select	*copy*	*paste*
enter	*delete*	*insert*
highlight	*undo*	

3 Ask students whether they normally use the library or the Internet to find information. Elicit the advantages and disadvantages of both. (There is so much emphasis on using computers nowadays, students often forget that there is a lot of information readily to hand in the library.)

Answers

Possible answers:

Library

+	–
easy to look things up in a dictionary or an encyclopedia	books can be out of date
you can find information in your own language	the book may not be in the library when you want it
information is usually correct	most books can't be accessed from home (though this is now starting to change)

Internet

+	–
a lot of information from different sources	difficult to find the right keywords
information is usually more up-to-date than books	difficult to know which results are the best
can be accessed from home	information is often not correct
you can quickly and easily get copies of books or journal articles not in your library	you may have to pay for the books/articles/information

Exercise A

Ask students to study the words in the box and elicit that they all relate to research.

Set for pairwork. If necessary, give an example of a pair: *index, search engine results*. Tell students to justify the pairs they choose. To help students understand what a database is, refer to ones they are familiar with in your college, e.g., student records, exam results, library catalogues, etc.

Students may argue that some terms are not exact equivalents, e.g., *catalogue/database*. Discuss any objections as they arise.

Answers

Model answers:

Research word or phrase	Common word or phrase for printed information
electronic resources	books
search engine results	index
hyperlink	cross-reference
database	catalogue
World Wide Web	library
menu	table of contents
browse/search	look up
web page	page
log in/log on	open
exit/log off	close

Language note

Log in and *log on*: these two verbs are used a little differently. *Log in* is used when accessing a closed system such as a college Intranet. Log on is used for open systems such as the Internet in general, as in *You can log on to the Internet with a hand-held computer*. Note also that the related noun has now become one word (*login*). The opposite of *log in* is *log out*, while the opposite of *log on* is *log off*.

Exercise B

Set for individual work and pairwork checking. Ensure that students read all the text and have a general understanding of it before they insert the missing words.

Feed back by reading the paragraph or by using an OHT or other visual display of the text. Discuss alternative ideas and decide whether they are acceptable. Verify whether errors are due to using new words or to misunderstanding the text.

Answers

Model answers:

You need to find out about careers in tourism, hospitality and leisure. If you want to access web pages on the World Wide Web, you must first log in to the university Intranet with your username and password. You can use any search engine but the default is Google. Browse/Search for web pages by typing one or more keywords in the search box and clicking on *Search*, or pressing *Enter*. When the results appear, click on a hyperlink (highlighted in blue) to go to the web page. Click on *Back* to return to the results listing. You can also use the university database of learning resources. Click on *Careers in Tourism* on the main menu.

Exercise C

1/2 Set for pairwork.

3/4 For abbreviations in box b, refer students to the *Career update* section on the opposite page. Monitor but do not assist. Feed back, building up the list on the board. These abbreviations are not necessarily exclusive to the tourism and hospitality sector, but are used in the *Career update*, which is industry-related.

For abbreviations in box c, tell students to pick out the ones they already know first (B&B is probably a familiar one, and perhaps VAT), then check with the table of abbreviations on the opposite page.

5 Set for pairwork. Feed back, eliciting ideas on pronunciation and confirming or correcting. Make sure students can say letter names and vowel sounds correctly.

Answers

1 They are all to do with jobs/job titles.

2 They are all to do with tourism – mostly with holidays.

3/4

CEO	chief executive officer
CFO	chief financial officer
COO	chief operations officer
DOO	director of operations
GM	general manager
HRD	human resources director
MD	managing director

AIT	air inclusive tour
APD	air passenger duty
ARR	average room rate
B&B	bed and breakfast
BABA	book-a-bed-ahead
F&B	food and beverage
(F)IT	(fully) inclusive tour
QA	quality assurance
T&T	tourism and travel
TIC/P	tourist information centre/point
VAT	value added tax

Exercise D

1 This exercise looks at some acronyms from the world of tourism. Set for pairwork. Students should be able to see the connection. If not, say they are all associations connected with tourism.

2 Students will probably struggle, but may recognize that A stands for Association in most cases.

3 Students check with the Internet. Note that each abbreviation will return several answers on the Internet. They must decide which is appropriate in each case. Feed back, building up the table on the board.

4 Establish that words with normal consonant/vowel patterns (as here) are *normally* pronounced as a word, and those with unusual patterns (e.g., AIT, CFO) are *normally* pronounced with single letters. Refer to the *Vocabulary bank* at the end of the Course Book unit.

Answers

1 They are all associations connected with tourism.

2/3/4

ACE	Association for Conferences and Events	/eɪs/
ANTOR	Association of National Tourist Office Representatives	/'æntɔː(r)/
BATO	British Association of Tourism Officers	/'bætəʊ/
ETOUR	European Tourism Research Institute	/'iːtʊə/
NAITA	National Association of Independent Travel Agents	/'naɪtə/
VISTA	Vision for Industry in Sustainable Tourism Action	/'vɪstə/

Note: An exhaustive list of acronyms and abbreviations used in the tourism and travel industry can be found (at the time of writing) on www.staruk.org.uk.

Language note

If students don't use acronyms or initial abbreviations in their language, a discussion about the reasons for using them is useful. They will then know how to find the meaning of new ones when they meet them. You might point out that abbreviations can sometimes be longer than the thing they abbreviate! For example, World Wide Web is three syllables, whereas WWW is six. It evolved because it is quicker to write, but it is longer, and harder, to say. It is also possible to mix acronyms with abbreviations: for example, JPEG – J/peg/.

Exercise E

Set for individual work and pairwork checking. Feed back, highlighting the changes from noun form to verb in the case of *identity/identify* and *machine/mechanize*.

Answers

Model answers:

Noun 1	Verb	Noun 2
class	classify	classification
computer	computerize	computerization
digit	digitize	digitization
identity	identify	identification
machine	mechanize	mechanization

Closure

Ask students whether they agree with the following statements.

1 Every college student must have a computer.

2 The college library uses a computer to help students find information.

3 College departments use computers to store research data.

4 Students can't do research without a computer.

5 College computers can access research data from other colleges and universities.

6 College computers can access research data from businesses and the media.

7 A personal computer can store information students think is important.

8 Computers can help us to talk with students from other colleges and universities.

9 Computers can help students access data from anywhere in the world.

10 A computer we can carry in our pocket can access worldwide data.

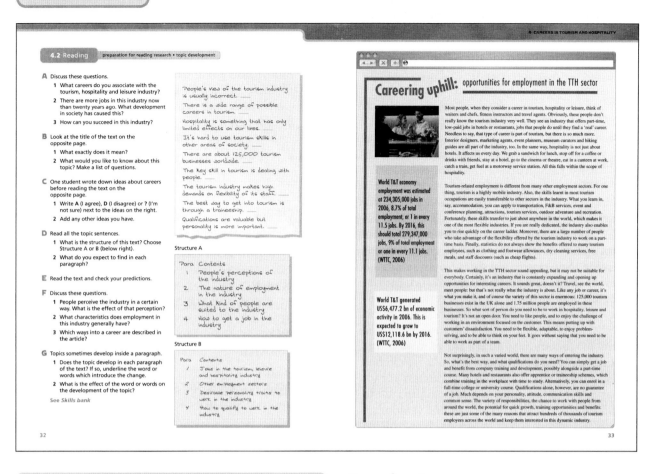

4.2 Reading

General note

Read the *Skills bank – Developing ideas in a paragraph* at the end of the Course Book unit. Decide when, if at all, to refer students to it. The best time is probably at the very end of the lesson or the beginning of the next lesson, as a summary/revision.

Lesson aims

- prepare to read a text by looking at title and topic sentences
- understand the purpose of discourse markers and stance markers in the development of a topic

Introduction

Ask students to talk about the career in tourism they have in mind for themselves and to describe the market they will be working in. Do not correct or criticize. They should answer in some detail with examples. Encourage them to use vocabulary, abbreviations and acronyms from Lesson 1.

Exercise A

Set for general discussion. Allow students to debate differences of opinion. Encourage them to give examples if they can.

Answers

Possible answers:

1 There is a wide range of possible careers. Some were mentioned in Lesson 1 but encourage students to extend the list with as many job names as they can think of. Categorize them on the board into *Tourism/travel*, *Hospitality* and *Leisure*.

2 Travel has become possible for a much larger number of people now, compared with 20 years ago. More people have more spare time, and earn more money to spend on travel. Technology allows easy access to travel arrangements and shorter travel and return times.

3 Encourage students to 'dream up' scenarios in pairs or groups. This can be a fairly creative exercise, leading to students coming up with a suggestion for an activity or describing what somebody in a specific position could achieve.

Exercise B

1 Write the title of the reading text on the board. Set the question for general discussion. Encourage students to define *careering* or speculate on what it might mean.

2 Set for pairwork. Tell students to think of four or five questions with different *Wh~* question words:

What ...?   *Why ...?*

Where ...?   *How ...?*

When ...?

Answers

Model answers:

1 *Careering* means moving fast and sometimes erratically; *uphill* refers to the concept of the career ladder. *Uphill* is also associated with a struggle – *it was an uphill task*. The title refers to the fact that it is possible in the sector to develop a career quickly and achieve many things, but you have to work hard.

2 Possible questions:

What types of jobs are there?

How can I qualify for jobs?

Where can I find information?

How big is the employment market?

What kind of person do I need to be?

Exercise C

1 Set for individual work and pairwork checking. Feed back, trying to get consensus on each point, but do not actually confirm or correct. Preface your remarks with phrases like *So most of you think ... You all believe ...* Remind students to look back at these predictions while they are reading the text (Exercise E).

2 Elicit some more ideas, but once again, do not confirm or correct.

Exercise D

Review paragraph structure – i.e., paragraphs usually begin with a topic sentence which makes a statement that is then expanded in the following sentences. Thus, topic sentences give an indication of the contents of the paragraph. You may wish to refer students to the *Skills bank* at this point.

1 Write the topic sentences from the text on an OHT, or use Resource 4B from the additional resources section. Students should use only the topic sentences for this exercise. Set for individual work and pairwork checking.

2 Set for pairwork. Tell students that close analysis of the topic sentences will help them. Feed back with the whole class. Point out any language features that led them to draw their conclusions.

Answers

Model answers:

1 Text structure A.

2

	Predicted content
Para 1	what people think the industry is like
Para 2	what types of jobs there are, how jobs differ from those in other sectors
Para 3	what kind of person you need to be in order to succeed in the industry
Para 4	what you need to do to start a career in the industry

Exercise E

Set the reading. Students should make notes on the differences between their predictions and the text.

Exercise F

Set for pairwork. Class feedback.

Answers

Model answers:

1 The effect of the perception is that people think the tourism market is one packed with fun or glamorous jobs like chefs or fitness instructors. The reality is different and there are many 'ordinary' jobs as well as jobs that you would at first perhaps not associate with the industry, such as marketing agents, event planners, museum curators, accountants, etc.

2 It is mobile; skills are transferable; it is worldwide; it allows quick career development; it allows for flexibility in working hours; there are many benefits (like discounts, etc.).

3 Possible ways:

- get a job (and take an in-company training course or part-time course)

- do an apprenticeship/traineeship

- do a college course

Exercise G

The purpose of this exercise is for students to try to identify the information structure of each paragraph and to see how a new step in the progression of ideas may be signalled by a rhetorical marker or phrase.

Refer also to the *Skills bank* at the end of this unit. Elicit more examples of discourse markers and stance markers.

Set for pairwork. Feed back. A good idea is to make an OHT or other visual display of the text and use a highlighter to indicate which are the relevant parts of the text. Students should notice that there is not a discernible topic development in every paragraph.

Answers

Model answers:

1/2 Students may underline the following words:

	Discourse marker	Stance marker	Effect
Para 1		Obviously	to draw a conclusion (and encourage the reader to agree)
		Needless to say	to inform the reader that the writer knows the reader is aware of these jobs as part of tourism
	but		to show contrast (yes, these careers of these are part of the industry but there are more)
	In the same way		to compare with what went before (tourism isn't just about travel agents, hospitality is not just about hotels)
Para 2	For one thing		to introduce a description and sum up
	Also		to introduce a description and sum up
		Fortunately	to highlight a positive aspect: not only do the skills transfer to other jobs, they apply worldwide
	Moreover		to introduce an additional point
Para 3		Certainly	to acknowledge that there is a strong appeal, implicitly introducing a contrast (which is touched upon in the next sentence)
	but		to indicate contrast/disagreement
	This means		to explain what 'an environment focused on the customer' actually means
		It goes without saying	to indicate that the writer believes this is obvious
Para 4		Not surprisingly	to refer back, and show that the writer is not surprised
	So		to indicate that the writer is about to ask a question or make a statement
	Alternatively		to introduce further explanation and development of ideas
	however		to express contrast (indicating that qualifications are not all that counts: personality is equally important)

Methodology note

Words like *but* and *however* do not fundamentally change the topic of a paragraph but they do develop it and sometimes take it off in an unexpected direction. Having read the topic sentence, a reader might assume, for example, that the whole paragraph would be positive. Then comes the word *However* …

Imagine a school report with the topic sentence: *John is an extremely able student* which then proceeded with a great deal of praise, but ended with the following: *Despite his many good qualities, however, John will have some difficulty in gaining high marks in his exams unless he concentrates more in class.* We could justifiably claim either that:

1 the whole paragraph is about John and his school work, or

2 the paragraph has two topics – John's positive aspects and his negative aspects.

Alternatively, divide the class into two teams. One team chooses a topic sentence and reads it aloud. The other team must give the information triggered by that topic sentence. Accept a prediction or the actual paragraph content. However, ask students which it is – prediction or actual.

Language note

There is no universal logic to the structuring of information in a text. The order of information is language-specific. For example, oriental languages tend to have a topic sentence or paragraph summary at the end, not the beginning, of the paragraph. Or students whose first language is Arabic might structure a particular type of discourse in a different way from native English speakers. So it is important for students to see what a native speaker writer would consider to be a 'logical' ordering.

Closure

1 Divide the class into groups. Write the topic sentences on strips, or photocopy them from the additional resources section (Resource 4B). Make a copy for each group. Students must put them into the correct order.

2 Refer students back to the sentences in Exercise C. Students should find it easier to comment on these now that they have read the text.

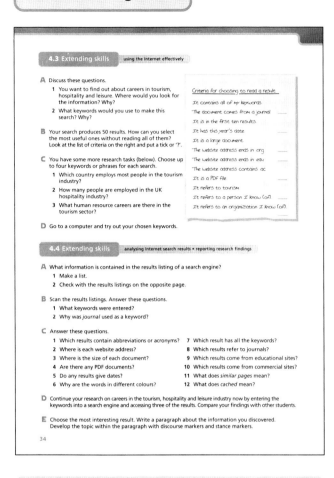

4.3 Extending skills

Key words to elicit: *search engine, keyword, website, web page, website address, search result, subject directory.*

Note: Where the subject is a new one or a fairly general topic, it is a good idea to start first with a **subject directory** which evaluates sites related to the topic and collects them in one place. Some examples are: Academic Info; BUBL LINK; INFOMINE; The WWW Virtual Library.

Exercise A

Write *researching careers* on the board.

1 Set for class discussion. Make sure students give reasons for their answers. Accept their answers at this stage.

2 Remind students that words in English often have more than one meaning, so care must be taken to get the desired result.

Answers

Possible answers:

1 Research can either be done online or in libraries, etc. Recruitment websites have actual information about positions. Academic journals are useful for the latest trends and HR developments. Tourism, hospitality or leisure journals are very useful, as recent articles give the latest information. The Internet is good if the correct keywords are used and a careful selection of results is made. Textbooks are useful if up-to-date, but books take time to publish, so even the latest may be out of date in these fast-moving times.

2 In this list of possible keywords, the bold ones are obvious starting points; others are also possible.

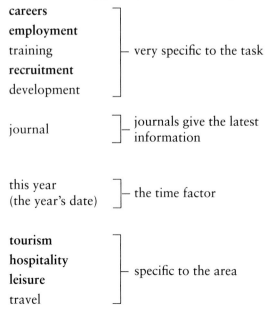

General note

Students will need access to a computer with an Internet connection. If computers are not available during the lesson, part of the lesson can be set for private study.

Lesson aim

- learn or practise how to use the Internet effectively for research

Introduction

Brainstorm the uses of the Internet. Then brainstorm what the important factors are when using the Internet. These should include:

- the search engines students use and why
- how to choose *and write* keywords in their preferred search engine
- how they extract the information they want from the results

Put students in groups and ask them to compare how they normally use a computer to find information. Ask each group to produce a set of advice for using the Internet. Then, as a class, produce an accepted set of advice.

64

Exercise B

Set for pairwork. Remind students of the research topic. Emphasize that we only know what *might* be useful at this stage. Feed back, encouraging students to give reasons for their decisions.

Answers

Possible answers:

✔ It contains all of my keywords. *(but check that the meaning is the same)*

✔ The document comes from a journal. *(current information)*

? It is in the first ten results. *(a web page can have codes attached to put it high in the list)*

✔ It has this year's date. *(current information)*

? It is a large document. *(size is no indication of quality)*

✔ The website address ends in .org *(because it is a non-profit organization)*

✔ The website address ends in .edu *(because it is an educational establishment)*

✔ The website address contains .ac *(because it is an educational establishment)*

? It is a PDF file. *(file type is no indication of quality)*

? It refers to tourism. *(may not be relevant)*

✔ It refers to a person I know (of). *(reliable)*

✔ It refers to an organization I know (of). *(reliable)*

Language note

PDF stands for *portable document format*. PDF documents look exactly like the original documents, and can be viewed and printed on most computers, without the need for each computer to have the same software, fonts, etc. They are created with Adobe Acrobat software.

Exercise C

Set for individual work and pairwork checking. Ask students to compare their choice of keywords with their partner, and justify their choice.

Exercise D

Students should try out different combinations to discover for themselves which gives the best results.

Answers

The information students find will depend on the keywords chosen. Also listings will vary over time in sometimes unpredictable ways, but the following is an indication of possibilities at the time of writing:

1 *employment tourism country statistics* will generate a few useful links to reports with either worldwide or country, or even region, specific data. Leaving out the word *statistics* leads to more generalist and regional results. Including *WTTC* or *World Travel and Tourism Council* will lead to this organization's website, which students should know about, and which contains a lot of statistical data.

2 Typing *UK hospitality employment statistics* leads to many useful sites. Leaving out *statistics* will lead to many recruitment agency sites that give useful information about types of jobs and employment in the industry.

3 *HR tourism career management* leads both to recruitment sites and to many educational sites (universities and colleges selling their programmes). Adding the word *journal* to these search criteria leads to many academic publications on HR and career development in the tourism sector.

Closure

Tell students to think of their own question for research, as in Exercise C, and find the best web page for the data by entering appropriate keywords. Ask students to write their question on a piece of paper and sign it. Put all the questions in a box. Students pick out one of the questions at random and go online to find the best page of search results. From those results they can find the most useful web page. They should ask the questioner for verification and then briefly present the information on the site.

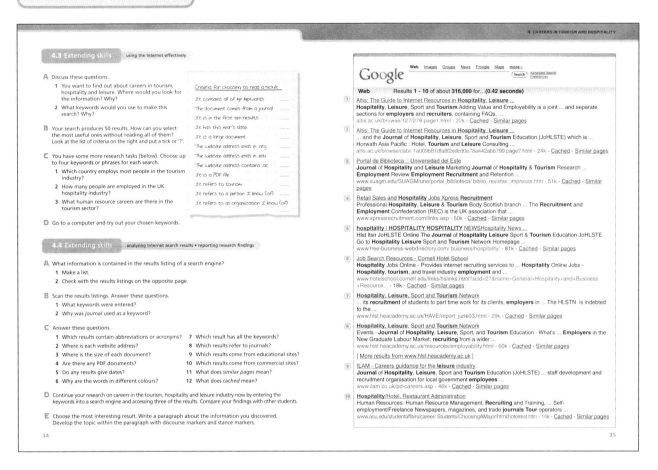

General note

Students will need access to a computer with an Internet connection. If computers are not available during the lesson, part of the lesson can be set for private study.

Lesson aims

- examine a page of Internet search results critically
- report Internet search findings in a short written summary

Introduction

Ask students what problems they had, what lessons they have learnt and what advice they can give from their Internet search experience in Lesson 3. Brainstorm the important factors when searching for information on the Internet and put them in order of importance.

Exercise A

Set for pairwork. Students should first make a list of information they expect to find in search engine results. (They should do this before they look at the search engine results on the right-hand page.) They should

then look at the page of results and identify any other information that is there.

Answers

Possible answers:

number of results
keywords used
time taken
title of document
type of document
quotations from the text with key words highlighted
date
web address/URL

Exercise B

This is further reinforcement on keywords. Set for pairwork or whole class discussion.

Answers

Model answers:

1 *hospitality leisure tourism recruitment employment journal*

2 Because journals give the most current/academic information.

Exercise C

This detailed examination of the results page should make students aware of the content, so that they can make an educated selection of a web page with useful information. Set for pairwork.

Answers

Possible answers:

1 Acronyms/Abbreviations:

Result 1: FAQs (Frequently Asked Questions)

Results 2, 5, 9: JoHLSTE (*Journal of Hospitality, Leisure, Sport and Tourism Education*)

Result 4: REC (Recruitment and Employment Confederation)

Result 7: HLSTN (Hospitality, Leisure, Sport and Tourism Network)

Result 9: ILAM (Institute of Leisure and Amenity Management)

Students may identify further abbreviations, e.g., in the website addresses: www, k, htm, etc.

2 At the end.

3 At the end (if it is given), e.g., 22k.

4 No.

5 Result 7.

6 Blue = titles and viewing information; green = website address; black = keywords.

7 Result 3.

8 Results 2, 3, 5, 8, 9, 10.

9 Results 1, 2, 3, 6, 7, 8, 10.

10 Results 4, 5, 9.

11 There were other very similar results, so the search engine ignored them. They are available if you click on the words.

12 It is a more efficient way of storing information. It means that you can go to a copy of the page stored by Google, in case the actual website happens to be down at the time of the search; of course, it could be a little out of date.

Exercise D

Set the search for individual work. Students should input the keywords again. They will not get exactly the same results page as here, but the results should be comparable. Tell them to take notes.

Feed back, getting students to tell the rest of the class about their most interesting findings. Encourage other students to ask questions.

Exercise E

Set for individual work. Students can complete it in class or for homework.

Closure

1 Focus on some of the vocabulary connected with tourism, hospitality and leisure on the Google page in the Course Book. List the words or phrases on the board. Decide on the meaning and pronunciation of the following (based on the search result at the time of writing):

employability (the extent to which a person and their skills are useful for a company)

recruiter (a person who looks for suitable staff and tries to hire them)

consulting (the activity of advising people and companies on their businesses)

retention (keeping staff that you have hired through training, development, etc.)

association (a group of people or organizations working together for mutual benefit)

graduate labour market (the number of students available for work after graduation)

tour operators (people who organize trips, tours and journeys for tourists)

2 The importance of the care needed when selecting keywords can be demonstrated by a simple classroom activity. Tell the class you are thinking of a particular student who you want to stand up. Say (for example):

It's a man. (all the men stand up and remain standing)

He has dark hair. (only those with dark hair remain standing)

He has a beard.

He has glasses.

He's tall.

His name begins with A.

And so on.

When only one student remains, ask the class to list the minimum number of keywords necessary to identify only that student. Make sure they discard unnecessary ones. For example, if all students have dark hair, that is unnecessary.

3 Finding the keywords for familiar topics is another activity, done in groups. For example, they could:

● find their own college record (name, ID number or date of entry)

● find their last exam results (name, class, subject, date)

● find a book in the library about the Grand Tour (Grand Tour, 18th century, Europe)

Extra activities

1 Work through the *Vocabulary bank* and *Skills bank* if you have not already done so, or as a revision of previous study.

2 Use the *Activity bank* (Teacher's Book additional resources section, Resource 4A).

   A Set the wordsearch for individual work (including homework) or pairwork.

   Answers

Verb	Noun
appoint	appointment/appointee
attract	attraction
browse	browser
curate	curator
discount	discount
employ	employment/employer/employee
find	finding(s)
operate	operation/operator
perceive	perception
plan	plan/planner
promote	promotion/promoter
qualify	qualification
recruit	recruitment/recruiter
refer	reference/referee
research	research/researcher
reserve	reservation
train	traineeship/trainee/trainer
transfer	transfer
transport	transport(ation)
update	update

B Set for pairwork. Teach students how to play noughts and crosses if they don't know – they take it in turns to say the abbreviation or acronym, and what it stands for. If they succeed, they can put their symbol – a nought 0 or a cross X – in that box. If a person gets three of their own symbols in a line, they win.

3 Write acronyms and abbreviations from the unit on cards, or photocopy them from the additional resources section (Resource 4C). Divide the class into two teams. A student selects a card and reads it correctly. (Speed is of the essence.) Alternatively, one team picks a card with an acronym or abbreviation; the other team gives the actual words.

4 Elicit other abbreviations and acronyms from the students – in particular, common/useful ones from the field of tourism, hospitality and leisure. Alternatively, give students some abbreviations/acronyms (for example, the ones below) and ask students to find out what they mean, using the Internet.

BHA	British Hospitality Association
ETOA	European Tour Operators Association
NRA	National Restaurant Association
NTA	National Tour Association
PATA	Pacific Asia Travel Association
TTRA	Travel and Tourism Research Association
WTO	World Tourism Organization
WTTC	World Travel & Tourism Council
YHA	Youth Hostels Association

5 Have a class debate on one of the following:

   a 'Tourism, hospitality and leisure are a luxury for the rich and powerful. Governments of developed countries should spend more on important issues, such as poverty, than on the travel habits of the rich.'

   b 'Tourism is a great opportunity for people to see the world. However, the environmental consequences of tourism are substantial and must be taken into account.' (This leads back to systems theory as discussed in the previous unit.)

   c 'The best way to enter the industry is by working in it, not by going to university'.

6 Ask students to work in small groups to research and feed back to the group on a top three of most successful tourism countries in the world. If students are going to do research on the Internet, suggest that they go to the WTTC site for data. Alternatively, you can do this research before the lesson and print off some pages for students to work from. Remind students that they can't possibly read everything they find, so they must use the topic sentences to decide if a paragraph is worth reading.

7 Write the following job titles on the board:

Tourism careers	Hospitality careers
travel agent	receptionist
overseas rep	chef
sales rep	housekeeper
events manager	food and beverage manager

Ask students to write one-sentence job descriptions for the jobs. You could do this as a communicative game, i.e., students describe the job and the other students have to guess the job title.

Answers

Possible answers:

A travel agent is somebody who organizes and books trips for tourists.

An overseas rep is somebody who helps travel agents and travel organizations to sell holidays, or who manages holidays overseas.

A sales rep is responsible for selling products and services.

An events manager is somebody who organizes activities for tourists or big events such as concerts.

A receptionist is somebody who welcomes and registers guests in a hotel.

A chef is the manager of a restaurant kitchen.

A housekeeper is the person responsible for the smooth running of a hotel.

A food and beverage manager is responsible for buying food and drinks for restaurants.

8 There are a number of fixed phrases which are often used to talk about jobs and changing jobs. Write the following on the board or display on an OHT. Ask students to match the two columns to make phrases that describe a career move.

Ask them if they know anybody who has made a career move and let them describe the move, using the phrases.

has been promoted	the role of DOO
has taken on	into the position of DOS
has moved	the rooms division
has been named/appointed	to HR Director
has joined	MD

Answers

has been promoted	to HR Director
has taken on	the role of DOO
has moved	into the position of DOS
has been named/appointed	MD
has joined	the rooms division

9 Give students one of the following two links. To be sure the link is still current, test it on the Internet before class:

www.otec.org/hrd/ocareers02.htm. This will lead to a site maintained by the Ontario Tourism Education Corporation (OTEC), a not-for-profit human resource development company that supports Ontario's tourism and hospitality industries. On the site, students can click the link for the career planning website, which will open in a separate window or at www.cthrc.ca/careerplanning. On that site students can research job profiles, do quizzes, look at FAQs, etc.

Tell students to browse the site and find their favourite job description. Do a short presentation on the job: what is the job title, what are the responsibilities, etc.

Alternatively, you could lead students to www.wttc.org. Students will be taken to the site of the World Travel & Tourism Council, which offers up-to-date reports and statistical data on tourism and travel. The site is generally useful for students but will not specifically give information on careers – it will, however, give data on employment worldwide.

5 TOURISM MARKETING

Marketing is covered in this unit, and also in Unit 6 and Unit 8, where the focus is on hospitality marketing. In Unit 5, the focus is on the nature of marketing, types of markets, market segmentation and market research. The first listening extract, from a lecture, looks at what marketing is and why it is important, and gives an overview of some key marketing concepts. The second listening extract is from a seminar about market mapping. This leads into work on the four types of market research: primary, secondary, qualitative and quantitative.

Skills focus

 Listening

- understanding 'signpost language' in lectures
- using symbols and abbreviations in note-taking

Speaking

- making effective contributions to a seminar

Vocabulary focus

- word sets: synonyms, antonyms, etc.
- the language of trends
- common lecture language

Key vocabulary

Note: Key marketing and research-related vocabulary is listed below. Useful lecture/seminar language is given in the *Vocabulary bank* and *Skills bank* in the Course Book.

Resort types	Marketing	Statistical/market trends	Research methods
beach resort	advertising	decline (n and v)	analyse
eco-resort	brand (n)	decrease (n and v)	data analysis
golf resort	consumer	drop (n and v)	interview (n and v)
health resort/spa	mailing	gradual	market research
ski resort	marketing	growth	primary research
	market leader	increase (n and v)	qualitative research
Market segmentation and target markets	market share	outperform	quantitative research
category	marketing mix	rise (n and v)	questionnaire
gender	product	steady (adj)	sample (n and v)
low-income	promotion	trend	secondary research
manual	satisfy (demand)		statistical
mass market	special offer		statistics
niche market	sponsorship		survey (n and v)
professional	strategy		
socio-economic status	target (n and v)		

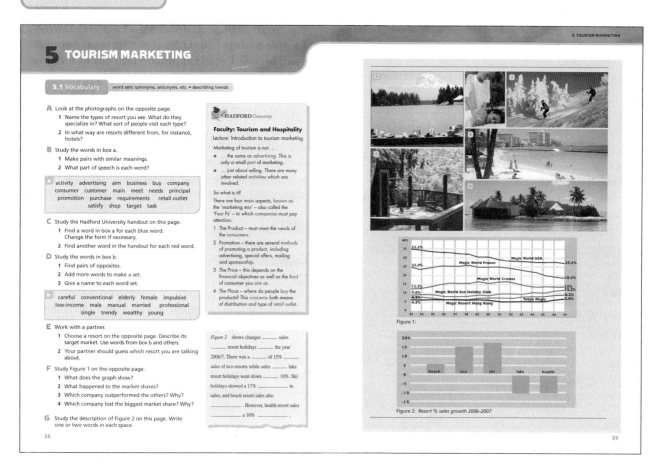

General note

Read the *Vocabulary bank – Vocabulary sets* and *Describing trends* at the end of the Course Book unit. Decide when, if at all, to refer your students to it. The best time is probably at the very end of the lesson or the beginning of the next lesson, as a summary/revision.

Lesson aims

- gain an understanding of lexical cohesion in texts through building word sets, synonyms and opposites/converses
- use appropriate language for describing trends

Introduction

Do some vocabulary revision from the previous units. For example:

1 Choose some prefixes and suffixes (see Units 1 and 4). Write them on the board. Ask students to give the meaning of the affix and an example of a word.

2 Dictate some of the key vocabulary from Unit 3. Ask students to check their spellings (with a dictionary) and group the words according to their stress patterns.

Exercise A

Set for pairwork discussion and whole class feedback. Do not comment or correct at this point. Talk about the word *resort* and that its meaning is derived from the verb *to resort*, i.e., 'to escape to'. When talking about the photographs, use and elicit general words such as *resort/tourism/hospitality*, *male/female*, *old/young*, *market/target* and write them on the board.

Answers

Model answers:

1   1 A lake resort.

    2 A health/spa resort.

    3 A ski resort.

    4 An eco-resort.

    5 A beach resort.

    6 An island resort.

Accept all reasonable answers to the second part of question 1.

2 *Resort* suggests something larger or with more facilities than a simple hotel. A resort could be a single hotel with extra facilities such as a spa or golf course. It could be a beach or ski resort, comprising several hotels and beach or ski facilities.

Exercise B

The purpose of this exercise is to build sets of synonyms. This not only helps in understanding textual cohesion, but is useful for paraphrasing.

Set both questions for pairwork. Students should look for pairs of words/items. Tell them to use their dictionaries if necessary to check the grammatical information, and to note if they find other words with similar meanings.

Feed back with the whole class, building up a table on the board, and eliciting other words which can be used with the same meaning.

Answers

Model answers:

Word 1/ part of speech		Word 2/ part of speech		Words with similar meanings/ notes
activity	n (C)	task	n (C)	job
advertising	n (U)	promotion	n (C/U)	a special promotion = a special offer to promote a product
aim	n (C) v (T)	target	n (C) v (T)	objective, goal if *aim* is a transitive verb it is followed by *at*
business	n (C/U)	company	n (C)	firm, organization business U = the activity
buy	v (T)	purchase	v (T)	get, acquire
consumer	n (C)	customer	n (C)	client (for services); shopper (for shops)
main	adj	principal	adj	major, chief, key
meet	v (T/I)	satisfy	v (T)	use with *needs* or *requirements*
needs	pl n	requirements	pl n	
retail outlet	n (C)	shop	n (C)	*shop* can also be a verb

Language note

The synonyms given here are those which can replace the words in Exercise C. *Meet* and *satisfy* are synonymous when used with *needs/requirements*, but not in other contexts.

Exercise C

1 Set for individual work and pairwork checking.

2 Set for pairwork. Students may need to change the part of speech.

Feed back with the whole class by reading the paragraph or by using an OHT, or other visual medium, of the text. The text is reproduced in the additional resources section (Resource 5B) for this purpose. Discuss alternative ideas and decide whether they are acceptable. Check the meaning of any unknown words in the text (e.g., *mailing*, *sponsorship*). Note that the blue words are marketing words whereas the red words are general purpose words frequent in academic contexts.

Answers

Model answers:

1 **Marketing is not ...**

- ... the same as (*advertising*) promotion. This is only a small part of marketing.

- ... just about selling. There are many other related (*activities*) tasks which are involved.

So what is it?

There are four (*main*) principal aspects, known as the 'marketing mix' – also called the 'Four Ps' – to which (*companies*) businesses must pay attention.

1 The **Product** – must (*meet*) satisfy the (*needs*) requirements of the (*consumers*) customers.

2 **Promotion** – there are several methods of promoting a product, including advertising, special offers, mailing and sponsorship.

3 The **Price** – this depends on the financial objectives as well as the kind of consumer you (*aim at*) target.

4 The **Place** – where do people (*buy*) purchase the products? This concerns both means of distribution and type of (*retail outlet*) shop.

2

part	aspect
known as	called
methods	means
kind	type
concern(s)	involve(d)

Exercise D

1 Set for pairwork. Feed back. Start the first column of the table as shown in the Answers section.

2 Do the first pair of words with the whole class as an example. Set the remainder for pairwork. Feed back, completing the second column of the table on the board.

3 Discuss with the whole class. Elicit a word or phrase which describes the whole set of words and add this to the table.

Answers

Model/possible answers:

Opposites	Other words	Word for set
careful, impulsive	cautious, risk-taker	personality
conventional, trendy	traditional, fashionable	style/lifestyle
elderly, young	old, middle aged, teenage, in his/her 20s etc., child, adult	age
female, male	woman, man	gender/sex
low-income, wealthy	high/middle/average income, poor, rich, well-off	income
manual, professional	managerial, clerical, skilled/unskilled/semi-skilled, casual, part-time, blue collar/white collar, unemployed, higher/lower professional/managerial*	occupation/type of job/socio-economic status
married, single	divorced, widowed, with/without children, parent	marital or family status

*other useful words: *housewife, retired*

Language note

There are a very large number of words which can be used to describe lifestyle or personality and which are used by marketers. The words in Exercise D are just a small selection. A quick search on the Internet for marketing language will get you to websites where useful terminology can be found.

Exercise E

Introduce the terms *market segmentation* and *target market*. Elicit or give definitions, e.g., *market segmentation is the division of a market for a product into groups of customers who have similar needs or characteristics. Each of the groups is likely to want different types of the product. Each market 'segment' can thus be a **target market**.*

Point out that the names for the word sets in Exercise D are actually categories that are used to segment markets. Choose one of the resorts and give a description of its possible target market (see table in Answers section), asking students to identify which type of resort you are talking about. Explain that resorts can have more than one target market and it's hard to generalize. Having said that, certain resorts seem to appeal to certain target groups more than to others.

Set the remainder for pairwork, telling students to use several of the categories in Exercise D for each resort, adding other words or ideas if they need to. Feed back as a class discussion.

Answers

Possible answers:

Type of resort	Gender	Age	Marital status	Occupation	Income	Personality/lifestyle
1 lake	male or female	20s, 30s–55s	young people (un)married couple (without children or with older children)	any profession	middle income	conventional, not adventurous
2 health/spa	male or female	middle-aged/elderly	probably single, or couple with no children	higher managerial, company director, rich, widow	wealthy	traditional, conventional
3 ski	male or female	20s–30s	single or couple	white collar, higher professional, managerial	middle to high income	risk-taker, fashionable, impulsive
4 eco	male or female	middle-aged (late 30s –late 50s)	married couple with older children	white collar, professional, managerial	middle to high income	concerned about environment, careful
5 beach	male or female	middle-aged (30s–40s)	married couple with children	any profession	middle income	conventional, not adventurous
6 island	male or female	middle-aged, elderly	may have family	high managerial (e.g., successful businessperson, company director)	rich	not practical, doesn't care about environment

Note: The above suggestions may not fit certain countries or cultures. While the segmentation categories should apply universally, the descriptors can be changed to suit students' culture.

Exercise F

Introduce *market share*. Elicit or give a definition, e.g., *market share is a company's sales of a product as a percentage of the total sales in the market*. With the whole class, discuss what the graph shows. Elicit some of the verbs and adverbs which students will need in order to discuss question 2. For example:

Go up	No change	Go down	Adverbs
rise	stay the same	fall	slightly
increase	remain at	decrease	gradually
grow	doesn't change	decline	steadily
improve	is unchanged	worsen	significantly
soar		drop	sharply
			dramatically

Note: These verbs are generally used in an intransitive sense when describing trends.

1 Discuss with the whole class. The answer to this question should be one sentence giving the topic of the graph.

2 Set for pairwork. Students should write or say a sentence about each company. Feed back by eliciting sentences from the students. Write correct sentences on the board or display the model answers below on an OHT or other visual medium. Make sure that students notice the prepositions used with the numbers and dates.

Answers

Possible answers:

1 The graph shows changes in market share for six companies in the resort business between 1993 and 2007.

2 Magic World USA's market share <u>fell steadily</u> from 35.5% in 1993 to 27.3% in 2007. Magic World France's market share <u>increased</u> between 1994 and 1998 and then <u>fell sharply</u> to 18.3% in 2007. Magic World Cruises' market share <u>rose</u> until 2001. Then it <u>fell significantly</u> from about 16% to 13% in 2007. Magic World Eco Holiday Club's market share fell slightly between 1995 and 1997, but then <u>increased steadily</u> to 12.2% in 2007. Tokyo Magic's market share <u>dropped</u> between 1994 and 1998. Then it <u>increased gradually</u> to 8.2% in 2007. Magic Resort Hong Kong's market share <u>increased slightly</u> between 1993 and 2007.

Underline the verbs and adverbs. Ask students to make nouns from the verbs and adjectives from the adverbs. Alternatively, you could reproduce the following table minus the noun and adjective forms on the board, on an OHT or on a handout. The incomplete table is reproduced in the additional resources section (Resource 5C) to facilitate this.

Verbs	Nouns	Adverbs	Adjectives
rise	a rise	gradually	gradual
increase	an increase	sharply	sharp
grow	growth*	slightly	slight
improve	improvement	markedly	marked
fall	a fall	significantly	significant
decrease	a decrease	rapidly	rapid
drop	a drop	steeply	steep
decline	a decline	steadily	steady

*usually (but not always) uncountable in this sense

Return to the original answer sentences and ask students to make sentences with the same meaning, using the nouns and adjectives in place of the verbs and adverbs. Note that when using the noun + adjective, sentences can be made using *there was ...* or *showed*. Do one or two examples orally, then ask students to write the remaining sentences. Feed back.

Answers

Model answers:

Magic World USA's market share <u>fell steadily</u> from 35.5% in 1993 to 27.3% in 2007.	<u>There was a steady fall</u> in Magic World USA's market share from 35.5% in 1993 to 27.3% in 2007.
Magic World France's market share <u>increased</u> between 1994 and 1998 and then <u>fell sharply</u> to 18.3% in 2007.	<u>There was an increase</u> in Magic World France's market share between 1994 and 1998 and then <u>a sharp fall</u> to 18.3% in 2007.
Magic World Cruises' market share <u>rose</u> until 2001. Then it <u>fell significantly</u> from about 16% to 13% in 2007.	<u>There was a rise</u> in Magic World Cruises' market share until 2001, and then <u>a significant fall</u> from about 16% to 13% in 2007.
Magic World Eco Holiday Club's market share fell slightly between 1995 and 1997, but then <u>increased steadily</u> to 12.2% in 2007.	Magic World Eco Holiday Club's market share <u>showed a slight fall</u> between 1995 and 1997, and then <u>a steady increase</u> to 12.2% in 2007.
Tokyo Magic's market share <u>dropped</u> between 1994 and 1998. Then it <u>increased gradually</u> to 8.2% in 2007.	Tokyo Magic's market share <u>showed a drop</u> between 1994 and 1998, and then <u>a gradual increase</u> to 8.2% in 2007.
Magic Resort Hong Kong's market share <u>increased slightly</u> between 1993 and 2007.	Magic Resort Hong Kong's market share <u>showed a slight increase</u> between 1993 and 2007.

3/4 Check the meaning of *outperformed*. Tell students to look at all the information on the right-hand page, i.e., the photographs as well as Figure 2. They should be able to think of *possible* reasons for the trends. Set for pairwork. Feed back with the whole class. You could take the discussion further by asking why students think these increases and decreases took place.

Answers

Possible answers:

3 Magic World Eco Holiday Club increased its market share by around 5%, possibly because of an increase in the number of people interested in environmentally sustainable holidays.

4 Magic World USA lost 8.2% of its market share, possibly because of rising fuel prices and the events of 9/11.

Exercise G

Ask students to look at Figure 2 and discuss in pairs the information it shows. Feed back. Elicit two types of sentence using a verb and a noun to express the changes. For example:

There was a rise of 15% in sales of eco-resort holidays.

Sales of eco-resort holidays rose by 15%.

Again, make sure that students notice the prepositions, especially the use of *by* to show the size of the increase. Set the text completion for individual work and pairwork checking.

Answers

Model answers:

Figure 2 shows changes in sales of resort holidays for/in the year 2006/7. There was a rise of 15% in sales of eco-resorts while sales of lake resort holidays went down by 10%. Ski holidays showed a 17% improvement/growth/rise/increase in sales, and beach resort sales also rose/went up/increased/grew/improved slightly. However, health resort sales showed a 10% drop/fall/decrease/decline.

Closure

Some students may have stayed in a resort at some point, or might have a desire to do so in the future. Let them talk in small groups or pairs and rank the features from most to least important when choosing a resort holiday.

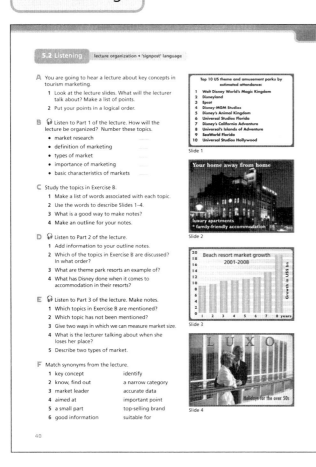

General note

Read the *Skills bank – Signpost language in a lecture* at the end of the Course Book unit. Decide when, if at all, to refer students to it. The best time is probably at the very end of the lesson or the beginning of the next lesson, as a summary/revision.

Lesson aims

- improve comprehension through understanding of signpost language and lexical cohesion
- deal with disorganization in lectures/fractured text

Further practice in:

- predicting content from own background knowledge and from the lecture introduction
- using the introduction to decide the best form of notes to use

Introduction

Review key vocabulary from this unit by writing a selection of words from Lesson 1 on the board and asking students to put the words in groups, giving reasons for their decisions.

Exercise A

Remind students about preparing for a lecture. If you wish, review Unit 1 *Skills bank – Making the most of lectures.*

Remind students that when lecturers begin their talks, they usually provide their listeners with an outline. Remind/tell students about the signpost language which speakers use at the beginning to list the areas they will cover. On the board, build the table below, eliciting suggestions from the students. Alternatively (or in addition), you could refer to the *Skills bank* at this point.

Sequencing words		Verbs
To start with, Firstly, Secondly, Then … After that, Finally,	I'll	begin/start by …ing discuss examine consider mention talk about look at define give a(n) outline/overview/ definition/summary of … end/finish/conclude by …ing

Language note

Speakers will usually avoid repeating words. So they would be unlikely to say *To start with, I'll start by … .*

Refer students to the lecture slides. Set the exercise for pairwork.

Ask students to feed back their possible lecture ideas to the whole class using the signpost language on the board to order their points. Accept any reasonable ideas. One possibility is given below.

Answer

Possible answer:

To start with, the lecturer will examine the US theme park market, including different types of accommodation in theme parks. After that he/she will talk about the market for beach resorts. Then he/she will mention holidays for older people.

Methodology note

If students are new to the subject of tourism marketing, they may only be able to make simple points about the slides, as in the model answer above. If they already know something about the subject they may realize that the slides illustrate the concepts which the lecturer will discuss, i.e., market size, market share and market leaders; creating new markets and maintaining market growth; mass and niche markets. These words will appear in the exercises that follow.

🎧 Exercise B

Tell students they are only going to hear the introduction to the lecture. Give students time to read the topics. Check that they understand the meaning. Remind them they will only hear the introduction once, as in a lecture. Tell them to listen out for the signpost language on the board. They should number the topics from 1–5 in the order in which the lecturer will talk about them.

Play Part 1. Allow students to compare answers. Feed back. Ask students to say what signpost language they heard related to each topic. Confirm the correct answer.

Answers

market research – 3
(*After that, I'll talk about …*)

definition of marketing – 1
(*to start with, we need to consider …*)

types of market – 5
(*I'll finish by mentioning …*)

importance of marketing – 2
(*And secondly, …*)

basic characteristics of markets – 4
(*So then I'll discuss …*)

Transcript 🎧 1.22

Part 1

Good morning, everyone. This morning we're going to start on the topic of tourism marketing. I'm sure you've covered some general marketing in other lectures, so some of this will be familiar to you.

In this first talk I'm just going to give you an overview of a few key concepts, and then other aspects will be dealt with in the next few lectures. Also, in your seminars and assignments you'll be able to cover all the important points in more detail. So … er … let's see – yes – to start with, we need to consider firstly what marketing is. In other words, why do businesses engage in marketing? And secondly, why is marketing so important for tourism? After that, I'll talk about market research,

because businesses – well, any business, not just businesses in the tourism and hospitality sector – need good information on which to base their marketing strategy. Part of this involves analysing markets. So then I'll discuss some basic characteristics of markets, and I'll finish by mentioning some different types of markets.

Exercise C

1 Set for pairwork. Divide the topics up among the pairs so that each pair concentrates on one topic. Feed back. Accept any reasonable suggestions.

2 Refer students to the lecture slides. Students should try to guess which of the topics each slide could refer to. Set for individual work and pairwork checking. Feed back but do not confirm or correct yet.

3 Elicit suggestions from the whole class. If you wish, refer students to Unit 1 *Skills bank*.

4 Set for individual work. Students should prepare an outline on a sheet of paper preferably using either numbered points (with enough space between the points to allow for notes to be added) or a mind map/spidergram (see example below).

Answers

Possible answers:

1 Some key words might be:

  market research – *survey, focus group, interview, qualitative, quantitative*

  definition of marketing – *promotion, satisfy customer needs*

  types of markets – any words from Lesson 1 concerned with market segmentation; also *niche* and *mass* (to be mentioned in the lecture)

  importance of marketing – *ensure company profits, help meet company objectives*

  basic characteristics of markets – *size, trends, growth, share, leader, brand, value, analysis*

2 Accept any reasonable answers with good justifications.

3/4 Example of spidergram:

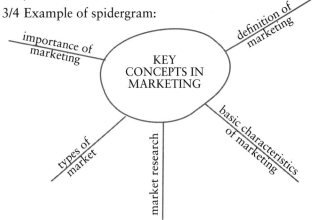

Methodology note

🎧 Exercise D

Tell students to use their outline from Exercise C to take notes. Which topics do they expect to hear in this section?

Play Part 2. Put students in pairs to compare their notes and discuss the questions.

Feed back. When it becomes clear that the lecturer did not actually stick to the plan in the introduction, say that this happens very often in lectures. Although it is a good idea to prepare outline notes, students need to be ready to alter and amend these. Discuss how best to do this. One obvious way is to use a non-linear approach such as a mind map or spidergram, where new topics can easily be added. After checking answers to questions 2, 3 and 4, build a complete set of notes on the board as a spidergram, as in the example in the Answers section.

Answers

Possible answers:

1 Example notes: see spidergram below.
2 Discussed first: definition of marketing; second: importance of marketing.
3 Creating new markets.
4 They have done market research, analysed the data carefully and developed accommodation which appeals to the tastes of different target groups. This allows them to target specific customers.

Transcript 🎧 1.23

Part 2

Well, what *is* marketing? We might define it as 'the process of identifying and targeting particular groups of people with the aim of selling them a product or a service'.

Actually, marketing is arguably *the* most important aspect of management. You can manage your staff and your production processes well, but if nobody buys your products your business will fail. So, it follows that marketing must ensure that a business can satisfy customers' needs and at the same time that it makes a profit. But what *are* the needs of customers? Of course, there are many products which people will always need, but really successful companies identify gaps in markets and create new markets with new products. What I mean is, they anticipate consumers' requirements. A good example of this is theme park resorts. Have a look at Slide 1. I don't think there are any surprises in this top ten. Most of you will be familiar with these names, I think? Already, in 1952, Disney realized the appeal that lies in fairy tales and fantasy, and that people love coming together for an unusual experience. What was missing were places for people to stay. Disney theme parks and resorts are now extremely popular, which is not surprising, because they appeal to young and old. And there is a type of accommodation for everyone, from luxury apartments to family hotels. They have really studied and analysed what their customers want to get out of the experience. Because of that, they cater for everyone's wishes: there's something for everyone. With their resorts, Disney have tried to turn the ordinary into the extraordinary, and 'making dreams come true every day' has become central to their global strategy.

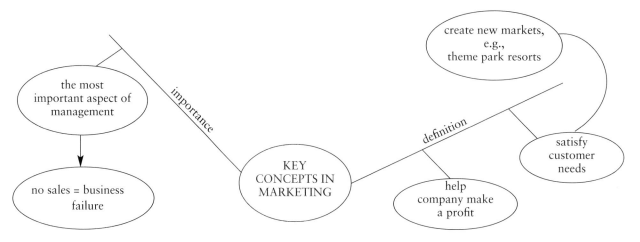

🎧 Exercise E

Ask students what they expect to hear about in the next part. Refer students to their outline again. Give them time to read the questions. Note that the final part of the lecture will be heard in Lesson 3, but there is no need to tell them this at this point. Play Part 3. Set the questions for pairwork. Students should use their notes to help them answer the questions.

Feed back. Note that there is no need to build a set of notes on the board at this point – this will be done in Lesson 3. Ask students if they can remember exactly what the lecturer said to indicate that she had lost her place.

Answers

Model answers:

1 Basic characteristics of markets and types of market.

2 Market research.

3 By what it is worth (value) and by number (volume) of sales.

4 The different types of customers for resort holidays (customer profiles). (*Er ... Where was I? Oh, yes.*)

5 Mass market and niche market.

Transcript 🎧 1.24

Part 3

Anyway, er ... to return to the main point – fundamentally, successful marketing is about having accurate data so that customers' needs can be met. So what is it that marketers need to know? Well, first, they must begin by analysing the market. For example, it's essential to identify basic characteristics of the market such as its size, and which companies are the market leaders; that is to say, we need to look at the share of the market which each company has. Naturally, it is the aim of all companies to become the market leader – or to have the top-selling brand in a particular field. If we take the beach resort market in the US as an example – you can see the statistics on Slide 3. As you can see, in 2006 this market was worth around $12 billion per year, and in terms of sales, it had annual sales of more than 2 million resort vacations worldwide. And what's more, it has been getting bigger. Just look at the figures ... Before the 1970s, going on vacation was a simple matter. But these days, there's a huge variety and choice. There are different resort vacations for men and women, families and singles, rich and not so rich people, different ages, and so on ... Er ... Where was I? Oh, yes. We also need to be clear about the type of

market. One way to categorize the type of market is to think about whether the product is aimed at a mass market, like ski resort or beach resort vacations, for example. Or is it more suitable for a niche market – by that I mean a small part of a larger market. For example, vacations for people over 50 are a niche market inside the huge vacation market. In other words, is the product aimed at just one narrow category of customer?

Exercise F

This gives further practice in identifying words and phrases used synonymously in a particular context. Set for individual work and pairwork checking.

Answers

1 key concept	important point
2 know, find out	identify
3 market leader	top-selling brand
4 aimed at	suitable for
5 a small part	a narrow category
6 good information	accurate data

Closure

1 Group work. Ask students to make a short list of three theme park resorts they know of, and to find out why these parks are probably successful. What marketing strategy have they used?

Most students will have heard of resorts in their area, region or country. They may need to do some research on the Internet. Even though students would not as yet be aware of the fine points of marketing strategy, information they can harvest from, for instance, a resort's website will usually give them a clue as to what marketing strategy a particular company has chosen. This could be to appeal to young kids, or to present themselves as an environmentally friendly organization, or to stress the fact that they are involved in helping the local community, etc.

Set students to work in groups, and make pairs within the groups. Ask each pair to draw up a list of three resorts which they are interested in. After this, they can compare their findings in their groups. The group results can be presented orally, using phrases such as:

The market leader for ... in our group is ...

The second most popular resort is ...

The least popular resort is ...

Their main marketing strategy is/seems to be/is probably ...

Alternatively, the results could be put into graphic form and written up.

2 Check that students understand some of the concepts and vocabulary in the unit so far, including *brand, market characteristics, market share, market leader, market segment, target market, market segmentation, market size, market trends.*

5.3 Extending skills

5.3 Extending skills note-taking symbols • stress within words • lecture language

A Look at the student notes on the right. They are from the lecture in Lesson 2.
1 What do the symbols and abbreviations mean?
2 The notes contain some mistakes. Find and correct them.
3 Make the corrected notes into a spidergram.

B 🎧 Listen to the final part of the lecture (Part 4).
1 Complete your notes.
2 Why does the lecture have to stop?
3 What is the research task?

C 🎧 Listen to some stressed syllables. Identify the word below in each case. Number each word.
Example: You hear: 1 sem /sem/
You write:

analyse	___	characteristics	___	seminar	_1_
anticipate	___	identify	___	strategy	___
assignment	___	overview	___	successful	___
category	___	qualitative	___	variety	___

D Study the extract from the lecture on the right.
1 Think of one word for each space.
2 🎧 Listen and check your ideas.
3 Match words or phrases from the blue box below with each word or phrase from the lecture.
4 Think of other words or phrases with similar meanings.

as I was saying   basically   clearly   crucial
in fact   in other words   obviously
of course   possibly   probably
some people say   that is to say
we can see that

E Discuss the research task set by the lecturer.
1 What kind of information should you find?
2 What do you already know?
3 Where can you find more information?

3) basic characteristics of markets
(i) size
e.g., beach resort market (UK)
• c. $12 m
• > 2 bn hols.
(ii) market share (newest brand = market leader)
4) types of market
e.g.,
(i) beach/ski resort = niche market
(ii) over 50s hols. = mass market

_____, marketing is _____ the most important aspect of management. So, *it* _____ *that* marketing must ensure that a business can satisfy customers' needs. *What I* _____ *is,* they anticipate consumers' requirements. _____, successful marketing is about having accurate data. Anyway, er … *to return to the main* _____, it's _____ to identify basic characteristics of the market. _____, it is the aim of all companies to become the market leader.

41

Lesson aims

- use symbols in note-taking
- understand and use lecture language such as stance adverbials (*obviously*, *arguably*), restatement (*in other words* …) and other commentary-type phrases

Further practice in:

- stress within words
- asking for information
- formulating polite questions

Introduction

1 As in Unit 3, encourage students to ask you questions about the information in the lecture in Lesson 2 as if you were the lecturer. Remind them about asking for information politely. If they can't remember how to do this, you could tell them to revise the *Skills bank* for Unit 3.

2 Put students in pairs. Student A must ask Student B about the information in the lecture in Lesson 2 to help him/her complete the notes from the lecture. Then they reverse roles. Again, they can revise language for this in the *Skills bank* for Unit 3.

Exercise A

1 Revise/introduce the idea of using symbols and abbreviations when making notes. Ask students to look at the student notes and find the symbols and abbreviated forms. Do they know what these mean? If not, they should try to guess.

If you wish, expand the table in the Answers section with more symbols and abbreviations that will be useful for the students. There is also a list at the back of the Course Book for students' reference.

2 Ask students to tell you what kind of notes these are (linear and numbered). Set the task for pairwork. Students will need to agree what the notes are saying and then make the corrections.

3 Set for individual work. Feed back with the whole class and build the spidergram in the Answers section on the board.

Answers

Model answers:

1

Symbol/abbreviation	Meaning
e.g.	(for) example
UK	United Kingdom
c.	around, approximately
$	dollars
m	million
>	more than
bn	billion
hols.	holidays
=	equals, is
over 50s	people over 50

2 Suggested corrections (underlined):
3) basic characteristics of markets
   (i) size
   e.g., beach resort market (<u>US</u>)
   c. $12 <u>bn</u>
   >2 <u>m</u> hols.
   (ii) market share (<u>top-selling</u> brand = market leader)
4) types of market
   e.g.,
   (i) beach/ski resort = <u>mass</u> market
   (ii) over 50s hols. = <u>niche</u> market

3

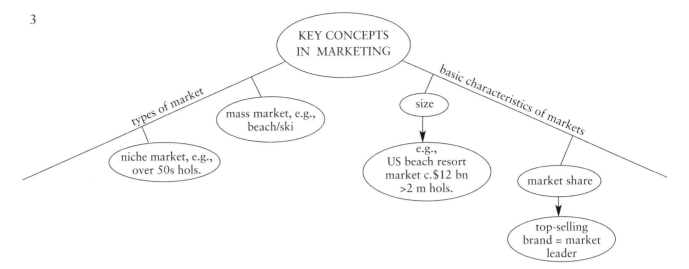

Language note

Some abbreviations are universal and some are personal. People often develop their own personal system of symbols and abbreviations. For example, *bn* for billion is used by everyone but *hols.* is an example of a longer word abbreviated by the individual who wrote these notes.

🎧 Exercise B

Tell students they will hear the final part of the lecture. Remind them that there is one topic which has not yet been covered, but don't say what it is. Put students in pairs to discuss what they think they might hear. Give them time to read the questions. They should complete the final leg of the spidergram.

Play Part 4. Put students in pairs to compare their notes and discuss the questions. Feed back. For question 2, ask students if they can remember the exact words used by the lecturer (*However, oh, dear … sadly, I see that we've run out of time.*).

Answers

Model answers:

1

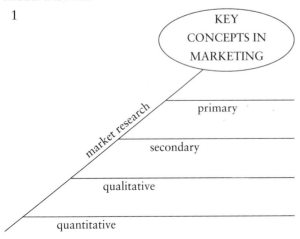

2 Because there is no more time.

3 The research task is to find out about the four different types of market research: primary, secondary, qualitative and quantitative.

Transcript 🎧 1.25

Part 4

So how does the marketer get the necessary information? By research, obviously. There are several ways to categorize market research. Let me see … one way is to distinguish between primary and secondary research. Another important distinction is between qualitative and quantitative research. However, … oh, dear … sadly, I see that we've run out of time. This means that I'll have to ask *you* to do some research. I'd like you to find out what is meant by the four types of research I've just mentioned, that is, primary and secondary research, and qualitative and quantitative research. We'll discuss what you've found out next time I see you.

🎧 Exercise C

Remind students of the importance of stressed syllables in words (see the teaching notes for Unit 3, Lesson 3, Exercise A). Play the recording, pausing after the first few to check that students understand the task.

Feed back, perhaps playing the recording again for each word before checking. Ideally, mark up the words on an OHT or other visual medium.

Answers

analyse	8
anticipate	7
assignment	3
category	11
characteristics	5
identify	10
overview	2
qualitative	9
seminar	1
strategy	4
successful	6
variety	12

Transcript 🎧 1.26

1 'seminar
2 'overview
3 a'ssignment
4 'strategy
5 character'istics
6 suc'cessful
7 an'ticipate
8 'analyse
9 'qualitative
10 i'dentify
11 'category
12 va'riety

🎧 Exercise D

This exercise gives students a chance to focus on some typical lecture language.

1 Set for pairwork. Students should try to think of a word for each of the blank spaces. Note that they should *not* try to use the words from the box at this stage. Do not feed back at this point.

2 Tell students they will hear the sentences from the lecture and should fill in the missing words as they listen. There will be pauses at the end of each sentence but you will play the recording straight through without stopping (as a kind of dictation).

Feed back with the whole class, playing the sentences again if necessary. Check the meanings and functions of the words and phrases. Point out the fixed phrases (in italics in the text) and encourage students to learn these. Ask students to repeat the sentences for pronunciation practice,

making sure that the stress and intonation is copied from the model.

3 Set for individual work and pairwork checking. Students should check in their dictionaries for meanings or pronunciations of words from the box that they don't know. Feed back, building the first two columns of the table in the Answers section on the board.

4 Elicit suggestions from the whole class for a third column: 'Other similar words'.

If you wish, students can practise saying the sentences in question 2 but this time with words from questions 3 and 4.

After completing Exercise D, students can be referred to the *Vocabulary bank – Stance* and the *Skills bank – Signpost language in a lecture* for consolidation.

Answers

Model answers:

1/2 <u>Actually</u>, marketing is <u>arguably</u> the most important aspect of management. So, *it <u>follows</u> that* marketing must ensure that a business can satisfy customers' needs. *What I <u>mean</u> is*, they anticipate consumers' requirements. <u>Fundamentally</u>, successful marketing is about having accurate data. Anyway, er … *to return to the main <u>point</u>*, it's <u>essential</u> to identify basic characteristics of the market. <u>Naturally</u>, it is the aim of all companies to become the market leader.

3/4

Word/phrase from the lecture	Words/phrases from the box	Other similar words/phrases
Actually	in fact	in reality
arguably	probably, possibly, some people say	perhaps
it follows that	we can see that	logically
What I mean is	that is to say, in other words	or, by that I mean, to put it another way
Fundamentally	basically	in essence, really
to return to the main point	as I was saying	
essential	crucial	important
Naturally	of course, obviously, clearly	certainly

Transcript 🎧 **1.27**

Actually, marketing is arguably *the* most important aspect of management.

So, it follows that marketing must ensure that a business can satisfy customers' needs.

What I mean is, they anticipate consumers' requirements.

Fundamentally, successful marketing is about having accurate data.

Anyway, er … to return to the main point, it's essential to identify basic characteristics of the market.

Naturally, it is the aim of all companies to become the market leader.

Language note

There are three main categories of language here:

1 Stance markers. These are words or phrases that speakers use to show what they feel or think about what they are saying. Adverbs used like this are generally (though not always) positioned at the beginning of the sentence.

2 Phrases used to indicate a restatement. It is very important for students both to understand and to be able to use these, since speakers frequently need to repeat and explain their points.

3 Phrases used to show that the speaker has deviated from the main point and is now about to return to it. Again, this type of phrase is very common in lectures and discussions.

Exercise E

Remind students of the task set by the lecturer at the end of Part 4. Set the questions for pairwork discussion. Students should first list the sort of information they will need to find, then discuss and make notes on what they already know. Then they should compile a list of possible sources of information.

Feed back on all three tasks with the whole class. Do not confirm or correct at this point, as the topic will be taken up in the next lesson.

Answers

Possible answers:

1 Definitions, methods and anything else that is relevant.

2 Answers depend on the students.

3 Internet, library, subject textbooks, encyclopedias, etc.

Closure

Play a version of the game 'Just a minute'. Put students in groups of four. Give them an envelope in which they will find topics written on slips of paper. Students take turns to take a slip of paper from the envelope and then talk for one minute on the topic. Encourage them to use as many of the words and phrases from Exercises C and D as they can. Each person should talk for up to a minute without stopping. If they can talk for one minute they get a point. If they deviate from their topic or can't think of anything more to say, they have to stop. The person who has the most points is the winner.

Suggestions for topics are: luxury holidays, beach resorts, ski resorts, spa resorts, eco-resorts, island resorts, lake resorts, mountain resorts, target markets, market leaders, customers' needs, advertising, market segmentation. (Or if they or you prefer you can use other topics unrelated to tourism or marketing.)

5.4 Extending skills

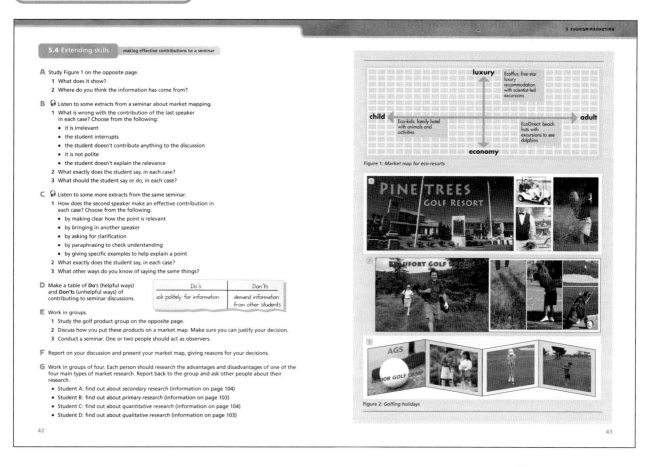

5.4 Extending skills · making effective contributions to a seminar

A Study Figure 1 on the opposite page.
1 What does it show?
2 Where do you think the information has come from?

B 🎧 Listen to some extracts from a seminar about market mapping.
1 What is wrong with the contribution of the last speaker in each case? Choose from the following:
  • it is irrelevant
  • the student interrupts
  • the student doesn't contribute anything to the discussion
  • it is not polite
  • the student doesn't explain the relevance
2 What exactly does the student say, in each case?
3 What should the student say or do, in each case?

C 🎧 Listen to some more extracts from the same seminar.
1 How does the second speaker make an effective contribution in each case? Choose from the following:
  • by making clear how the point is relevant
  • by bringing in another speaker
  • by asking for clarification
  • by paraphrasing to check understanding
  • by giving specific examples to help explain a point
2 What exactly does the student say, in each case?
3 What other ways do you know of saying the same things?

D Make a table of **Do's** (helpful ways) and **Don'ts** (unhelpful ways) of contributing to seminar discussions.

Do's	Don'ts
ask politely for information	demand information from other students

E Work in groups.
1 Study the golf product group on the opposite page.
2 Discuss how you put these products on a market map. Make sure you can justify your decision.
3 Conduct a seminar. One or two people should act as observers.

F Report on your discussion and present your market map, giving reasons for your decisions.

G Work in groups of four. Each person should research the advantages and disadvantages of one of the four main types of market research. Report back to the group and ask other people about their research.
  • Student A: find out about *secondary research* (information on page 104)
  • Student B: find out about *primary research* (information on page 103)
  • Student C: find out about *quantitative research* (information on page 104)
  • Student D: find out about *qualitative research* (information on page 103)

42

luxury

EcoPlus: five-star luxury accommodation with scientist-led excursions

child ← → **adult**

Eco-kids: family hotel with animals and activities

EcoDirect: beach huts with excursions to see dolphins

economy

Figure 1: *Market map for eco-resorts*

PINE TREES GOLF RESORT

BEAUFORT GOLF

AGS JUNIOR GOLF CAMP

Figure 2: *Golfing holidays*

43

Lesson aims

• make effective and appropriate contributions to a seminar

Further practice in:

• speaking from notes
• reporting information

Introduction

Revise stance words and restatement/deviation phrases from the previous lesson. Give a word or phrase and ask students to give one with a similar meaning. Alternatively, give a sentence or phrase from the lecture in Lessons 2 and 3 and ask students to tell you the accompanying stance word or restatement phrase, e.g., *Marketing is … (arguably) the most important aspect of management.*

Exercise A

1 Tell students to look at the market map. Set for pairwork discussion.

2 Ask students to use what they know about marketing of tourism and resorts to speculate on the answer. Feed back, accepting any reasonable suggestions.

Answers

Possible answers:

1 It shows how the eco-resort market could be segmented according to two variables: luxury/economy and adult/child. It also shows three brands that could be offered by a travel organization/tour operator, and where each brand is positioned according to the two criteria.

2 The information has probably come from some form of market research, maybe carried out by a travel operator – for example, by asking travellers, guests or travel agents, or by reading or observing.

Subject and methodology note

Market mapping is a technique which is based on surveys of customers' attitudes and profiles. Two main variables are identified which enable products in a particular market to be distinguished from each other, and then the existing brands in a market are put on the map using knowledge about customers' attitudes and their profiles. Companies can use the technique to help spot gaps in a market which could be filled. They can also see if their target market is being reached or if they need to reposition a brand with extra advertising or, for instance, a different image. Students do not need to know the ins and outs of the technique: the concept is fairly easy to use.

In this lesson, students will be asked to make market maps based on their own ideas rather than by using statistics from a survey.

🎧 Exercise B

In this exercise, students will hear examples of how *not* to contribute to a group discussion.

1/2 Allow students time to read the questions. Tell them they will hear five extracts. They should choose a different answer for each one. Set for individual work and pairwork checking. Play all the extracts through once.

Play the extracts a second time, pausing after each one. Students should write down the actual words, as in a dictation, then check in pairs. When students have completed questions 1 and 2, feed back with the whole class, maybe building up columns 1 and 2 of the table in the Answers section on the board.

3 Set for pairwork discussion. Feed back, adding a third column to the table on the board.

Answers

Model answers:

	Contribution is poor because	Exact words	How to improve
Extract 1	it is irrelevant	MAJED: I love using the Internet!	say something relevant: for example, something about the eco-resorts they found
Extract 2	it is not polite	MAJED: That's rubbish. She obviously didn't want to talk to us.	use polite (tentative) language when disagreeing, e.g., *Actually, that's not quite right. I don't think she really wanted to talk to us.*
Extract 3	the student doesn't contribute anything to the discussion	EVIE: Well, erm … I'm not sure really.	be ready to contribute something when brought into the discussion by the lecturer or other students
Extract 4	the student doesn't explain the relevance	JACK: So it's secondary.	the comment is relevant to the topic but he doesn't explain why. He should say, for example, what he said later after the lecturer asked him to explain (i.e., it's an example of secondary research)
Extract 5	the student interrupts	EVIE: (interrupting) Actually, that's primary.	she should wait until the speaker has finished

Transcript 🎧 1.28

Extract 1

LECTURER: Right, Leila and Majed, what did you find out about the segmentation of the eco-resort market?

LEILA: Well, first of all, we looked on the Internet to see what resorts there were.

MAJED: I love using the Internet!

Extract 2

LECTURER: And what else did you do?

LEILA: We talked to the manager of a tour operator who specializes in resorts. She was quite helpful.

MAJED: That's rubbish. She obviously didn't want to talk to us.

Extract 3

LECTURER: Can you give us an explanation of your market map?

LEILA: Well, yes, it has a vertical and a horizontal axis: children versus adults, and economy versus luxury. And as you can see, we've put some different eco-resort types on it.

LECTURER: What do the rest of you make of this? Evie, what about you?

EVIE: Well, erm … I'm not sure really.

Extract 4

LECTURER: Majed, can you explain how you decided where to place the different resorts on your map?

MAJED: Well, yes, it's based on what the tour operator told us.

JACK: So it's secondary.

Extract 5

LECTURER: What do you mean by 'secondary', Jack?

JACK: I mean it's an example of secondary research. They did two things – they asked someone for information and …

EVIE: [interrupting] Actually, that's primary.

🎧 Exercise C

1/2 This time students will hear good ways of contributing to a discussion. Follow the same procedure as for 1 and 2 in Exercise B above. Make sure students understand they should listen for the second speaker in this case.

Again, when students have completed 1 and 2, feed back with the whole class, maybe building up a table on the board. If you wish, students can look at the transcript in the Course Book.

3 Ask the whole class for other words or phrases that can be used for the strategy and add a third column to the table on the board.

Answers

Model answers:

	Helpful strategy	Exact words	Other ways to say it
Extract 6	bringing in another speaker	LEILA: Didn't they, Majed?	What do you think, Majed?/What do you make of this, Majed?
Extract 7	asking for clarification	JACK: Sorry, I don't follow. Could you possibly explain …?	I don't quite understand. Could you say a bit more about …?
Extract 8	giving specific examples to help explain a point	LEILA: Well, the manager said that … For example, they say that …	For instance …
Extract 9	paraphrasing to check understanding	JACK: If I understand you correctly, you're saying that the travel operators …	So what you are saying is …
Extract 10	making clear how the point is relevant	EVIE: Yes, but if we could just go back to the market map, the EcoKids programme …	Thinking about …/If we can go back to … for a moment, …

Transcript 🎧 1.29

Extract 6

LECTURER: Let's go back to the market map for the moment to see how it can help with segmentation. First of all, tell us about the dimensions you chose.

LEILA: Well, the tour operator we talked to used price and age group as the main ways to distinguish their services. Didn't they, Majed?

MAJED: Absolutely. Those were really the only criteria they used. So that's why we chose them.

Extract 7

MAJED: In their brochure they put the product aiming at families with children next to the EcoDirect product which, according to the lady, is aimed at couples without children. What's quite important is that they put the EcoPlus product, aiming at wealthy, elderly people, on a different page of the brochure, in smaller type and with no photos.

JACK: Sorry, I don't follow. Could you possibly explain why that's important?

MAJED: Well, basically they're trying to aim for the mass market first, I think. They don't seem to be as interested in the EcoPlus market.

Extract 8

EVIE: I don't understand how travel agents know exactly which eco-holidays are suitable for which market.

LEILA: Well, the manager said that as a tour operator they give very specific information about their target markets to the agents. For example, they say that the EcoDirect holiday shouldn't really be offered to families with young children.

Extract 9

MAJED: Yes, they tell travel agents exactly about the ins and outs of each product, so agents can achieve maximum sales.

JACK: If I understand you correctly, you're saying that the travel operators supply their travel agents with information about how to market their products.

MAJED: Yes, that's right.

Extract 10

LECTURER: This is all very interesting, isn't it?

EVIE: Yes, but if we could just go back to the market map, the EcoKids programme is for families with children so it goes on the left, and it's in the cheap to middle price range, so it goes around the middle on the vertical axis.

LEILA: Correct!

Exercise D

Set for group work. Tell students to brainstorm suggestions for more good and bad seminar strategies. They should think about what helps a seminar discussion to be successful. It may help to think about having seminar discussions in their own language, but they should also think about what is involved in having a seminar discussion in English. Aspects to consider include language, how to contribute to discussions and how to behave.

Feed back, making a list on the board.

Answers

Possible answers:

Do's	Don'ts
ask politely for information	demand information from other students
try to use correct language	
speak clearly	mumble, whisper or shout
say when you agree with someone	get angry if someone disagrees with you
contribute to the discussion	sit quietly and say nothing
link correctly with previous speakers	
build on points made by other speakers	
be constructive	be negative
explain your point clearly	
listen carefully to what others say	start a side conversation
allow others to speak	dominate the discussion

Exercise E

Set students to work in groups of five or six. All groups look at the pictures of golfing holidays.

In each group there should be one or two observers and three or four discussing. Groups should appoint one person to take notes on the discussion, since they will have to present their solution to another group. During the discussion, they will need to identify two key variables (consisting of a pair of antonyms) for the market map. (They may choose the same variables as in Figure 1 in Exercise A.) They will then need to decide where to place each product on the map and be able to justify their decisions. If you wish, give each group a large sheet of paper on which to draw their market map. While students are talking, you can listen in and note where students may need help with language, and where particularly good examples of language are used.

The students acting as observers for the discussion should use a checklist of things to watch for. One observer can concentrate on poor contributions and the other on good contributions. Sample checklists are provided in the additional resources section (Resource 5D) – students simply mark in each cell whenever the behaviour occurs.

Exercise F

For this exercise, groups can join together to make one larger group. Alternatively, if the groups are already large, divide each group in half and send one half plus one observer to another group.

First, the observers should give an overview of how the seminar discussion went and should highlight especially good practice. They can also report on poor contributions, but this needs to be done carefully and constructively (possibly without mentioning names), so that individuals are not embarrassed or upset.

Then the person who took notes should present the decisions of their group to the other group.

Finally, feed back to the whole class on what you heard as you listened in to the groups. Suggest improvements for words and phrases, and highlight good practice.

Exercise G

With the whole class, revise asking for information, opinions and clarification, and agreeing or disagreeing in a seminar. Also remind students about reporting information to people (see Unit 3 *Skills bank*). For this discussion exercise, students will make use of the information at the back of the Course Book, plus the information they have already found on the four research types, as set in Lesson 3, Exercise B. Each student should have found out information about one type of research (primary, secondary, qualitative, quantitative) and be able to give the source reference for their information.

Set students to work in groups of four. Each student is allocated one type of research and reads this information. Students should not write anything down: instead they should read and try to remember the information, and then close their books. It is best to discuss each type of research in turn. Student A asks Student C *What did you find out about …?* Student A explains, while the others ask questions and take notes.

While students are discussing, 'eavesdrop' the conversations, noting where students are having difficulty with language and where things are going well. When everyone has finished, feed back with the class on points you have noticed while listening in to the discussions.

Closure

1 If you wish, refer students to the *Skills bank – Seminar language* for consolidation.

2 Focus on the meaning of some of the vocabulary connected with research from Lessons 2 and 4. For example:

   analysis
   attitudes
   beliefs
   data
   definition
   identify
   research
   qualitative
   quantitative
   sources
   statistics
   survey
   trend

Extra activities

1 Work through the *Vocabulary bank* and *Skills bank* if you have not already done so, or as a revision of previous study.

2 Use the *Activity bank* (Teacher's Book additional resources section, Resource 5A).

  A Set the crossword for individual work (including homework) or pairwork.

  Answers

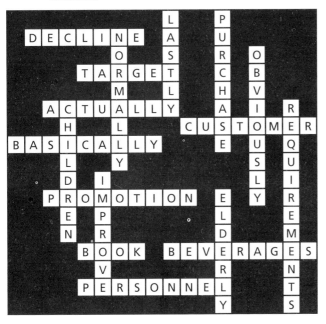

  B Students should select any six words from the box in their book, listed here in alphabetical order.

  accurate
  anticipate
  appeal
  brand
  categorize
  characteristics
  data
  ensure
  fail
  mass
  needs
  niche
  quantitative
  requirements
  research
  segment
  strategy
  variety

Call out words at random, not forgetting to note which words you have called. Ask students who have the word on their card to define it and/or give an example sentence. When someone has managed to cross out all the words on his/her bingo card, he/she should call out 'Bingo.' Check to see if all the words are correctly crossed out. If the student has made a mistake, they are out of the game. The first person to correctly cross out all the words on his/her bingo card is the winner.

An alternative is to put students in groups to play the game, with one student acting as the teacher.

3 Students can choose a suitable tourism product for which they can try to identify the target markets and/or segmentation. This can be anything they wish. Some suggestions: snorkelling holidays in the Caribbean, polar expeditions to the Arctic, a spa resort in Sri Lanka. Inspiration for products can be had by looking at the Internet, particularly travel sites. Students can present their findings to the whole class or in groups.

6 THE BUSINESS OF EVENTS TOURISM

Unit 6 continues the theme of marketing and focuses on the product, which is central to the marketing mix. Lesson 1 looks at typical life cycles of events such as festivals in terms of costs, sales and cash flow. The reading text in Lesson 2 discusses the attraction of large-scale events. The unit finishes with a case study of a marketing strategy in a mature market: how a city art gallery used sponsorship to increase visitor numbers.

Skills focus

Reading
- locating key information in complex sentences

Writing
- writing complex sentences
- reporting findings from other sources: paraphrasing

Vocabulary focus
- synonyms, replacement subjects, etc. for sentence-level paraphrasing

Key vocabulary

attend	fair (n)	participate
attendance	festival	peak (n and v)
availability	frequent	regional
cash flow	hallmark event	scope
celebrate	income	sponsor (n and v)
celebration	investment	themed weekend
convention	logistics	trend
corporate	mega event	value (n)
event	one-off	venture (n)
exhibition	participant	virtual

6.1 Vocabulary

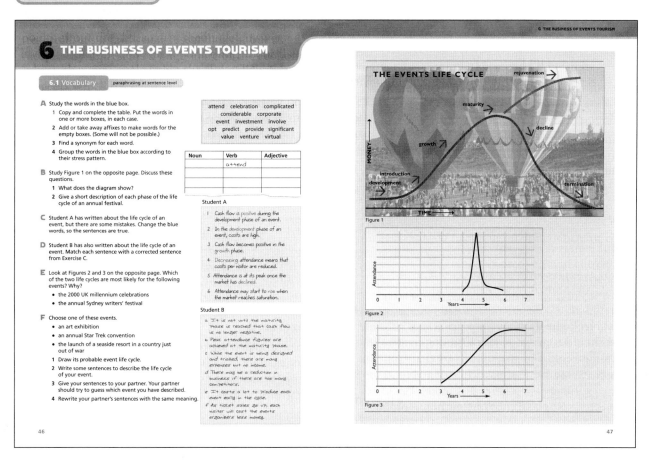

6 THE BUSINESS OF EVENTS TOURISM

6.1 Vocabulary — paraphrasing at sentence level

A Study the words in the blue box.
1 Copy and complete the table. Put the words in one or more boxes, in each case.
2 Add or take away affixes to make words for the empty boxes. (Some will not be possible.)
3 Find a synonym for each word.
4 Group the words in the blue box according to their stress pattern.

attend celebration complicated considerable corporate event investment involve opt predict provide significant value venture virtual

B Study Figure 1 on the opposite page. Discuss these questions.
1 What does the diagram show?
2 Give a short description of each phase of the life cycle of an annual festival.

Noun	Verb	Adjective
	attend	

Student A
1 Cash flow is positive during the development phase of an event.
2 In the development phase of an event, costs are high.
3 Cash flow becomes positive in the growth phase.
4 Decreasing attendance means that costs per visitor are reduced.
5 Attendance is at its peak once the market has declined.
6 Attendance may start to rise when the market reaches saturation.

C Student A has written about the life cycle of an event, but there are some mistakes. Change the blue words, so the sentences are true.

D Student B has also written about the life cycle of an event. Match each sentence with a corrected sentence from Exercise C.

E Look at Figures 2 and 3 on the opposite page. Which of the two life cycles are most likely for the following events? Why?
• the 2000 UK millennium celebrations
• the annual Sydney writers' festival

Student B
a It is not until the maturity phase is reached that cash flow is no longer negative.
b Peak attendance figures are achieved at the maturity phase.
c While the event is being designed and trialled, there are many expenses but no income.
d There may be a reduction in business if there are too many competitors.
e It costs a lot to produce each event early in the cycle.
f As ticket sales go up, each visitor will cost the events organizer less money.

F Choose one of these events.
• an art exhibition
• an annual Star Trek convention
• the launch of a seaside resort in a country just out of war
1 Draw its probable event life cycle.
2 Write some sentences to describe the life cycle of your event.
3 Give your sentences to your partner. Your partner should try to guess which event you have described.
4 Rewrite your partner's sentences with the same meaning.

46

47

General note

Read the *Vocabulary bank* at the end of the Course Book unit. Decide when, if at all, to refer students to it. The best time is probably at the very end of the lesson or the beginning of the next lesson, as a summary/revision.

Lesson aims

• paraphrase at sentence level using passives, synonyms, negatives, replacement subjects

Further practice in:

• affixes
• stress within words
• word sets – synonyms, antonyms

Introduction

1 Revise affixes, *e.g., re~, un~, in~, out~, ~ize, ~al, ~ty, ~ly, ~ion, ~ive, ~ent, ~ance.* Do this by dividing the class into small groups. Give each group one affix. Allow three or four minutes. The group which can list the most words is the winner.

2 Revise words describing graphs (from Unit 5). Draw a line graph on the board. The line should rise and fall, sharply and gradually, have a peak and a point where it levels off. Point to each part of the line and ask students to give you the appropriate verb and adverb. Alternatively, draw your own line graph on a piece of paper and describe it. Students should try to draw an identical line graph from your description while you are talking.

Exercise A

1 Tell students to make a table with three columns in their notebooks. Go through the example in the Course Book. Set the exercise for individual work and pairwork checking. Tell students to use their dictionaries if they need to check meanings, grammatical category, etc. Feed back with the whole class, building the first three columns of the table in the Answers section on the board. Ask students to say what meanings they can give for the words.

2 Refer to the example in the Course Book. Ask students to suggest a form of *attend* which is a noun (*attendance*). Set for pairwork. Students

Noun	Verb	Adjective	Possible synonym
attendance	<u>attend</u>	attended	participate in (v)
<u>celebration</u>	celebrate	celebratory	party (n)
complication	complicate	<u>complicated</u>	difficult, complex (adj)
consideration	consider	<u>considerable</u>	big (adj)
corporation	incorporate	<u>corporate</u>	business (n)*
<u>event</u>	–	eventful	happening (n)
<u>investment</u>	invest	invested	funds (n)
involvement	<u>involve</u>	involved	include, comprise (v)
option	<u>opt</u>	opted	choose (v)
prediction	<u>predict</u>	predicted, predictable	expect (v)
provision	<u>provide</u>	provided	deliver (v)
–	signify	<u>significant</u>	important (adj)
<u>value</u>	value	valued, valuable	worth (n)
<u>venture</u>	venture	–	project (n)
–	–	<u>virtual</u>	web-based (adj)

* this is a noun but common in noun noun constructions

should try to fill as many empty boxes as possible. They should continue to use their dictionaries to check meanings and spellings. Note that it is possible to use the past participle of a verb as an adjective if there is no other possibility. Feed back with the whole class, checking meanings of the words added to the table.

3 Add a fourth column on the board and give it the heading 'Possible synonym'. Ask students to suggest (or find in their dictionaries) synonyms or near synonyms for these words. Limit the synonyms to those for the underlined words. Accept all reasonable suggestions.

4 Set for pairwork. Feed back with the whole class, checking pronunciation.

Answers

Model answers:

1–3 See table above.

4

one syllable	opt
Oo	value, venture
oO	attend, event, involve, predict, provide
oOo	investment
Ooo	corporate, virtual
Oooo	complicated
oOoo	significant
ooOo	celebration
oOooo	considerable

Exercise B

1 Set for pairwork discussion. Monitor but don't assist. Feed back with the whole class, checking that students can give the topic of the diagram, and the meanings of the vertical and horizontal axes.

2 Set for pairwork discussion. Remind students about words they have already studied for describing trends in graphs. Feed back with the whole class. Make sure that students use the present simple tense to talk about the stages, as this is a *process*.

Answers

Possible answers:

1 Figure 1 shows the concept of the events life cycle. (This is very similar, if not identical, to the general product life cycle in marketing.) The vertical axis represents money and the horizontal axis represents time. As can be seen, a product goes through a series of stages over time and the cost and income vary with each stage.

2 The stages can be described as follows:

Development: ideas for the event are developed. The event is designed and possibly tested.

Introduction: the event is launched.

Growth: people become aware of the event and start to attend it. Attendance and income grow.

Maturity: at this point the event is doing well. It has become established and the market has stabilized. (At this point it may be decided that **rejuvenation** of the event is needed, to prevent a decline.)

Decline: as more and more companies enter the market, or people get used to and perhaps bored with the event, a saturation point may be reached where there are either too many companies offering something similar or people feel that the event is no longer exciting. In the final phase, fewer and fewer people attend until eventually it is no longer viable to organize the event.

Termination: the event is no longer held.

Exercise C

As well as requiring the use of antonyms, this exercise is a check to see if students have understood the diagram in Exercise B. Set for individual work and pairwork checking. Feed back with the whole class. A good way to do this is to use an OHT or other visual medium with blanks for the blue words (see additional resources section, Resource 6B).

Answers

Model answers:

1 Cash flow is <u>negative</u> during the development phase of an event.
2 In the <u>introduction</u> phase of an event, costs are high.
3 Cash flow becomes positive in the <u>maturity</u> phase.
4 <u>Increasing</u> attendance means that costs per visitor are reduced.
5 Attendance is at its peak once the market has <u>stabilized</u>/<u>matured</u>.
6 Attendance may start to <u>fall</u>/<u>drop</u>/<u>decline</u> when the market reaches saturation.

Exercise D

Introduce the idea of paraphrasing – or restating. Elicit from the students the main ways to do this at sentence level, namely:

- using different grammar
- using different words
- reordering the information

Write these points on the board. Also make the point very strongly that a paraphrase is not a paraphrase unless 90% of the language is different. There are some words which must remain the same, but these are very few, and are likely to be words specific to the subject, such as *cash flow*. It is best to try to use all three of the above strategies, if possible.

Students should look carefully at the corrected sentences from Exercise C and then compare them with the paraphrases. The first step is to identify which

sentences match. Set for individual work and pairwork checking. It may be helpful for the students if you reproduce the corrected sentences from Exercise C and the sentences in Exercise D on strips of paper that they can move around. Both sets of sentences are reproduced in the photocopiable resources section (Resource 6C) to facilitate this.

Feed back with the whole class. A good way to do this is to reproduce the sentences on overhead transparencies or other visual medium, with each sentence cut into a separate strip. Display the sentences one at a time, as you agree what is the correct match.

Once the sentences are correctly paired, ask students to locate the parts of each sentence which seem to match. They will need to look at the overall meaning of each phrase, using what they know about the subject, to make sure that the phrases are similar. Set for pairwork. Feed back with the whole group, using the sentence strips and highlighting the matching parts with coloured pens.

Answers

Model answers:

1 **Cash flow is negative** *during the development phase of an event.*
c *While the event is being designed and trialled,* **there are many expenses but no income.**
2 **In the introduction phase of an event,** *costs are high.*
e *It costs a lot to produce each event* **early in the cycle.**
3 *Cash flow becomes positive* **in the maturity phase.**
a **It is not until the maturity phase is reached** *that cash flow is no longer negative.*
4 **Increasing attendance means that** *costs per visitor are reduced.*
f **As ticket sales go up,** *each visitor will cost the events organizers less money.*
5 *Attendance is at its peak* **once the market has stabilized/matured.**
b *Peak attendance figures are achieved* **at the maturity phase.**
6 *Attendance may start to fall* **when the market reaches saturation.**
d *There may be a reduction in business* **if there are too many competitors.**

A final step is to discuss the changes that have been made in detail. Students should refer to the list of types of changes you have written on the board. Look at each paraphrase with the class and ask students what changes have been made. Be specific about the types of vocabulary or grammar changes.

	Types of change in paraphrase
1 Cash flow is negative … c … there are many expenses but no income.	reorder grammar: replacement subject *there* vocab: all words different
1 … during the development phase of an event. c While the event is being designed and trialled, …	reorder grammar: time clause instead of phrase; use of passive vocab: all words different
2 In the introduction phase of an event, … e … early in the cycle.	reorder vocab: different time phrase
2 … costs are high. e It costs a lot to produce each event …	reorder vocab: all words different, except *costs* and even that has changed from noun to verb grammar: replacement subject *it*
3 Cash flow becomes positive … a … that cash flow is no longer negative.	reorder vocab: antonyms. Note *cash flow* and *maturity phase* are not changed as they are technical words grammar: negatives
3 … in the maturity phase. a It is not until the maturity phase is reached …	reorder vocab: *maturity phase* not changed here; use of *reached* grammar: phrase expanded to clause – cleft sentence construction
4 Increasing attendance means that … f As ticket sales go up, …	no reorder vocab: all words different; possibly a slight change in meaning with *mean*, but this still preserves the overall sense grammar: noun phrase *increasing attendance* changes to verb phrase
4 … costs per visitor are reduced. f … each visitor will cost the events organizers less money.	no reorder vocab: all words different, except *visitor* grammar: passive changes to active
5 Attendance is at its peak … b Peak attendance figures are achieved …	no reorder vocab: all words different apart from *peak* and *attendance* grammar: active changes to passive
5 … once the market has stabilized. b … at the maturity phase.	no reorder vocab: all words different grammar: clause to phrase
6 Attendance may start to fall … d There may be a reduction in business …	no reorder vocab: all words different grammar: replacement subject (*there*) is used
6 … when the market reaches saturation. d … if there are too many competitors.	no reorder vocab: all words different grammar: *if* in place of *when*; replacement subject *there*

Exercise E

Put students in pairs to discuss the two figures, and which event is most likely to have which type of cycle. Feed back with the whole group. If you wish, you could write some descriptive sentences on the board.

Answer

Model answer:

These two graphs show extremes of event life cycles. Figure 2 shows a four-year development phase, a rapid increase in attendance following introduction and an extremely rapid decline – the likely product is the millennium celebration event. Figure 3 shows a development phase of around three years, and a rapid introduction and growth phase. The product is still selling well in a mature market. The likely product is the annual Sydney writers' festival.

Exercise F

1/2 Set for individual work.

3 Set for pairwork. Go round and check what students have written, giving advice if necessary.

4 Set for individual work or for homework. Tell students to try to follow the advice for paraphrasing in Exercise D, i.e., to reorder the information and to change vocabulary and grammar as far as possible. You may wish to refer students to the *Vocabulary bank* at this point to provide a reminder for grammar structures to use.

Answers

1 Possible answers:

- an art exhibition is likely to be like Figure 2
- an annual Star Trek convention is likely to be like Figure 3

- the launch of a seaside resort in a country just out of war: this is likely to have a short introduction period, followed by a slow growth period (a few years) and maturity for a longer time (like Figure 1 but no decline visible)

2–4 Answers depend on the students.

Closure

Get students to work in small groups and list as many (local, regional or international) events they can think of. After this, get them to indicate how important they think these events are in terms of (local, regional or international) tourism.

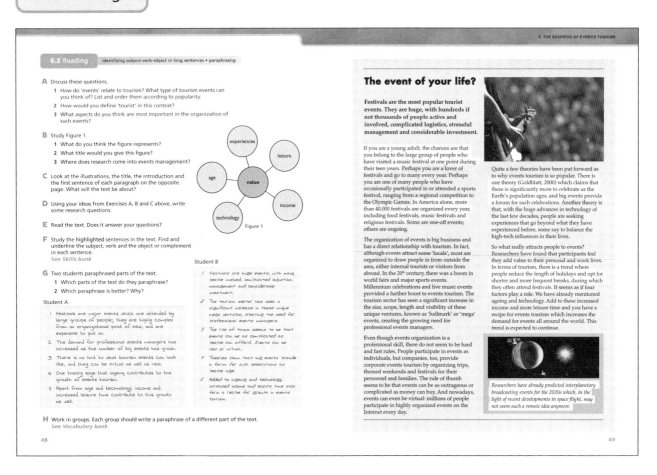

General note

Read the *Skills bank* at the end of the Course Book unit. Decide when, if at all, to refer students to it. The best time is probably Exercise F, or at the very end of the lesson or the beginning of the next lesson, as a summary/revision.

Lesson aims

- identify the kernel SVC/O of a long sentence

Further practice in:

- research questions
- topic sentences
- paraphrasing

Introduction

Remind the class about techniques when using written texts for research. Ask:

What is it a good idea to do:

- *before reading?* (think of research questions)
- *while you are reading?* (look for topic sentences)
- *after reading?* (check answers to the research questions)

What words in a text signal the development of a topic in a new direction? (markers showing contrast such as *but*, *however*, *at the same time*, *on the other hand*, etc.).

If you wish, refer students to Unit 4 *Skills bank*.

Exercise A

Set for general discussion. Allow students to debate differences of opinion. Encourage them to give examples if they can. Do not correct or give information at this point, as these topics will be dealt with in the text. However, for your information only at this stage, research has shown that music events are most popular, followed closely by food, culture and recreation. In turn these are followed by entertainment, history, creative arts and education. 'Tourists' can be local, regional and international.

Exercise B

1 Set for pairwork discussion. Feed back with the whole class. Accept any reasonable answers. If students don't know, don't tell them, but say they may find out in the reading text.

2 Set for pairwork. Feed back with the whole class.

3 Discuss with the whole class. Accept any sensible suggestions. Don't elaborate further at this point, as more information will be found in the text.

Answers

Model answers (do not expect students to produce these answers at this stage; return to the questions after students have read the text):

1 The figure shows the contributory factors that play a role in people's desire for tourism events: age, income, leisure, technology and experiences. All these together form the added value that events tourists are looking for.

2 Possible title: *Contributory factors to popularity of tourism events*.

3 Events organizers need to know about their 'demographic' (target audience) as well as about leisure trends in society. They also need to be knowledgeable in the areas of finance (sponsorship), organization (planning), human resources (volunteer management), etc.

Exercise C

Set for individual work. Elicit ideas, but do not confirm or correct.

Exercise D

Set for individual work and pairwork checking.

Exercise E

Set for individual work. Feed back with the whole class.

Exercise F

Draw a table with the headings from the Answers section on the board. If you wish, students can also draw a similar table in their notebooks. Explain that in academic writing, sentences can seem very complex. This is often not so much because the sentence structure is highly complex in itself, but that the subjects and objects/complements may consist of clauses or complex noun phrases. Often the verb is quite simple. But in order to fully understand a text, the grammar of a sentence must be understood. Subject + verb + object or complement is the basic sentence structure of English. Students need to be able to locate the subjects, main verbs and their objects or complements.

Elicit from the students the subject, main verb and object for the first sentence. Ask students for the *head word* of each subject, main verb and object (underlined in the table in the Answers section). Write them in the table on the board. The idea is that students should be able to extract something which contains the kernel even if it does not make complete sense without the full phrase. Add the leading prepositional/adverbial phrase, pointing out that this part contains information which is extra to the main part of the sentence. The sentence can be understood quite easily without it.

Set the remainder of the exercise for individual work followed by pairwork checking. Finally, feed back with the whole class. You may wish to refer students to the *Skills bank – Finding the main information*.

Answers

Model answers:
See table below.

Note: Conjunctions linking main and sub clauses have been placed in the first column in brackets.

Leading (prepositional/ adverbial) phrases	Subject	Verb	Object/complement (Head noun)
If you are a young adult, the chances are that	you	belong to	the large <u>group</u> (of people who have visited a music festival at one point during their teen years).
In America alone,	more than 40,000 <u>festivals</u>	are organized	–
	one <u>theory</u> (Goldblatt, 2000)	claims*	–
	more	is (to celebrate)*	–
(and)	big <u>events</u>	provide	a forum for such celebrations.
In terms of tourism,	people	reduce	the <u>length</u> of holidays
	(people)	opt for	shorter and more frequent breaks
during which (often)	they	attend	festivals.
	Researchers	have (already) predicted	interplanetary broadcasting <u>events</u> for the 2020s
in the light of recent developments in space flight,	which (= the events)	may not seem	such a remote <u>idea</u> anymore.

*note that the replacement subject makes it harder to find the subject, e.g.,
There is one theory which claims = One theory claims
There is more to celebrate = More (S) is to celebrate (V)

Exercise G

Set for individual work and pairwork checking. Make sure that students identify the original phrases in the text first before looking at the paraphrases.

Feed back with the whole class. A good way to demonstrate how Student B's text contains too many words from the original is to use an OHT or other visual medium and highlight the common words in colour. (A table giving the sentences is included in the additional resources section – Resource 6D.) Check that students are able to say which parts of the paraphrase match with the original, and which structures have been used.

Answers

Model answers:

1 1 = paragraph 1 (introductory paragraph)

   2 = the last part of paragraph 3

   3 = the middle of paragraph 4

   4 = paragraph 5, sentence 2

   5 = the last part of paragraph 6

2 Student A's paraphrase is better, because it uses fewer words from the original text.

Language note

It is important that students understand that when paraphrasing, it is not sufficient to change a word here and there and leave most of the words and the basic sentence structure unchanged. This approach to paraphrasing is known as 'patch-writing' and is considered to be plagiarism. It is also important when paraphrasing not to change the meaning of the original – also quite hard to do.

Exercise H

Refer students to the *Vocabulary bank* at this stage. Review paraphrasing skills with the whole class before starting this exercise.

Divide the text into parts. Give each section to different students to work on. Alternatively, you could choose one part of the text for all students to work on. This can be done in class or if you prefer as individual work/homework. If students are doing the work in class in groups or pairs, a good way to provide feedback is to get students to write their paraphrase on an OHT or other visual medium. Show each paraphrase (or a selection) to the class and ask for comments. Say what is good about the work. Point out where there are errors and ask for suggestions on how to improve it. Make any corrections on the OHT or other visual medium with a different coloured pen.

Closure

1 Divide the class into two teams. Write the topic sentences from the reading text on strips, or photocopy them from the additional resources section (Resource 6E). One team chooses a topic sentence and reads it aloud. The other team must give the information triggered by that topic sentence. Accept only the actual paragraph content.

2 Dictate the following to the class:

Think of a tourism event which …

… has a large share of a mature market

… has just been launched

… includes travel as part of its core product

… is international in scope

Students work in pairs to think of events which fit the descriptions. The first pair to find a product for each category are the winners. Feed back with the whole class.

6.3 Extending skills

[Reproduced student book pages 50–51]

6.3 Extending skills — understanding complex sentences

A Study the words in box a from Lesson 2.
1 What part of speech are they in the text?
2 Think of one or more words that have a similar meaning to each word.

> participate in ongoing
> boost put forward claim seek
> trend reduce frequent

B Complete the summary with words from Exercise A. Change the form or part of speech if necessary.

> An increasing number of people _____ mega events. These events _____ tourism in an area. Researchers _____ that participants are _____ new experiences in our age of technology. Other theories have been _____ which show that the _____ is for people to _____ the number of long holidays they have and opt for more _____ short breaks. Hallmark events seem to top the list of tourists' preferences. Some are one-off events, others are _____ .

C Study the words in box b.
1 What is each base word?
2 How does the affix change the part of speech?
3 What is the meaning in the text in Lesson 2?

D Study sentences A–E on the opposite page.
1 Copy and complete Table 1. Put the parts of each sentence in the correct box.
2 Rewrite the main part of each sentence, changing the verb from active to passive or passive to active.

E Look at the 'Other verbs' column in Table 1.
1 How are the clauses linked to the main part of the sentence?
2 In sentences A–C, what does each relative pronoun refer to?
3 Make simpler versions of the original sentences.

> stressful regional
> visibility professional themed
> outrageous population interplanetary

6.4 Extending skills — writing complex sentences

A Make one sentence for each box on the right, using the method given in red. Include the words in blue. Write the sentences as one paragraph.

B Study the notes on the opposite page which a student made about a case study. Write up the case study.
1 Divide the notes into sections to make suitable paragraphs.
2 Decide which ideas are suitable topic sentences for the paragraphs.
3 Make full sentences from the notes, joining ideas where possible, to make one continuous text.

> Vodafone made a deal with the Summadayze music festival in Australia and New Zealand.
> Vodafone sponsored the festival.
> relative, passive In 2006

> The stages displayed Vodafone's name.
> The entrance tickets displayed Vodafone's name.
> passive, ellipsis In the deal

> People attending the festival had access to special mobile phone services.
> These services gave information about the bands performing.
> These services gave information about the latest gigs.
> relative, passive, ellipsis In addition

> Vodafone created new added value.
> Vodafone attracted a new range of customers.
> participle As a result

50

A In the UK the name of the annual music festival which was previously known as Music on the Sea was changed to the International Shanty Festival.

B Three of the many ways in which an event can be evaluated will be described here.

C You can also post messages on the Internet blog, which is so useful that this benefit has played an important part in the rate at which this event has developed.

D As well as understanding its target audiences, an events management company must fully understand the qualities of its products.

E Having taken these steps as part of an integrated events management approach, the organizers saw a satisfactory increase in attendance.

Table 1: Breaking a complex sentence into constituent parts

	Main S	Main V	Main O/C	Other V + S/O/C	Adv. phrases
A	the name (of the annual music festival)	was changed	(to) the International Shanty Festival	which was known as Music on the Sea	In the UK; previously
B					

> Marketing strategy in a mature market:
> A case study - Organizing Fundays at the City Art Gallery
> • art gallery operating in a small market - needs to maintain a competitive edge - how?
> • good e.g. of this situation = City Art Gallery sponsorship programme
> • analysis of figures → museum attendance low, market reached maturity
> • gallery developed 2 major new activities:
>   1) activities for families on Sunday afternoon - many attractions
>   2) online gallery - pre/during/after visit - show all collection + many other features
> • parents saw benefits quickly
> • sharp increase in web hits → people get interested in gallery/activities
> • → attendance up
> • Sunday afternoon events - v.well attended
> • after making changes, gallery did research:
>   - attracted new (esp. younger) customers
>   - kept existing customers
>   - increased awareness of gallery
>   - new activities v.important for young visitors
> • long-term issue - finance - how to keep events going?
> • sponsorship - good marketing strategy
> • family performance activities attracted interest of media
> • Sunday Telegraph newspaper → aim: younger readership
> • to keep ahead paper had to look at poss. extra benefits → attract existing + new readers
> • deal made = Sunday Telegraph sponsored 'Funday Afternoon Family Activities'
> • arrangement - beneficial to both parties
> • both gallery and newspaper achieved aims + created added value

51

Lesson aims

- study sentence structure in more detail
- identify the main information in:
  an active sentence
  a passive sentence
  a complex sentence with participles
  a complex sentence with embedded clauses

Further practice in:

- vocabulary from Lesson 2

Introduction

Ask students how many phrases or compound nouns they can make with the word *market*. Tell them to brainstorm a list in pairs. Feed back with the whole class.

Possible answers: *market share, market research, market leader, market segment, target market, market size, market trends, growth/growing market, over 50s market, gap in the market*, etc.

Exercise A

Ask students to study the words in box a and to find the words in the text. Set for individual work and pairwork checking. Tell students not to use their dictionaries to begin with but to use what they know to guess meanings and parts of speech. If necessary, they should use dictionaries when checking in pairs. Deal with any common problems with the whole class.

Answers

Model answers:

Word	Part of speech	Similar meaning
participate (in)	v	attend
ongoing	adj	recurrent, regular, continuing
boost	v	increase
put forward	v (T)	advance, suggest
claim	v (I)	say, be of the opinion (that)
seek	v (T)	look for
trend	n (C)	tendency
reduce	v (T)	decrease, shorten
frequent	adj	happening more often

Exercise B

Set for individual work and pairwork checking. Students can make use of all the words they have discussed in Exercise A (i.e., the synonyms as well as the words in box a). Feed back with the whole class.

Answers

Model answers:

An increasing number of people <u>participate in/attend</u> mega events. These events <u>boost/increase</u> tourism in an area. Researchers <u>claim/are of the opinion</u> that participants are <u>seeking/looking for</u> new experiences in our age of technology. Other theories have been <u>put forward/advanced/suggested</u> which show that the <u>trend/tendency</u> is for people to <u>reduce/decrease</u> the number of long holidays they have and opt for more <u>frequent</u> short breaks. Hallmark events seem to top the list of tourists' preferences. Some are one-off events, others are <u>ongoing</u>.

Exercise C

Set for pairwork. Feed back with the whole class.

Answers

Model answers:

Word	Base	Effect of affix	Meaning in text
stressful	stress	~*ful* = changes a noun into an adjective, meaning 'having a particular quality'	causing stress/tension
regional	region	~*al* = adjective ending, meaning 'relating to' regions	for a particular region
visibility	visible	~*ility* = noun ending, meaning 'relating to' being visible	prominence, importance; how aware people are of these events
professional	profession	~*al* = adjective ending, meaning 'relating to' jobs/positions/people in work	dedicated, trained
themed	theme	~*d* = changes a verb to an adjective, meaning 'having this thing or quality'	based on a particular activity or interest
outrageous	outrage	~*ous* = changes a noun into an adjective, meaning 'having that quality'	shocking*
population	populate	~*(at)ion* = changes a verb into a noun, meaning 'the process of the action described by the verb'	inhabitants, people who live on Earth
interplanetary	planet	*inter*~ = between or among ~*ary* = adjective ending, meaning 'relating to' planets	between planets

*the word *shocking* is rather strong; here the writer may be using *outrageous* in the sense of attention-grabbing, rather than offensive

Exercise D

1 Copy the table headings onto the board and complete the example with the students. Tell them that when they look at the 'Other verbs' column they may well find several, and should number each verb and subject/object/complement section separately. Point out that the order of each part of the sentence is not reflected in the table: the table is just a way to analyse the sentences.

Set the rest of the sentences for individual work and pairwork checking. Feed back with the whole class. Draw their attention to the 'main' parts of the sentence: it is very important in reading that they should be able to identify these. Notice also that the main parts can stand on their own and make complete sentences.

2 Set for individual work. If the clause is active it should be changed to passive, and vice versa. Students may need to devise a subject (e.g., in sentence A, the events management company).

Answers

Model answers:

See next page.

1 Model answers:

	Main subject	Main verb	Main object/ complement	Other verbs + their subjects + objects/complements	Adverbial phrases
A	the name (of the annual music festival)	was changed	(to) the International Shanty Festival	which* was known as Music on the Sea	In the UK previously
B	Three of the many ways	will be described		in which an event can be evaluated	here.
C	You	can (also) post	messages	1. ... which is so useful 2. ... that this benefit has played an important part in the rate 3. ... at which this event has developed.	on the Internet blog,
D	an events management company	must understand	the qualities of its products.	As well as understanding its target audiences, ...	fully
E	the organizers	saw	a satisfactory increase in attendance.	Having taken these steps as part of an integrated events management approach, ...	

*underlined text = means by which dependent clause is joined to main clause

2 Possible answers:

A The events management company changed the name of the event to the International Shanty Festival.

B I/the author will describe three (of the many) ways (to evaluate events).

C Messages can also be posted on the Internet blog.

D The qualities of (its) products must be fully understood (by an events management company).

E A satisfactory increase in attendance was seen (by the organizers).

Exercise E

This exercise involves looking carefully at the dependent clauses in sentences A–E.

1 Say that these clauses have special ways to link them to the main part of the sentence. Do this exercise with the whole class, using an OHT or other visual medium of the table in Exercise D, and a highlighter pen to mark the relevant words. Go through the clauses asking students what words or other ways are used to link the clauses to the main part of the sentence.

2 Set for individual work and pairwork checking. Students should look at each sentence and identify the antecedents of the relative pronouns. You could ask them to use a highlighter pen or to draw circles and arrows linking the words.

3 Students must be able to get the basic or kernel meaning of the clause. Take sentence A as an example and write it on the board. Point out that the relative pronouns and other ways of linking these clauses to the main clause will need to be changed or got rid of. Students should aim to write something that makes good sense as a complete sentence. They can break a sentence into shorter sentences if necessary.

Set the remaining clauses for individual work. Feed back with the whole class. Accept anything that makes good sense.

Answers

Model answers:

1 A–C use relative clauses. D and E use participle clauses.

2 A *which* = the music festival

   B *which* = ways

   C 1 *which* = using the Internet blog
   3 *which* = rate

3 Possible answers:

A The festival was previously known as Music on the Sea.

B An event can be evaluated in many ways.

C You can also post messages on the Internet blog. This benefit has played an important part in the development of this event.

D A(n events management) company must (also) understand its target markets and its products.

E The organizers took these steps as part of an integrated events management approach, and attendance increased.

Language note

A dependent clause contains a verb and a subject and is a secondary part of a sentence. It is dependent because it 'depends' on the main clause. A main clause can stand by itself as a complete sentence in its own right (usually). A dependent clause always goes with a main clause and cannot stand by itself as a sentence in its own right.

Dependent clauses are typically joined to main clauses with certain types of words: for example, relative pronouns (e.g., *who*, *which*, etc.), linking adverbials (e.g., *if*, *when*, *before*, *although*, *whereas*, etc.); words associated with reporting speech (e.g., *that*, a *Wh~* word such as *what* or *why*) and so on.

Some dependent clauses are non-finite, that is, they don't have a 'full verb' but a participle form (e.g., *having* *taken*) and the subject may not be stated.

Closure

Write the following underlined beginnings and endings of words on the board or dictate them. Ask students to give the (or a) complete word. Accept alternatives and other parts of speech.

avail(ability)

cele(bration)

corpor(ate)

(freq)*uent*

invest(ment)

opt (for)

out(rageous)

partici(pate)

profess(ional)

signi(ficant)

6.4 Extending skills

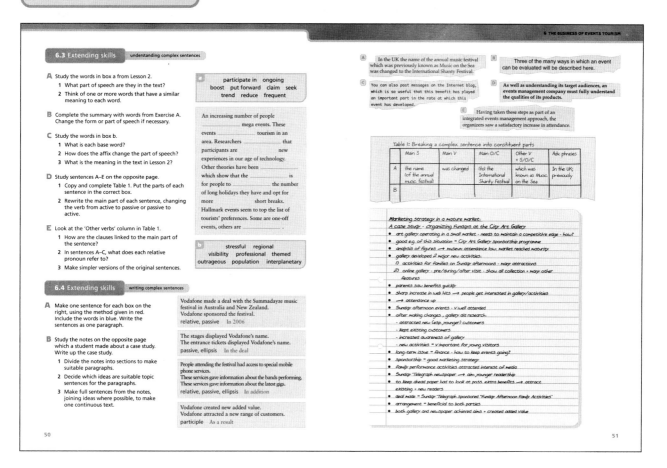

Lesson aims

- write complex sentences:

  with passives

  joining with participles

  embedding clauses

  adding prepositional phrases

Further practice in:

- writing topic sentences
- expanding a topic sentence into a paragraph

Introduction

Ask students to think about and discuss the following questions:

1 Give some examples of well-known events.

2 Is the way these events are organized more likely to be product-led or market-led? In other words, are these companies more likely to develop products in response to perceived market needs (= market-led) or are they more likely to develop new products and then try to promote them (= product-led)?

3 Why?

4 What are some of the marketing strategies an events management company might use?

Exercise A

Set for individual work and pairwork checking. If necessary, do the first box with the whole class. Make sure students understand that they should write the four sentences as a continuous paragraph.

Feed back with the whole class. Accept any answers that make good sense. Point out where the phrases in blue act as linkers between the sentences to make a continuous paragraph.

Answer

Possible answer:

In 2006, a deal was made by Vodafone with the Summadayze music festival in Australia and New Zealand in which the company sponsored the festival. In the deal, Vodafone's name was displayed on the stages and on the tickets. In addition, people attending the festival had access to special mobile phone services through which they were given information about the bands performing and the latest gigs. As a result, having created new added value, Vodafone attracted a new range of customers.

Note: Vodafone's sponsorship deal with Australia/New Zealand Summadayze music festival began in 2006. It can be read about (at the time of writing) on www.summadayze.com or www.vodafone.com.au.

Exercise B

In this exercise, students are required to use all they have practised about sentence structure as well as revise what they know about topic sentences and paragraphing.

Set for pairwork. Do not feed back after each question but allow students to work through the questions, proceeding to write up the whole text. Students can change the wording and add extra phrases to help the flow of the text, as long as the sense remains the same.

If possible, pairs should write their text on an OHT or other visual medium. Select two or three texts for display and comment by the whole class. Make any corrections on the text yourself with a coloured pen. Alternatively, circulate the transparencies to other pairs to correct and comment on. These pairs then display the corrected work and explain why they have made the corrections.

Answers

Possible answers:

1/2 Paragraph divisions are given below, with possible topic sentences underlined. Note that other answers may be possible.

- <u>art gallery operating in a small market – needs to maintain a competitive edge – how?</u>
- good e.g. of this situation = City Art Gallery sponsorship programme
- analysis of figures → museum attendance low: market reached maturity

---

- gallery developed 2 major new activities:
  1) activities for families on Sunday afternoons – many attractions
  2) online gallery – pre / during / after visit – show all collection + many other features

---

- <u>parents saw benefits quickly</u>
- sharp increase in web hits → people get interested in gallery/activities
- → attendance up
- Sunday afternoon events – v. well attended

- <u>after making changes, gallery did research:</u>
  – attracted new (esp. younger) customers
  – kept existing customers
  – increased awareness of gallery
  – new activities = v. important for young visitors

- <u>long-term issue = finance – how to keep events going?</u>
- sponsorship = good marketing strategy
- family performance activities attracted interest of media
- Sunday Telegraph newspaper → aim: younger readership
- to keep ahead paper had to look at poss. extra benefits → attract existing + new readers
- deal made = Sunday Telegraph sponsored 'Funday Afternoon Family Activities'
- arrangement = beneficial to both parties
- both gallery and newspaper achieved aims + created added value

---

3 <u>An art gallery operating in a small market needs to maintain a competitive edge to keep its attendance figures up.</u> A good example of this situation is the City Art Gallery sponsorship programme. Having analysed its figures, the Art Gallery realized attendance was too low, and that the market for what they were offering had reached maturity.

<u>The gallery developed two major new activities.</u> Firstly, they organized activities on Sunday afternoons for families with many attractions. Secondly, they developed an online gallery which visitors could look at before, after or even during their visit to the gallery. The online gallery showed the entire collection and had many other attractive features.

<u>Parents quickly saw the benefits of these developments.</u> There was a sharp increase in web hits, and people became interested in the gallery and activities. This resulted in increased attendance. The Sunday afternoon events were especially well attended.

<u>After making these changes, the gallery carried out some research.</u> This showed that the gallery had attracted new (especially younger) customers, kept existing customers and increased awareness of the gallery. It showed that the new activities were especially important in appealing to young visitors.

<u>The long-term issue was finance: how to keep the events going.</u> It was thought that sponsorship would be a good marketing strategy. The family performance activities had drawn the attention of the media. The *Sunday Telegraph* newspaper was aiming to reach a younger readership, which it needed to keep the paper ahead of its competitors.

Having decided on that strategy, it was looking for benefits it could offer to attract existing and new readers. A deal was made in which the *Sunday Telegraph* sponsored 'Funday Afternoon Family Activities'. The arrangement was beneficial to both parties: both the gallery and newspaper achieved their aims and created added value.

Closure

Give students some very simple three- or four-word SVO/C sentences from the unit (or make some yourself) and ask them to add as many phrases and clauses as they can to make a long complex sentence. Who can make the longest sentence?

For example:

Attendance grew.

→ *It was not until the maturity phase, when attendance was at its peak and demand for the event was established, that* **income became more positive** *and the company created extra funds to start investing in a new event which they will develop over the next few years* … (47 words)

Extra activities

1 Work through the *Vocabulary bank* and *Skills bank* if you have not already done so, or as a revision of previous study.

2 Use the *Activity bank* (Teacher's Book additional resources section, Resource 6A).

A Set the wordsearch for individual work (including homework) or pairwork.

Answers

B With the class, decide on an event that has the potential to draw many tourists. Imagine you are the organizers. Students work in pairs or small groups first to familiarize themselves with the names of committees, services and people involved in organizing the event. They should be able to explain the meaning of these.

Assign one of the responsibilities to each pair or group. Let each pair/group explain what their responsibilities are and how they will contribute to the success of the event.

3 Tell students to do some research into a local/regional/national event in the country where you teach, drawing regional/national or international tourists. Let them describe the target group (in terms of the criteria presented in Lesson 2).

4 After students have completed Exercise B in the *Activity bank*, tell them to work in groups to set up a tourism event for the city or region where you teach. Tell them to describe:

- the event itself
- the reason for holding it
- the aims
- what they hope to achieve/what they expect in each stage in the life cycle
- how they intend to market it.

7 THE BUSINESS OF FUN

In this unit, the focus is on theme parks. Lesson 1 looks at the process of setting up a park, and highlights the importance of planning and scheduling. The first listening extract, from a lecture, identifies factors that make for a successful theme park. The second listening extract is from a seminar in which criteria for choosing a location for a theme park are debated.

Skills focus

 Listening

- understanding speaker emphasis

Speaking

- asking for clarification
- responding to queries and requests for clarification

Vocabulary focus

- compound nouns
- fixed phrases from business and tourism
- fixed phrases from academic English
- common lecture language

Key vocabulary

See also the list of fixed phrases from academic English in the *Vocabulary bank* (Course Book page 60).

(add) value	design (n and v)	maintenance
advertising campaign	entertain	marketing
amusement park	entertainment	operate
appeal (n and v)	experience (n and v)	operation
attract	fantasy	retail (n)
benefit (n and v)	finance (n and v)	ride (n)
business plan	generate	simulator
cash flow	investment	theme park
construction	leisure	themed
corporate	life cycle	(TV) exposure
demand (n and v)	location	venture (n)

7.1 Vocabulary

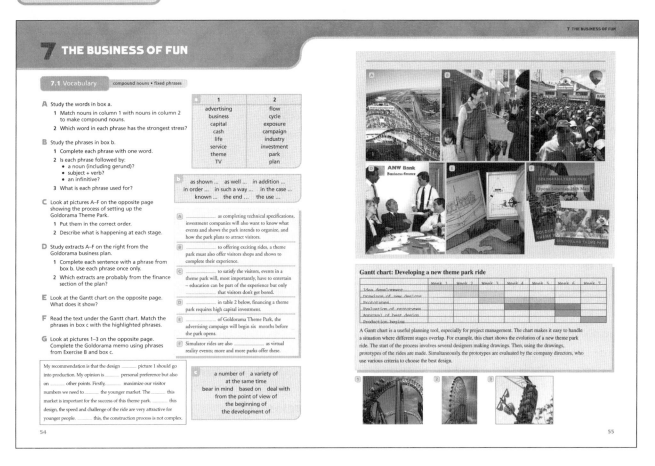

7 THE BUSINESS OF FUN

7.1 Vocabulary compound nouns • fixed phrases

General note

Read the *Vocabulary bank* at the end of the Course Book unit. Decide when, if at all, to refer your students to it. The best time is probably at the very end of the lesson or the beginning of the next lesson, as a summary/revision.

Lesson aims

- understand and use some general academic fixed phrases
- understand and use fixed phrases and compound nouns from the discipline

Introduction

Explain that some of the documents students will study/see/hear about relate to a (fictitious) business plan for a theme park called Goldorama. This places the unit in its context – that is, tourism/theme parks as business.

1 Revise some noun phrases (noun + noun, adjective + noun) from previous units. Give students two or three minutes to make word stars with a base word, trying to find as many possible combinations as they can (preferably without having to look at dictionaries).

For example:

Other base words which could be used are *company, tourism, hospitality, management.* If they are stuck for ideas, tell them to look back at previous units.

2 Introduce the topic of the lesson by looking at the photos throughout the unit. Discuss what students know about theme parks. How do they think ventures like these are set up?

111

Exercise A

Set for individual work and pairwork checking. Feed back with the whole class, making sure that the stress pattern is correct.

Answers

Model answers:

'advertising campaign

'business plan

capital in'vestment

'cash flow

'life cycle

'service industry

'theme park

T'V exposure

Exercise B

1/2 Set for individual work and pairwork checking. Feed back with the whole class, building the first three columns of the table in the Answers section on the board.

3 Add the fourth column with the heading 'Use to …'. Give an example of the kind of thing you are looking for, i.e., a phrase which can describe why you would choose to use this fixed phrase. Elicit suggestions from the students to complete the table, supplying the information yourself if students don't know the answer. If students are not sure about the meaning of some of the phrases, give them some example sentences and tell them that you will look further at how they are used shortly. Leave the table on the board as you will return to it.

Answers

Model answers:

Phrase		Followed by …	Use to …
as shown	in/by	noun/gerund	indicate a diagram or table
as well	as	noun/gerund	add information
in addition	to	noun/gerund	add information
in order	to	infinitive	give the purpose for doing something
in such a way	that*	subject + verb	give the result of doing something
in the case	of	noun/gerund	mention something
known	as	noun	give the special name for something
the end	of	noun	refer to the end of something
the use	of	noun	refer to the use of something

*as to is also possible after in such a way, although in this exercise, one word is required

Exercise C

Refer students to the photographs at the top of the page. Set for pairwork. Students should try to identify what each picture represents. One pair can describe each picture to the whole class. Build up on the board as many key words to describe the process as students can come up with. If students don't know some important words, tell them they will meet them shortly.

Answers

Possible answers:

1 1 B
  2 D
  3 E
  4 A
  5 F
  6 C

2 A Construction phase.
  B Research phase.
  C Opening (day).
  D Securing finance/Financing.
  E Design phase.
  F Marketing (campaign).

Exercise D

Establish that A–F are extracts from the business plan drawn up by Goldorama, who are considering entering the theme park market.

1 Set for individual work. Tell students to check words they can't guess in the dictionary. Feed back. If you wish, ask students to return to the table used in Exercise B and write one sentence for each of the fixed phrases to show their meaning. If you can put this into the context of the process of setting up a theme park that students are a bit more familiar with, so much the better.

2 Set for pairwork. Feed back with the whole class. Add any key words which might have been useful in Exercise C to the board.

Answers

Model answers:

1 A <u>As well</u> as completing technical specifications, investment companies will also want to know what events and shows the park intends to organize, and how the park plans to attract visitors.

  B <u>In addition</u> to offering exciting rides, a theme park must also offer visitors shops and shows to complete their experience.

  C <u>In order</u> to satisfy the visitors, events in a theme park will, most importantly, have to entertain –

education can be part of the experience but only <u>in such a way</u> that visitors don't get bored.

D <u>As shown</u> in table 2 below, financing a theme park requires high capital investment.

E <u>In the case</u> of Goldorama Theme Park, the advertising campaign will begin six months before the park opens.

F Simulator rides are also <u>known</u> as virtual reality events; more and more parks offer these.

2 Answers will vary, but extracts A and D are most likely to be from the finance section.

Exercise E

Introduce the Gantt chart – if students have not seen one before – by saying that it is a highly important tool in project management and extremely useful in any complicated project. It shows how different stages in a process follow each other and/or overlap. Set for pairwork discussion. Feed back with the whole group, making sure that students understand the concept behind the chart, and how this chart might relate to the development of a theme park. Do not correct or confirm students' views of the content at this point.

Subject note

The Gantt chart was the invention of Henry Laurence Gantt (1861–1919), who was a mechanical engineer. Gantt developed his charts in the early 20th century. His invention was hugely important in management then as well as now. It can be used for large-scale construction projects as well as for small pieces of work that an individual person may have to do.

Exercise F

Set for individual work and pairwork checking. Students should use their dictionaries if they are not sure of the meaning of the phrases. Note that some phrases can be used for the same thing – it is a good idea to use a different word to avoid repetition. Ask students to say which sentence goes with which part of the chart. Which part of the diagram is not mentioned?

Answers

Model answers:

A Gantt chart is a useful planning tool, especially (*for*) <u>from the point of view of</u> project management. The chart makes it easy to (*handle*) <u>deal with</u> a situation where (*different*) <u>a number of</u> stages overlap. For example, this chart shows (*the evolution of*) <u>the development of</u> a new theme park ride. (*The start of*) <u>The beginning of</u> the process involves (*several*) <u>a number of</u> designers making drawings. Then, (*using*) <u>based on</u> the drawings, prototypes of the rides are made.

(*Simultaneously*) <u>At the same time</u>, the prototypes are evaluated by the company directors, who (*use*) <u>bear in mind</u> (*various*) <u>a number of/a variety</u> of criteria to choose the best design.

Language note

The fixed phrases here are used in a situation which describes a series of chronological stages. However, the same words can be used when writing or talking in more general abstract academic terms, for example when introducing an essay or lecture or piece of research. This use of these words will be covered later in the unit.

Exercise G

Set for pairwork. Feed back with the whole class.

Answers

Model answers:

My recommendation is that the design <u>(as) shown in</u> picture 1 should go into production. My opinion is <u>based on</u> personal preference but also on <u>a number of</u> other points. Firstly, <u>in order to</u> maximize our visitor numbers we need to <u>bear in mind</u> the younger market. The <u>development of</u> this market is important for the success of this theme park. <u>In the case of</u> this design, the speed and challenge of the ride are very attractive for younger people. <u>In addition to/as well as</u> this, the construction process is not complex.

Closure

Tell students to look through the lesson once more and note down key words and phrases (or use the information on the board if you have written key words and phrases there). Tell them to close their Course Books and describe the typical main stages of setting up a theme park using as many of the words and phrases as they can remember.

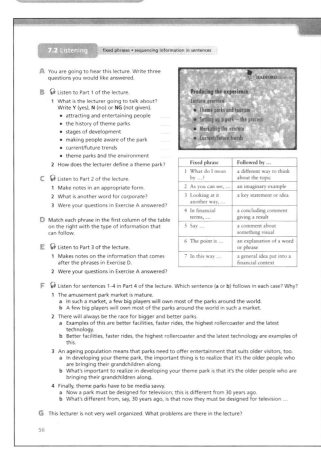

Lesson aims

- improve comprehension through recognition of fixed phrases and what follows them in terms of words/type of information

- understand how information can be sequenced in different ways within a sentence, e.g., for emphasis (see *Skills bank*)

    Further practice in:

- understanding fractured text

General note

Read the *Skills bank – 'Given' and 'new' information in sentences* at the end of the Course Book unit. Decide when, if at all, to refer students to it. The best time, as before, is probably at the very end of the lesson or the beginning of the next lesson, as a summary/revision. Alternatively, use the *Skills bank* in conjuction with Exercise F.

Introduction

Review key vocabulary by writing a selection of words from Lesson 1 on the board and asking students to put them into phrases of two or more words.

Exercise A

Remind students about preparing for a lecture. If you wish, review Unit 1 *Skills bank – Making the most of lectures*. Remind students that, when they begin their talks, lecturers usually provide their listeners with an outline in order to aid comprehension. Elicit from the students the kinds of signpost words lecturers might use (e.g., *To start with, … , Firstly, … , I'll begin/start by …ing, discuss, examine*, etc.). If necessary, refer students to Unit 5.

Refer students to the lecture slide. Tell them to look at the title and bullet points and to list ideas/make questions for each bullet point. At this stage do not explain any words from the slide, or allow students to check in their dictionaries, as the meanings will be dealt with in the lecture. Set the exercise for pairwork.

Feed back with the whole class: ask several students to read out their questions. Write some of the questions on the board.

🎧 Exercise B

Tell students they are going to hear the introduction to the lecture – not the whole thing. Give students time to read questions 1 and 2. Remind them they will only hear the recording once. Play Part 1. Allow students to compare their answers.

Feed back. Confirm the correct answers; discuss why N is probably the best option for 'the history of theme parks' (irrelevant to the lecture content).

Answers

Model answers:

1

attracting and entertaining people	Y
the history of theme parks	N
stages of development	Y
making people aware of the park	Y
current/future trends	Y
theme parks and the environment	NG

2 The lecturer defines a theme park as follows:

- needs to appeal to families
- often has a themed environment
- almost always offers some form of free entertainment, such as musicians and performers
- provides a high standard of service
- offers enough activities to make the average visitor stay for five to seven hours

Transcript 🎧 1.30

Part 1

Good morning, everyone. Do the names Disney World, SeaWorld, Movie World and Six Flags mean anything to you? I'm Craig Horton and I run a theme park. I was asked to talk about theme parks and tourism, and to show you how these businesses work. I'm sure many of you will have visited a theme park at some stage in your lives. People often consider amusement parks, also called theme parks, American inventions. However, amusement parks were first created in the 'old world'. Did you know that it was in 1853 that the first amusement park was opened in Copenhagen, Denmark? We've come a long way since then.

You probably won't be surprised to hear that theme parks need to appeal to families, often have a themed environment, almost always offer some form of free entertainment, such as musicians and performers, and provide a high standard of service. Plus there's the fact that they must offer enough activities to make the average visitor stay for, typically, five to seven hours.

What I'm going to talk about today is one of the core features of tourism: that is, attracting people and entertaining them. I would like to trace the process with you of developing a park from beginning to end. What I mean is, we'll be looking at how a tourism business, in this case a theme park, does what it does. Bearing in mind that, in a way, a theme park is like any other company, big or small, it will become clear that it has a production process that it needs to manage, and that this depends on many other parts of the operation. I mean, it's everything from doing the research, designing the park, financing, building the park, and running it. It's a continuous process. Getting the name of your park to the public is one of the most important steps to take, and we'll be taking a close look at that. Near the end, I'll be making some predictions about the future.

Theme parks are a service industry, and yet they are very much like any other manufacturing company. I agree, a theme park hasn't actually got an assembly line, but it does have to produce the same experience over and over again. Would you call that mass production?

Anyway, we'll look at that later on.

🎧 Exercise C

Refer students to the second point on the lecture slide ('Setting up a park – the process'). Ask students to suggest an appropriate type of notes. The key word here is *process*, which should instantly trigger the idea of a flowchart (see Unit 1). Other parts of the lecture may require different notes.

Give students time to read the questions. Play Part 2. Put students in pairs to compare their notes and discuss the questions. Feed back, establishing the key stages in the process of setting up a theme park.

Finally, with the whole class, ask students how many answers to their questions in Exercise A they heard.

Answers

Model answers:

1 A flowchart is an appropriate form of notes, showing the stages of the process as they follow each other.

2 Business/related to business.

3 Answers depend on students' questions.

Transcript 🎧 **1.31**

Part 2

It was Walt Disney who came up with the idea of starting a theme park in the 1950s. As is commonly acknowledged, Disneyland in Anaheim, California, which opened in 1955, was the first real modern theme park. Since then, the theme park industry in the United States, Europe and Asia has grown dramatically. The industry is now a multi-billion dollar business. Dozens of new parks are built every year. We have a few large corporate owners, and you've probably heard of most of them: Disney, Six Flags, Universal Studios, SeaWorld and Paramount.

I've been told that, in previous lectures, you've become familiar with the life cycle of tourism activities. The process of setting up a theme park can be thought of as a similar process. As you have seen before, there are many steps to this process. The first stage of the development cycle is coming up with an original idea and understanding the economic feasibility of the project. Like a regular business, a theme park has a cash flow, and needs capital investment. Another term for this is drawing up the master plan. Many ideas fail and never get off the drawing board.

What follows are the other ingredients, and even though these stages often overlap, they do happen in a more or less fixed sequence: design, financing, construction, buying the rides and other equipment for the park, installing those rides and the equipment, and organizing the show facilities. And then, finally, there is the actual opening of the park and operating and expanding the park over time. Typically, it can take three to four years to get from the idea to opening the gates.

Exercise D

Explain that these are common phrases in an academic context such as a lecture. Knowing the meaning of the phrases will help a lot with comprehension. Make sure students understand that the items in the second column are not in the correct order.

Set for individual work and pairwork checking. Tell students to check the meaning of any words they don't know in a dictionary. They should be able to guess the meanings of the phrases, even if they don't actually know the phrases.

Feed back with the whole class, completing the first two columns of the chart in the Answers section for Exercise E on the board. (Alternatively, make an OHT or other visual medium from Resource 7D in the additional resources section.) Once the 'Followed by …' column is completed, this will act as a predictive support for Part 3 of the lecture.

> **Methodology note**
>
> Two-column activities are good for pair checking and practice. Once students have got the correct answers they can test each other in pairs, i.e., student A covers the first column and tries to remember the phrases, then B covers the second column and tries to remember the purpose of each phrase. You can then check memory by getting students to close their books and giving first a phrase and students (as a group or individually) must give its purpose, then vice versa.

🎧 Exercise E

1 Tell students that in the next part of the lecture they will hear the phrases in Exercise D. They know now what *type* of information is likely to follow. Now they must try to hear what *actual* information is given. If you wish, photocopy the table in the additional resources section (Resource 7D) for students to write their answers on.

Do the first one as an example. Play the first sentence and stop after '*marketing*'. Ask students: *What is the important phase?* (Answer: '*marketing*'.) Play the rest of the recording, pausing if necessary to allow students to make notes. Put students in pairs to check their answers.

Feed back with the whole class, asking questions based on the words in the 'Followed by …' column. For example:

After phrase number 1, what is the word or phrase that is explained?

After phrase number 2, what is the brochure that is commented on?

2 Refer back to students' questions in Exercise A. Discuss with the whole class whether they heard any answers to their questions.

Answers

Model answers:

1

	Fixed phrase	Followed by ...	Actual information (suggested answers)
1	What do I mean by ... ?	an explanation of a word or phrase	explanation of 'important phase'
2	As you can see, ...	a comment about something visual	the Goldorama advertising brochure
3	Looking at it another way,	a different way to think about the topic	creating an experience = keeping people happy
4	In financial terms, ...	a general idea put into a financial context	added value can be calculated financially
5	Say ...	an imaginary example	an example of how you can neglect an aspect of running the business (which will make people feel unhappy)
6	The point is ...	a key statement or idea	to a large extent the way in which the park is run makes or breaks it (i.e., is responsible for its success or failure)
7	In this way ...	a concluding comment giving a result	the benefits of all people and departments working together

2 Answers depend on students' questions.

Transcript 🎧 1.32

Part 3

An important phase in theme park development is marketing. What do I mean by 'important phase'? Well, let's take a look at the brochure I've given you for the new Goldorama Theme Park in Bristol, UK. This will open in six months' time from now. Marketing is a key area which must begin well before you open a park. You need to develop public relations programmes, get group sales going, and advertise. As you can see, Goldorama is doing all that, so everybody already knows about the park before it has even opened its doors.

In terms of marketing, it's very important to add value. Add value for the visitors and for the company. The ingredients for making a theme park – location, rides, events, staff, catering, etcetera – create something much more than just a day's visit to an amusement park. They create an experience which visitors will remember for a long time.

Looking at it another way, when you run a theme park, you are in the business of keeping people happy. It's a funny business, hey? In financial terms, value can be added for the company. It's easy to calculate: the lower the cost of 'production', the higher the added value or profit can be. The happier people are, the quicker they'll come back or tell their friends.

The difference between a successful and an unsuccessful theme park lies not only in the choice of theme and the rides and events it offers. Say you don't pay enough attention to staffing. You'll soon find your customers are unhappy because there aren't enough people to pay attention to them. In fact, the point is that to a large extent the way in which the park is run makes or breaks it, and to run a park successfully, finance, marketing, sponsorship, sales, operations, entertainment, administration, personnel, maintenance and general services need to work together. In this way, theme parks keep on developing and offering attractions to people which make them return.

And don't forget: typically, people living or staying within one and a half to two hours from any park will account for 80 per cent of visitors. So there's a lot of work to do to also attract tourists from abroad and maximize their enjoyment.

🎧 Exercise F

The purpose of this exercise is to look at how information tends to be structured in sentences. It also requires very close attention to the listening text. Before listening, allow students time to read through the sentences. In pairs, set them to discuss which sentence (a or b) they think will follow the numbered sentences.

Play Part 4 all the way through. Students should choose sentence a or b. Put them in pairs to check and discuss why a or b was the sentence they heard.

Feed back with the whole class. Deal with sentences 1 and 2 first. Tell students that all the sentences are correct, but sentence a 'sounds better' when it comes after the first sentence. This is because of the way that sentences go together and the way in which information is organized in a sentence. Draw the table on the next page on the board. Show how the underlined words in the second sentence link back to the first sentence. In the second sentence the underlined words are 'old' or 'given' information. When sentences follow each other in a conversation (or a piece of writing), usually the 'given' information comes in the first part of a sentence.

Now look at sentences 3 and 4. These are different. The normal choice would be the **a** sentences. However, here the speaker wanted to emphasize the idea of 'important' and 'different'. So a *Wh~* cleft sentence structure was used, which changes the usual order of information. Show this on the table as below. This 'fronting' of information has the effect of special focus for emphasis.

Further examples of different ways to 'front' information and more practice will be given in Lesson 3.

Answers

Model answers:

First sentence		Second sentence	
		Given information	New information
1 The amusement park market is mature.		a In such a market, …	… a few big players will own most of the parks around the world.
2 There will always be the race for bigger and better parks.		a Examples of this …	… are better facilities, faster rides, the highest rollercoaster and the latest technology.
3 An ageing population means that parks need to offer entertainment that suits older visitors, too.	normal order	a In developing your theme park, …	… the important thing is to realize that it's the older people who are bringing their grandchildren along.
	special focus	b What's important to realize …	… in developing your theme park is that it's the older people who are bringing their grandchildren along.
4 Finally, theme parks have to be media savvy.	normal order	a Now a park must be designed for television; …	… this is different from 30 years ago.
	special focus	b What's different …	… from, say 30 years ago, is that now they must be designed for television …

Language note

In English, important information can be placed at the beginning or at the end of sentences. There are two types of important information. The first part of the sentence contains the topic and the second part contains some kind of information, or 'comment', about the topic. Usually the comment is the more syntactically complicated part of the sentence.

Once a piece of text or a piece of conversation (i.e., a piece of discourse) has gone beyond the first sentence, a 'given'/'new' principle operates. Information which is 'given', in other words that has already been mentioned, goes at the beginning of the sentence. Normally speaking, information which is new goes at the end of the sentence. So in the second sentence of a piece of discourse, an aspect of the comment from the previous sentence may become the topic. Thus the topic of the second sentence, if it has already been mentioned in the previous sentence, is also 'given'. Of course, the given information may not be referred to with exactly the same words in the second sentence. Other ways to refer to the given information include reference words (*it, he, she, this, that, these, those,* etc.) or vocabulary items with similar meanings.

Information structure is covered in the *Skills bank* in the Course Book unit.

Transcript 🎧 1.33

Part 4

Now ... er ... let's see ... oh dear, I see we're running short of time ... Maybe I should skip a few slides. On the other hand, perhaps I should just say something about some trends in amusement and theme park development. A lot of research has been done into this area and there are a few trends that stand out.

First of all, you can see that, in terms of life cycle, the amusement park market is mature. In such a market, a few big players will own most of the parks around the world. I've already mentioned companies like Disney and Paramount.

Secondly, there will always be the race for bigger and better parks. Examples of this are better facilities, faster rides, the highest rollercoaster and the latest technology. More and more parks offer visitors the benefits of technology: virtual reality shows, 3D cinema experiences, ride simulators ...

An ageing population means that parks need to offer entertainment that suits older visitors, too, and not just kids. What's important to realize in developing your theme park is that it's the older people who are bringing their grandchildren along.

Finally, and this is more marketing than anything else, theme parks have to be media savvy. What's different from, say, 30 years ago, is that now they must be designed for television and should be able to serve as locations for filming, celebrity events, competitions and conferences. After all, TV exposure will make tourists aware of your park.

Now ... oh dear, I was going to mention the relationship between theme parks and the environment. More and more people will travel to visit theme parks and ... well, but ... ah ... I see that time is moving on. So instead, I'm going to ...

Exercise G

Set for pairwork discussion. Feed back with the whole class. Note that the lecture has not yet finished. The last part will be heard in Lesson 3.

Answers

The lecturer is running out of time. The lecturer has not had time to talk about theme parks and the environment, but neither was this mentioned on the opening slide.

Closure

Encourage students to discuss a theme park they are familiar with. They should say how the theme park attracts and entertains its visitors, and how well they think the park does this. They can also discuss any recent changes to the park (new rides, new facilities, etc.) and evaluate how successful these have been.

The worksheet reproduction (page 57):

7.3 Extending skills — stress within words • fixed phrases • giving sentences a special focus

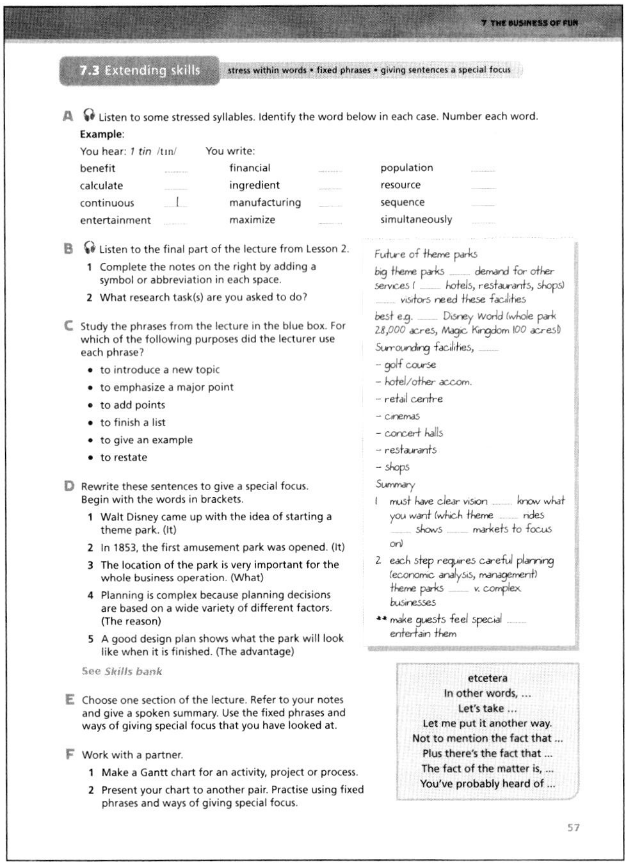

A Listen to some stressed syllables. Identify the word below in each case. Number each word.
Example:
You hear: 1 tin /tɪn/   You write:

benefit ___	financial ___	population ___
calculate ___	ingredient ___	resource ___
continuous ___	manufacturing ___	sequence ___
entertainment ___	maximize ___	simultaneously ___

B Listen to the final part of the lecture from Lesson 2.
1 Complete the notes on the right by adding a symbol or abbreviation in each space.
2 What research task(s) are you asked to do?

C Study the phrases from the lecture in the blue box. For which of the following purposes did the lecturer use each phrase?
• to introduce a new topic
• to emphasize a major point
• to add points
• to finish a list
• to give an example
• to restate

D Rewrite these sentences to give a special focus. Begin with the words in brackets.
1 Walt Disney came up with the idea of starting a theme park. (It)
2 In 1853, the first amusement park was opened. (It)
3 The location of the park is very important for the whole business operation. (What)
4 Planning is complex because planning decisions are based on a wide variety of different factors. (The reason)
5 A good design plan shows what the park will look like when it is finished. (The advantage)
See *Skills bank*

E Choose one section of the lecture. Refer to your notes and give a spoken summary. Use the fixed phrases and ways of giving special focus that you have looked at.

F Work with a partner.
1 Make a Gantt chart for an activity, project or process.
2 Present your chart to another pair. Practise using fixed phrases and ways of giving special focus.

Notes box:
Future of theme parks
big theme parks ___ demand for other services (___ hotels, restaurants, shops) ___ visitors need these facilities
best e.g. ___ Disney World (whole park 28,000 acres, Magic Kingdom 100 acres!)
Surrounding facilities,
– golf course
– hotel/other accom.
– retail centre
– cinemas
– concert halls
– restaurants
– shops
Summary
1 must have clear vision ___ know what you want (which theme ___ rides ___ shows ___ markets to focus on)
2 each step requires careful planning (economic analysis, management) theme parks ___ v. complex businesses
** make guests feel special ___ entertain them

Blue box:
etcetera
In other words, …
Let's take …
Let me put it another way.
Not to mention the fact that …
Plus there's the fact that …
The fact of the matter is, …
You've probably heard of …

57

Lesson aims

- extend knowledge of fixed phrases commonly used in lectures
- give sentences a special focus (see *Skills bank*)

Further practice in:

- stress within words

Introduction

As in Units 3 and 5, tell students to ask you questions about the information in the lecture in Lesson 2 as if you were the lecturer. Remind them about asking for information politely. If they need to revise how to do this, tell them to look back at the *Skills bank* for Unit 3.

🎧 Exercise A

Remind students of the importance of stressed syllables in words (see the teaching notes for Unit 3, Lesson 3, Exercise A). Play the recording, pausing after the first few to check that students understand the task.

Feed back, perhaps playing the recording again for each word before checking. Ideally, mark up an OHT or other visual medium of the words. Finally, check students' pronunciation of the words.

Answers

benefit	4
calculate	9
continuous	1
entertainment	11
financial	5
ingredient	3
manufacturing	7
maximize	8
population	12
resource	2
sequence	10
simultaneously	6

Transcript 🎧 1.34

1 con'tinuous
2 re'source
3 in'gredient
4 'benefit
5 fi'nancial
6 simul'taneously
7 manu'facturing
8 'maximize
9 'calculate
10 'sequence
11 enter'tainment
12 popu'lation

🎧 Exercise B

Write these words on the board and ask students to say what symbols you can use for them when taking notes. Put the symbols on the board.

because	∵
for example	e.g.
is, means	=
leads to*	→
therefore, so	∴
and	& +
a list	numbers, dashes or bullet points
or	/

*the arrow has a wide range of possible meanings, including *made*, *produced*, *did*, *causes*, *results in*, etc.

Tell students they will hear the final part of the lecture. Ask them to read the notes through. Remind them also to listen for their research task. Play Part 5.

Put students in pairs to compare their symbols. Feed back with the whole class, if possible using an OHT or other visual medium of the notes. Discuss acceptable alternatives (e.g., in summary point 1, slashes, plus signs and ampersands would all be acceptable).

Answers

Model answers:

1 Future of theme parks

 big theme parks → demand for other services

 (e.g. hotels, restaurants, shops) ∵ visitors need these facilities

 best e.g. = Disney World (whole park 28,000 acres, Magic Kingdom 100 acres!)

 Surrounding facilities, e.g.

 – golf course

 – hotel/other accom.

 – retail centre

 – cinemas

 – concert halls

 – restaurants

 – shops

 Summary

 1 must have clear vision = know what you want (which theme / rides / shows / markets to focus on)

 2 each step requires careful planning (economic analysis, management)

 theme parks = v. complex businesses

 **make guests feel special & entertain them

2 They must choose a theme, a location and a design for a new theme park in their country and develop an advertising campaign.

Transcript 🎧 1.35

Part 5

I'm going to finish with some more comments about the future of theme parks. The development of a big theme park often creates a demand for other tourism and hospitality services such as hotels, restaurants and shops. This is especially true of a park aiming at tourists. Why is this? Well, it's simple, really – tourists have to stay somewhere, they need to eat and drink, and they want to shop. So, theme parks generate demand for motel and hotel accommodation, entertainment attractions, and commercial and retail development. The best example of this is, again, Walt Disney World in Florida. The whole park is some 28,000 acres, although the Magic Kingdom itself is not that big. It's only about 100 acres! But surrounding the site are many other tourism-related facilities, such as a

golf course, a resort hotel and other types of accommodation, a retail centre and an entertainment village with cinemas, concert halls, restaurants and shops.

I'll finish by reviewing the key factors for successful development of theme parks. To sum up, then, the first factor is that you must have a clear vision of what you want to accomplish. In other words, you must know what you want. You need to know which theme, which rides, which shows, and which markets you want to focus on.

The second key success factor is that each step of the process requires careful planning. Let me put it another way. Without careful economic analysis, careful planning and careful management, it won't work and you won't draw tourists in. Theme parks may appear simple, but the fact of the matter is, they are highly complex businesses. Not to mention the fact that you must make each guest feel special and entertain them to the best of your ability, day in, day out.

OK … oh, I almost forgot to mention the research task. Er … your lecturer has given me a research task for you to do for next time. We would like you to choose a theme, a location, the design and an advertising campaign promoting a new theme park in your country. The campaign centres on the idea of fun and getting what you want when you want it. It needs to communicate three main ideas: the extreme rides, the family rides, and the entertainment. Your target group are visitors within a 90-minute drive time. Research which steps you should take, what the park should look like, and how you should communicate with your target visitor group. Good luck.

Exercise C

Set for pairwork. Feed back with the whole class. Ask for other phrases which have similar meanings, particularly from Lesson 3, and also from Unit 5. Build the table in the Answers section on the next page on the board. Accept any suitable words or phrases for the third column.

Language note

The phrases are appropriate in speaking. Many are not suitable for written language, for which different phrases should be used.

Answers

Model answers:

Use	Fixed phrase	Other phrases
to introduce a new topic	You've probably heard of …	Now, an important concept is …
to emphasize a major point	The fact of the matter is, …	Actually, … In fact, … The point is that …
to add points	Not to mention the fact that … Plus there's the fact that …	also, and, too
to finish a list	etcetera	and so on
to give an example	Let's take …	For example, … e.g., … Let's look at an example of this. For instance, …
to restate	Let me put it another way. In other words, …	What I mean is … That is to say, … By that I mean … To put it another way, …

Exercise D

Students need to decide which word(s) should receive the particular focus and then try to rewrite the sentences. Depending on the class, they can work in pairs or individually first.

Feed back with the whole class. Take each sentence in turn. Ask for suggestions as to which aspect could receive special emphasis. Accept any reasonable answers. If you wish, replay Part 5 of the lecture for students to check their answers. Note that:

- sentences 1 and 2 use an *It* construction to give the special focus
- sentence 3 uses a *Wh~* cleft sentence already seen in Lesson 2
- sentences 4 and 5 introduce new, general words (often found in academic contexts) followed by *is* plus a *that* clause

Answers

Model answers:

1 It was Walt Disney who came up with the idea of starting a theme park.

2 It was in 1853 that the first amusement park was opened.

3 What is very important for the whole business operation is the location of the park.

4 The reason (why) planning is complex is that planning decisions are based on a wide variety of different factors.

5 The advantage of a good design plan is that it shows what the park will look like when it is finished.

After completing Exercises C and D, students can be referred to the *Vocabulary bank* and the *Skills bank* for consolidation and preparation for Exercise E.

Exercise E

Set the initial preparation for individual work. Students can refer to their notes in Lesson 2 or the notes for completion in Lesson 3 (Exercise B). They should think about how they can use the phrases they have looked at, and ways of giving special focus/emphasis. (Note: They should not write out exactly what they are going to say in complete sentences and then read!)

Put students in pairs to give their oral summaries to each other, preferably pairing students who have chosen different sections to summarize.

Go around the class noting any problems or especially good examples of language use. You may wish to choose one or two individuals to give their summary to the whole class.

With the whole class, feed back any language or other difficulties which you noticed.

Exercise F

1 Set for pairwork. Suggest simple activities like making a cup of tea or a sandwich or writing an essay. Students should first list all the different processes and then decide how to order them and which processes overlap. They should draw a copy of the Gantt chart and put the activities in it. They should also decide what time units to use.

2 Put the pairs in groups of four to present their charts to each other.

Closure

Dictate some words for which students have learnt note-taking symbols or abbreviations such as *and, minus, approximately, less than, results in, therefore, because, etc., as, since, for example, approximately*. Students should write the symbol or abbreviation.

7.4 Extending skills

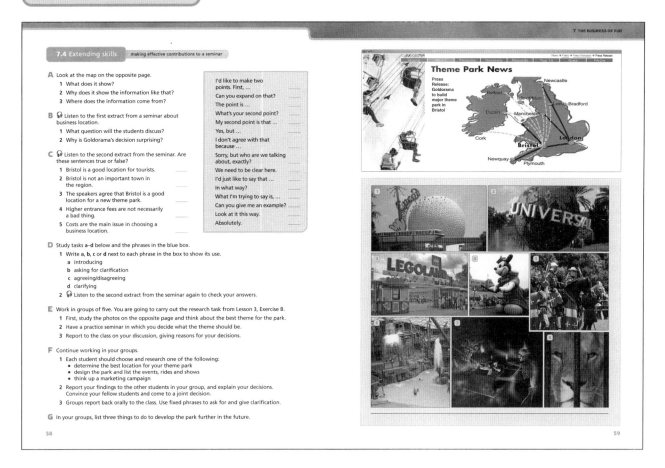

Lesson aims

- make effective contributions to a seminar:

  using pre-organizers – *I'd like to make two points;
  I don't agree with that because …*

  responding to queries by clarifying – *What I'm
  trying to say is …/What I meant was …*

Introduction

Revise phrases from the previous lessons. Give a word
or phrase and ask students to give one with a similar
meaning. Ask for phrases from the previous lesson
which can be used to:

- introduce a new topic
- emphasize a major point
- add a point
- finish a list
- give an example

Exercise A

Set for pairwork discussion. Feed back.

Answers

Possible answers:

1 It shows Bristol and other major cities in the UK
   and the transport links between them.

2 The aim is to show that Bristol is a city within easy
   travelling distance of other major cities.

3 The information comes from a press release about a
   new theme park.

🎧 Exercise B

Allow students time to read the two questions. Play
Extract 1 once only. Check answers in pairs. Feed back
with the whole class.

Answers

Model answers:

1 Why are Goldorama establishing a new theme park
   near Bristol?

2 They already have theme parks near major UK
   cities such as London and Birmingham. These
   places are not too far from Bristol. There are also
   other competitors in the market such as zoos and
   water parks.

Transcript 🎧 1.36

Extract 1

Now, as we know, what's very important for the whole operation is the location of a theme park: it's one of the most important decisions that companies have to make. I asked you to look at the case of Goldorama, who have decided to establish a new park near Bristol in the south-west of the UK. Why are they doing this? They already have parks near several other big cities in the UK, including London and Birmingham, which are not so far away from Bristol. Also, there are many medium-sized competitors, like zoos and water parks, in the area. So, let's have some views.

🎧 Exercise C

Allow students time to read the questions. Play the recording straight through once while they mark the answers true or false. Check in pairs and/or as a whole class.

Answers

Model answers:

1 true	Bristol gives easy access to several popular tourist destinations.
2 false	Bristol is an important regional centre.
3 false	The speakers do not agree that Bristol is a good location.
4 true	Even if the Goldorama park is more expensive, many customers will save on travel costs and may spend more on retail in the park.
5 false	There are other factors such as income and investment potential.

Transcript 🎧 1.37

Extract 2

JACK: Well. <u>I'd like to make two points. First,</u> Bristol gives easy access to several popular tourist destinations.

LEILA: <u>Can you expand on that,</u> Jack?

JACK: Sure, Leila. Bristol is near Wales and the south-west peninsula of the UK.

LEILA: So?

JACK: <u>So the point is</u> that both areas are famous for their beaches and natural beauty. Visitors to the park will want to extend their stay and see more of the UK.

LECTURER: OK. So, <u>what's your second point,</u> Jack?

JACK: I was coming to that! <u>My second point is that</u> Bristol is an important regional centre.

LEILA: <u>Yes, but</u> that's true for London, too. Even more so. I don't think it's a good idea to be so far away from London.

MAJED: Well, <u>I don't agree with that,</u> Leila, because from what I've read, there's huge potential for tourism based in or near Bristol.

EVIE: <u>Sorry, but who are we talking about, exactly?</u> People from the UK, or people flying into the UK from abroad? Goldorama must see enough opportunities here to make this investment.

LEILA : Yes, <u>we need to be clear here.</u> It must be both. Anyway, <u>I'd just like to say that</u> according to what I've read, in the case of a service industry, convenience for customers is a major factor in location.

EVIE: <u>In what way?</u>

LEILA: Well, if you can bring your service nearer to the customer, you can charge a bit more. Also, you may be able at the same time to offer a more attractive service than the competitors.

EVIE: I don't get that. How can it be more attractive if it's more expensive?

LEILA: <u>What I'm trying to say is,</u> the company can charge more for their product but actually the customer might get the product more cheaply overall.

EVIE: I still don't understand. <u>Can you give me an example,</u> Leila?

LEILA: OK. <u>Look at it this way.</u> Theme park visitors typically come from no more than about an hour and a half away. People who live near Bristol would have to travel to London or Birmingham to get to the closest theme park. That would cost them time and money – say, £100 per person? If there is a theme park near Bristol they won't have to spend that money. If Goldorama charge, say, £25 more for the entry fee than London competitors do, the customers may still end up spending less. And what they don't spend on transport, they can spend in the retail areas of the theme park …

MAJED: So everybody wins! It's all about money, in fact.

LECTURER: <u>Absolutely.</u> In making a decision on location, companies have to think about their fixed and variable costs, as well as the income they are likely to get from a particular site. There are other factors, of course, and we'll come on to these later.

MAJED: Yes, and I'd just like to say something else. As I mentioned before, there are potentially a lot of tourists who might come to this park. So it's a good investment, as visitor numbers are likely to increase in the future.

🎧 Exercise D

Check the meaning of 'introducing' phrases. This means a phrase to use before your main statement to announce that you are going to say something. It may also signal how much you are going to say, or how important you think what you are going to say is.

1 Set for individual work and pairwork checking. Feed back.

2 Play Extract 2 from Exercise C. Ask students to tell you to stop when they hear each phrase (underlined in the transcript above). Check what kind of phrase they think it is. Get students to repeat the phrase to copy the intonation.

Answers

Model answers:

I'd like to make two points. First, …	a
Can you expand on that?	b
The point is…	d
What's your second point?	b
My second point is that …	a
Yes, but …	c
I don't agree with that because …	c
Sorry, but who are we talking about, exactly?	b
We need to be clear here.	d
I'd just like to say that …	a
In what way?	b
What I'm trying to say is, …	d
Can you give me an example?	b
Look at it this way.	d
Absolutely.	c

Exercise E

Move on from Exercise D to the simulation in Exercises E, F and G. Encourage students to make this as realistic as possible by choosing a theme that they know or can identify with. The location could be in your area, or it could be elsewhere. If students decide on an international location, remind them that there will be other factors to consider such as language barriers, political stability, exchange rate fluctuations, and so on. If you wish, the whole class could work on the same theme park, but with the location decision (Exercise F) discussed in groups.

You may want to let students listen to the end of the last extract from the lecture in Lesson 3 once more, to refresh their memory about the research task the guest lecturer sets.

With the whole class, revise asking for information. Remind students of the questions used by the lecturer

in Unit 5, Lesson 4. Remind students also about reporting information to people (see Unit 3 *Skills bank*).

Set students to work in their groups of five to discuss the theme for their theme park. Tell them to study the photos on the opposite page to generate some ideas and, if necessary and possible, do some more Internet research on theme parks. A useful Internet link is www.123world.com/amusement/ which provides an overview of theme parks worldwide with links to the parks' websites.

Give them 15–20 minutes for their 'seminar' and then let each group present their theme and the reasons why they have chosen this theme. Encourage students to ask for clarification and to use the appropriate phrases when giving clarification. Note where students are having difficulty with language and where things are going well. When everyone has finished, feed back to the class on points you have noticed while listening in to the discussions.

For reference, the photos show:

1 space (Epcot, Florida, USA)

2 movies (Universal Studios, USA)

3 toys (Legoland, Windsor, UK)

4 cartoons (Disneyland, Hong Kong, China)

5 history (Camelot, Lancashire, UK)

6 water (Cariba Creek, Alton Towers, UK)

7 fantasy (The Haunted House Strikes Back, Alton Towers, UK)

8 animals (Animal Adventure Land, UK)

Exercise F

1 Each student should choose and research one of the three aspects (location, design, marketing). Make sure at least one student in each group is looking at each of these.

2 Tell students to exchange information and notes after, say, 20 minutes. The groups then discuss each of the three aspects and come to a joint decision on each one.

3 When all groups are ready they should feed back to the class, giving an oral report on their findings and decisions. It is important that they do not simply read their information aloud, but use it to inform their speaking.

Alternatively, you could have a 'pyramid discussion' on one of the aspects, e.g., location. Choose one theme for the whole class to debate and put students in pairs to discuss a suitable location for the park. After a short while, the pair should join together with another pair. This group of four should then come to an agreement on a suitable location. The group of four should then join another group of four. One or two people from each group of eight should then present the decision and the reasons for the decision to the class. It will help their presentation if they use visual aids such as maps or diagrams. Finally, the whole class should try to reach agreement on the site decision, taking a vote if necessary. Remind students about agreeing and agreeing, and about good and bad ways to contribute to seminar discussions (refer to Unit 5 if necessary).

While the representatives are presenting their group decisions, you should occasionally interrupt with a wrong interpretation so that students are forced to clarify their statements. Or you could ask for clarification.

Exercise G

Refer back to where the guest lecturer talked about trends and the future of theme parks. Thinking about the theme park the groups or the class have agreed on, tell students to discuss, in their groups, how they would develop the park to ensure its future viability.

Closure

Choose three cities in your country. Ask students to first discuss and then describe and evaluate the characteristics of each city according to the following:

- location
- logistics and transport systems
- people
- industries
- economy
- environment
- quality of life
- image
- cost of living

Then decide whether any of these cities would be suitable for a theme park, and why.

Extra activities

1 Work through the *Vocabulary bank* and *Skills bank* if you have not already done so, or as a revision of previous study.

2 Use the *Activity bank* (Teacher's Book additional resources section, Resources 7A–C).

   A Set the wordsearch (7A) for individual work (including homework) or pairwork. Uncountable nouns are only uncountable in the context in which they are used here; they may be countable in other contexts. Most but not all the words are from Unit 7.

Answers

   B Put students in pairs to play 'word battleships'. The idea behind this game is that each word represents a battleship, which is 'sunk' when all the letters of the word have been located; the aim of the game is to be the first to sink all the ships.

   Give Resource 7B to Student A; give Resource 7C to Student B. Make sure they can't see each other's information. Students take turns to ask about individual squares, e.g., *Is there a letter in (1C)?* The other student answers either *No* or *Yes, it's (F)*. They mark their empty grid accordingly – either putting a letter or a cross in each square. If a student finds a letter, he/she can continue asking until he/she gets a negative answer (i.e., an 'empty' square). Students continue asking one question each until one of them thinks they have found a word, when they

can say *Is the word … ?* The first student to find all their words is the winner.

The words for each category are:

Student A:

- two words for things you can find in an amusement park: *restaurants, rides*
- two nouns ending in *~ment*: *development, investment*
- two verbs ending in *~ate*: *evaluate, generate*
- two words which can be nouns or verbs: *experience, benefit*

Student B:

- two types of tourist accommodation: *apartment, motel*
- two possible themes for theme parks: *space, history*
- two verbs ending in *~ize*: *maximize, organize*
- two words which can be nouns or verbs: *finance, design*

3 Make some statements about what you're going to do after the class and ask students to transform them into *Wh~* cleft sentences. For example:

I'm going to have a coffee after the class.

➔ *What you're going to do after the class is have a coffee.*

I might go to a film tonight.

➔ *What you might do tonight is go to a film.*

Put students in pairs to practise.

8 HOSPITALITY MARKETING

This unit looks at how small hospitality businesses in particular can market themselves effectively. It examines different marketing strategies that can be applied in the small business context, and introduces the concepts of external and internal marketing.

Skills focus

Reading
- understanding dependent clauses with passives

Writing
- paraphrasing
- expanding notes into complex sentences
- recognizing different essay types/structures:
  descriptive
  analytical
  comparison/evaluation
  argument
- writing essay plans
- writing essays

Vocabulary focus
- synonyms
- nouns from verbs
- definitions
- common 'direction' verbs in essay titles (*discuss, analyse, evaluate,* etc.)

Key vocabulary

advertising	external marketing	perception
attract	gain (v)	promote
boost (v)	innovation	promotion
consistency	intangible	retain
cost-effective	internal marketing	strategy
direct mail	localization	tangible
effective	objective (n)	turnover
efficiency	opportunity	word of mouth
establish	outlet	
expense	outsource	

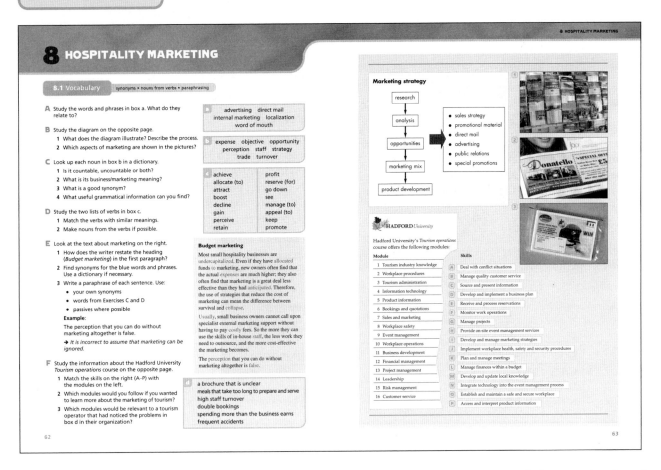

Lesson aims

- extend knowledge of synonyms and word sets (enables paraphrasing at word level)
- make nouns and noun phrases from verbs (enables paraphrasing at sentence level)

Further practice in paraphrasing at sentence level with:

- passives
- synonymous phrases
- negatives
- replacement subjects

Introduction

Revise ways of paraphrasing sentences. Write the following sentences from Unit 6 on the board and ask students to say what changes have been made to the paraphrased sentences.

Original sentence: *While the event is being designed and trialled, there are many expenses but no income.*

Paraphrase: *Costs are high when organizers are in the process of planning and trialling the event, and there is not a lot of money coming in.*

(answer: change in word order, passive to active, use of synonyms)

Original sentence: *It is not until the maturity phase is reached that income is no longer negative.*

Paraphrase: *When the event has become well-known and popular, income will become positive.*

(answer: change in word order, use of synonyms, replacement subject)

Exercise A

Set for pairwork or class discussion. Feed back. Discuss/clarify the difference between marketing and advertising at this stage if you wish. Establish that some words (*advertising*, *word of mouth* and *direct mail*) are marketing **tools**; others refer to specific **strategies** (*localization* – ensuring that events, services and products are embedded in local/regional/national settings; *internal marketing* – making sure that staff within the organization market the organization well through behaviour, activities, etc.). These marketing tools and strategies will be discussed throughout the unit.

Answers

Model answer:

They relate to marketing.

Exercise B

Set for pairwork discussion. Tell students to bear in mind the points they have just discussed. Feed back with the whole class. This could be quite a long discussion about the process of deciding on a strategy and the benefits/drawbacks of each marketing option, if the class is interested enough.

Answers

Model answers:

1 It's a diagram showing the steps marketing people go through to set up a marketing plan (the flowchart on the left), and the range of marketing options (on the right). One stage leads to the next in the flowchart.

2 1 promotional material
   2 advertising
   3 direct mail

Subject note

The term *marketing mix*, used in the diagram, is a key marketing term which refers to the 'four Ps' of product, price, place and promotion. By offering the right 'mix' of the four Ps, a company is thought to optimize its chances of success.

Exercise C

Set for pairwork. You may wish to divide the work up between different pairs. For question 4 (useful grammatical information), tell students to look out for words that can have the same form when used as a noun or verb, nouns that can be only singular or only plural, nouns that change their meaning when used as U or C, etc.

Feed back, building up the table in the Answers section on the board.

Answers

Model answers:

Word	C/U	Meaning in business/marketing	Synonym	Useful grammatical information
expense	C/U	cost	cost, outlay, spending, investment	U = refers to business expenses in general C = refers to costs claimed back by employees
objective	C	something you set out to do	aim, target	
opportunity	C	a possibility that you see in the market	chance	plural: ~y changes to ~ies
perception	C/U	the way people look at services and products; there is sometimes an implication that this view is wrong, e.g., *There is a perception that A is true, whereas, in fact ...*	view, idea	
staff	U	people who work for a company	personnel (U), employees (C)	tends to be used with plural verb (*the staff are*) in BrE and singular verb (*the staff is*) in AmE
strategy	C/U	a plan, or the process of planning, to ensure the success of a business or a product; can be short-term or long-term	plan	adj = *strategic*
trade	U/(C)	the area of business you are in	business	usually uncountable in a business context, but can be countable when used to refer to specific, often manual, labour (*trades such as carpentry*)
turnover	U	the amount of money earned by a business in a period of time (can also refer to the rate at which staff leave a company and are replaced – *staff turnover*)	(volume of) sales, income	v = two words (*turn over*)

Exercise D

Set for individual work and pairwork checking. Make sure students understand that they should find a verb in the right-hand column with a similar meaning to one of the verbs in the left-hand column.

Feed back with the whole class, discussing the extent to which the verbs are exact synonyms, and if not, identifying any differences in meaning.

Answers

Model answers:

Verb	Noun	Verb	Noun
achieve	achievement	manage (to)*	–
allocate (to)	allocation	reserve (for)	reservation
attract	attraction	appeal (to)	appeal
boost	boost	promote	promotion
decline	decline	go down	–
gain	gain	profit	profit profitability
perceive	perception	see	–
retain	retention	keep	–

*point out that *manage to* has a different meaning from *manage*. *Manage to* has an element of difficulty: *The company managed to make a profit in the first year of business.*

Exercise E

This is an exercise in paraphrasing based on word and sentence level techniques. As well as finding their own synonyms from memory and using some of the synonyms already discussed in Exercises C and D, students will use noun phrases in place of verb phrases as a technique in paraphrasing. Students should also make passive sentences wherever they can.

1 Set for individual work. Feed back with the whole class.

2 Set for individual work and pairwork checking.

3 Set for pairwork; pairs then check with other pairs. Alternatively, tell some students to write their answers on an OHT or other visual medium for discussion by the whole class.

Answers

Model answers:

1 Budget marketing = strategies that reduce the cost of marketing

2 Possible synonyms:

Budget marketing

Most small hospitality businesses are (*undercapitalized*) short of capital. Even if they have (*allocated*) reserved funds (*to*) for marketing, new owners often find that the actual (*expenses*) costs are much higher; they also often find that marketing is a great deal less effective than they had (*anticipated*) thought/expected. Therefore, the use of strategies that reduce the cost of marketing can mean the difference between survival and (*collapse*) failure.

(*Usually*) Generally, small business owners cannot call upon specialist external marketing support without having to pay (*costly*) expensive/high fees. So the more they can use the skills of in-house (*staff*) employees/personnel, the less work they need to outsource, and the more cost-effective the marketing becomes.

The (*perception*) idea/view that you can do without marketing altogether is (*false*) incorrect.

3 Possible paraphrases:

Budget marketing

It is common for small hospitality businesses to be short of capital.

New businesses may have reserved funds for marketing, but they frequently find that things are more expensive than they had expected.

So budget marketing techniques may be important to ensure the survival of the business.

Small hospitality companies generally do not have the funds to hire marketing people or companies.

If these things can be done by the company's own employees, less money will need to be spent on marketing.

It is incorrect to assume that marketing can be ignored.

Exercise F

Set for pair or small group discussion. Feed back with the whole class. Accept any reasonable suggestions. Alternative answers are given in brackets, because different courses will in real life address more than one skill.

Answers

Possible answers:

1

1	Tourism industry knowledge	M
2	Workplace procedures	A (O, F, J)
3	Tourism administration	C (E, F)
4	Information technology	N (P, C, E)
5	Product information	P (C)
6	Bookings and quotations	E
7	Sales and marketing	I (B)
8	Workplace safety	O (J)
9	Event management	H (G)
10	Workplace operations	F
11	Business development	D
12	Financial management	L
13	Project management	G
14	Leadership	A (K, D)
15	Risk management	J (O)
16	Customer service	B

2 Modules: 5, 7, 11, 16.

3 a brochure that is unclear – 5 Product information

meals that take too long to prepare and serve – 16 Customer service

high staff turnover – 10 Workplace operations

double bookings – 6 Bookings and quotations

spending more than the business earns – 12 Financial management

frequent accidents – 8 Workplace safety, 15 Risk management

Closure

Tell students to devise sentences using the following words or phrases, ideally making the meaning of each one clear:

cost-effective
direct mail
marketing
outsource
promotion
strategy
word of mouth

8.2 Reading

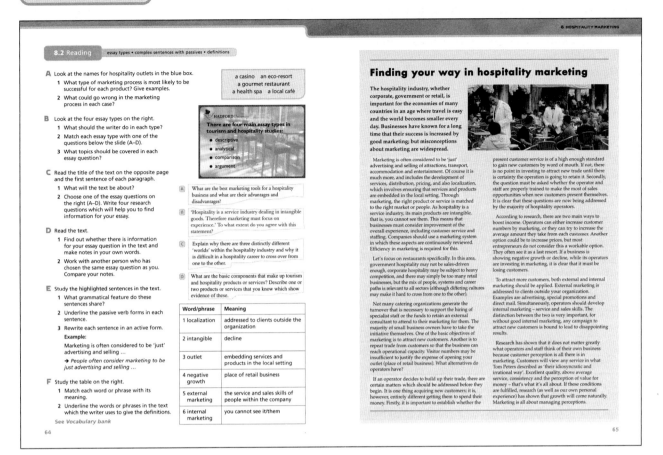

8 HOSPITALITY MARKETING

8.2 Reading   essay types • complex sentences with passives • definitions

A Look at the names for hospitality outlets in the blue box.
1 What type of marketing process is most likely to be successful for each product? Give examples.
2 What could go wrong in the marketing process in each case?

a casino   an eco-resort
a gourmet restaurant
a health spa   a local café

B Look at the four essay types on the right.
1 What should the writer do in each type?
2 Match each essay type with one of the questions below the slide (A–D).
3 What topics should be covered in each essay question?

There are four main essay types in tourism and hospitality studies:
• descriptive
• analytical
• comparison
• argument

C Read the title of the text on the opposite page and the first sentence of each paragraph.
1 What will the text be about?
2 Choose one of the essay questions on the right (A–D). Write four research questions which will help you to find information for your essay.

D Read the text.
1 Find out whether there is information for your essay question in the text and make notes in your own words.
2 Work with another person who has chosen the same essay question as you. Compare your notes.

E Study the highlighted sentences in the text.
1 What grammatical feature do these sentences share?
2 Underline the passive verb forms in each sentence.
3 Rewrite each sentence in an active form.
Example:
Marketing is often considered to be 'just' advertising and selling ...
→ People often consider marketing to be just advertising and selling ...

F Study the table on the right.
1 Match each word or phrase with its meaning.
2 Underline the words or phrases in the text which the writer uses to give the definitions.
See Vocabulary bank

64

A What are the best marketing tools for a hospitality business and what are their advantages and disadvantages?

B 'Hospitality is a service industry dealing in intangible goods. Therefore marketing must focus on experience.' To what extent do you agree with this statement?

C Explain why there are three distinctly different 'worlds' within the hospitality industry and why it is difficult in a hospitality career to cross over from one to the other.

D What are the basic components that make up tourism and hospitality products or services? Describe one or two products or services that you know which show evidence of these.

Word/phrase	Meaning
1 localization	addressed to clients outside the organization
2 intangible	decline
3 outlet	embedding services and products in the local setting
4 negative growth	place of retail business
5 external marketing	the service and sales skills of people within the company
6 internal marketing	you cannot see it/them

Finding your way in hospitality marketing

The hospitality industry, whether corporate, government or retail, is important for the economies of many countries in an age where travel is easy and the world becomes smaller every day. Businesses have known for a long time that their success is increased by good marketing; but misconceptions about marketing are widespread.

Marketing is often considered to be 'just' advertising and selling of attractions, transport, accommodation and entertainment. Of course it is much more, and includes the development of services, distribution, pricing, and also localization, which involves ensuring that services and products are embedded in the local setting. Through marketing, the right product or service is matched to the right market or people. As hospitality is a service industry, its main products are intangible, that is, you cannot see them. This means that businesses must consider improvement of the overall experience, including customer service and staffing. Companies should use a marketing system in which these aspects are continuously reviewed. Efficiency in marketing is required for this.

Let's focus on restaurants specifically. In this area, government hospitality may not be sales-driven enough, corporate hospitality may be subject to heavy competition, and there may simply be too many retail businesses, but the mix of people, systems and career paths is relevant to all sectors (although differing cultures may make it hard to cross from one to the other).

Not many catering organizations generate the turnover that is necessary to support the hiring of specialist staff or the funds to attract an external consultant to attend to their marketing for them. The majority of small business owners have to take the initiative themselves. One of the basic objectives of marketing is to attract new customers. Another is to repeat trade from customers so that the business can reach operational capacity. Visitor numbers may be insufficient to justify the expense of opening your outlet (place of retail business). What alternatives do operators have?

If an operator decides to build up their trade, there are certain matters which should be addressed before they begin. It is one thing acquiring new customers; it is, however, entirely different getting them to spend their money. Firstly, it is important to establish whether the present customer service is of a high enough standard to gain new customers by word of mouth. If not, there is no point in investing to attract new trade until there is certainty the operation is going to retain it. Secondly, the question must be asked whether the operator and staff are properly trained to make the most of sales opportunities when new customers present themselves. It is clear that these questions are now being addressed by the majority of hospitality operators.

According to research, there are two main ways to boost income. Operators can either increase customer numbers by marketing, or they can try to increase the average amount they take from each customer. Another option could be to increase prices, but most entrepreneurs do not consider this a workable option. They often see it as a last resort. If a business is showing negative growth or decline, while its operators are investing in marketing, it is clear that it must be losing customers.

To attract more customers, both external and internal marketing should be applied. External marketing is addressed to clients outside your organization. Examples are advertising, special promotions and direct mail. Simultaneously, operators should develop internal marketing – service and sales skills. The distinction between the two is very important, for without good internal marketing, any campaign to attract new customers is bound to lead to disappointing results.

Research has shown that it does not matter greatly what operators and staff think of their own business because customer perception is all there is in marketing. Customers will view any service in what Tom Peters described as 'their idiosyncratic and irrational way'. Excellent quality, above average service, consistency and the perception of value for money – that's what it's all about. If these conditions are fulfilled, research (as well as our own personal experience) has shown that growth will come naturally. Marketing is all about managing perceptions.

65

General note

Read the *Vocabulary bank* and *Skills bank* at the end of the Course Book unit. Decide when, if at all, to refer students to them. The *Vocabulary bank* section *Understanding new words: using definitions* is relevant to Lesson 2; the *Skills bank* will be more relevant to Lessons 3 and 4.

Lesson aims
- understand essay types
- interpret essay titles
- find the main information in a passive clause
- understand internal definitions (see *Vocabulary bank*)

Further practice in:
- reading research
- finding the kernel of a long sentence

Introduction

With the whole class, discuss how to use written texts as sources of information when writing an answer for an essay question. Ask students:

1 *How can you choose useful sources?* (to get an idea of whether a text might be useful, survey the text, i.e., look at the title, look at the beginning and the end and the first line of each paragraph; in other words, skim-read to get an approximate idea of the text contents)

2 *If you decide that a text is going to be useful, what is it a good idea to do ...*
   - *... before reading?* (think of questions related to the essay question to which you would like to find some answers)
   - *... while reading?* (identify useful parts of the text; make notes **in your own words**)
   - *... after reading?* (check answers to the questions)

Exercise A

Revise concepts from Lesson 1 of this unit: ask for suggestions of areas in which companies can market themselves better. Elicit the words *sales strategy, promotion(al) material, direct mail, word of mouth, advertising, public relations, special promotions*. Set the questions for pairwork discussion with whole class feedback.

Answers

Possible answers:

1

Product	Type of marketing process	Notes
a casino	advertising, special promotions	casinos are usually part of a chain organization that will often work with special promotional offers (e.g., through tour operators) and advertising
an eco-resort	advertising, special promotions, public relations	still fairly elite hospitality outlets, so often advertising through eco-magazines and tour operators; also could need exposure through lobbying with local/regional government and eco-organizations
a gourmet restaurant	word of mouth	such outlets are usually well-known among a select group of people who will meet each other regularly
a health spa	special promotions, direct mail	seeing as health spas are no longer considered elite establishments, you often see them using direct mail combined with special offers (linked to credit card companies, for instance)
a local café	word of mouth	regulars will talk about the café and bring their friends, relatives and business associates

2 Accept any reasonable answers, e.g., advertisement is placed in the wrong section of a magazine; people spreading bad stories about the food in a restaurant; difficult questions being asked at a press conference; wrong dates being printed on billboards; fight in a café stopping people from coming; bad press/reviews.

Exercise B

1 Discuss this question with the whole class before they embark on the second part of the task. Build up the table in the Answers section on the board.

2 Set for pairwork. Feed back with the whole class. Ask the class to say which are the key words in each title which tell you what type of writing it is.

3 Set for pairwork. Feed back using the second table in the Answers section, discussing with the whole class which topics will need to be included in each essay. Add the notes in the third column.

Answers

Possible answers:

1 See table below.

2/3 See table on the opposite page.

Essay type	What the writer should do
Descriptive	describe or summarize key ideas/key events/key points. Give the plain facts. Could involve writing about: a narrative description (a history of something); a process (how something happens); key ideas in a theory; main points of an article (answers the question *What is/are …?*)
Analytical	try to analyse (= go behind the plain facts) or explain something or give reasons for a situation; may also question accepted ideas and assumptions (answers the question *Why/how …?*)
Comparison	compare two or more aspects/ideas/things/people, etc.; usually also evaluate, i.e., say which is better/bigger, etc.
Argument	give an opinion and support the opinion with evidence/reasons, etc.; may also give opposing opinions (= counter arguments) and show how they are wrong

Essay type	Question	Topics
Descriptive	D What are the basic components that make up tourism and hospitality products or services? Describe one or two products or services that you know which show evidence of these.	• listing of the components, e.g., attraction, transport, accommodation • examples of companies and what they did
Analytical	C Explain why there are three distinctly different 'worlds' within the hospitality industry and why it is difficult in a hospitality career to cross over from one to the other.	• different types of hospitality industries: what are they? • the extent and reasons for their differences • examples of current types of organizations that represent each 'world'
Comparison	A What are the best marketing tools for a local hospitality business and what are their advantages and disadvantages?	• examples of marketing tools for a local hospitality business (e.g., a restaurant) • examples of advantages • examples of disadvantages
Argument	B 'Hospitality is a service industry dealing in intangible goods. Therefore marketing must focus on experience.' To what extent do you agree with this statement?	• definition of intangible goods in a hospitality context • examples of marketing focusing on experience • evaluation of how successful this strategy is

Exercise C

1 Set for individual work. Feed back with the whole class.

2 If necessary, remind students of the purpose of research questions and do one or two examples as a class. Set for individual work and pairwork checking. Feed back, getting good research questions for each essay topic on the board.

Answers

Possible answers:

1 The title of the text suggests that the text will look at marketing for the hospitality sector. The words *Finding your way* suggest these techniques may be a matter of trial and error, or at least development.

Paragraph 1 will introduce the topic.

Paragraph 2 will explain the true nature of marketing.

Paragraph 3 will talk about restaurants as an example of marketing.

Paragraph 4 will deal with financing aspects of marketing.

Paragraphs 5 and 6 are about how you can make income grow.

Paragraph 7 will explain the concepts of external and internal marketing.

Paragraph 8 will suggest that the way customers perceive things determines success.

2 Answers depend on the students.

Exercise D

1 Set for individual work. Monitor but do not assist. Tell students to make notes of general points, adding information from their own experience and knowledge if they can.

2 Put students into pairs, or possibly groups. Monitor and assist.

Feed back from each group on the answers they have found. Some groups will have found more information in the text than others. Discuss where they might go to find further information.

Exercise E

1 Set for individual work and pairwork checking. Feed back orally.

2 Set for pairwork. Feed back, ideally with an OHT, or other visual medium, of the text.

3 Set for individual work and pairwork checking.

Answers

Model answers:

1 All the sentences contain passive verb forms.

2 Marketing <u>is</u> often <u>considered</u> to be 'just' advertising and selling of attractions, transport, accommodation and entertainment.

Through marketing, the right product or service <u>is matched</u> to the right market or people.

Efficiency in marketing <u>is required</u> for this.

If an operator decides to build up their trade, there are certain matters which <u>should be addressed</u> before they begin.

To attract more customers, both external and internal marketing <u>should be applied</u>.

3 Possible sentences:

Many people consider marketing to be 'just' advertising and selling of attractions, transport, accommodation and entertainment.

Marketing matches the right product or service to the right market or people.

This requires efficiency in marketing.

If an operator decides to build up their trade, they should address certain matters before they begin.

To attract more customers, operators/companies should apply both external and internal marketing.

Language note

The choice of whether to use an active or a passive construction often depends on how the writer wants to structure the information. Refer to Unit 7 *Skills bank* for a note on information structure.

Exercise F

Set for individual work and pairwork checking. In question 2, tell students to look for the actual words used and the punctuation, grammatical and vocabulary devices which are used to indicate meanings.

Feed back with the whole class, pointing out the structures given in the 3rd column of the table in answer to question 2. If you wish, refer students to the *Vocabulary bank – Understanding new words: using definitions.*

Answers

Model answers:

1

Word/phrase	Meaning
1 localization	embedding services and products in the local setting
2 intangible	you cannot see it/them
3 outlet	place of retail business
4 negative growth	decline
5 external marketing	addressed to clients outside the organization
6 internal marketing	the service and sales skills of people within the company

2 See table below.

Closure

Tell students to make a list of hospitality outlets in the local or regional environment, e.g., theatres, events, cafés, museums, camp-sites, theme parks, etc. Students should work in small groups and choose one or two. Then they should discuss the following:

1 How is the product or service marketed?

2 What can you say about a) the external marketing and b) the internal marketing?

3 How could the marketing be improved?

Word/phrase	Actual words giving the meaning	Punctuation/vocab/structure
localization	… , which involves ensuring that services and products are embedded in the local setting.	word/phrase followed by comma + *which involves* (= explanation)
intangible	… , that is, you cannot see them.	word/phrase followed by comma + *that is* + comma + paraphrase
outlet	… (place of retail business).	word/phrase followed by explanation in brackets
negative growth	… or decline, …	word/phrase followed by *or* + synonym
external marketing	… is addressed to clients outside your organization.	word/phrase followed by *is* + explanation
internal marketing	… – service and sales skills.	word/phrase followed by a dash + explanation

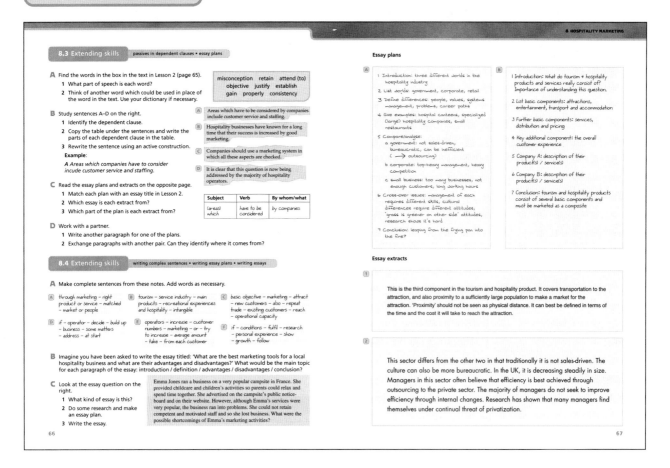

Lesson aims

- find the main information in a passive dependent clause
- recognize appropriate writing plans for essay types

Further practice in:

- vocabulary from Lesson 2

Introduction

Choose about 10–15 words from the previous unit which you think that students should revise. Write them in a random arrangement and at different angles (i.e., not in a vertical list) on an OHT or other visual medium. Allow students two minutes to look at and remember the words, and then take them away. Students should write down all the words they can remember.

Exercise A

Refer students back to the reading text in the previous lesson. Set for individual work and pairwork checking. Feed back with the whole class.

Answers

Model answers:

1/2

Word	Part of speech	Another word/phrase	Notes
misconception	n (C)	misunderstanding	
retain	v	hire, employ OR keep	meaning depends on context, e.g., *He was retained to give marketing advice* = employed *Companies must retain customers* = keep
attend (to)	v	take care of	*attend* without the preposition means *go to*, e.g., *He attended the meeting.*
objective	n (C)	aim, target, purpose	
justify	v	provide a reason for, support	
establish	v	find out	*establish* is often used when something is found out after research
gain	v	acquire, get, attract	
properly	adv	enough (after noun), suitably	
consistency	n (U)	maintaining good standards	not exact synonym

Exercise B

Set for individual work and pairwork checking. Make sure that students can correctly identify the main clause, the dependent clause and the linking word. Do the first transformation with the class to check that they know what to do. Note that they do not need to rewrite the main clauses. Also, if no agent is given they will need to supply one themselves.

Answers

1/2

Main clause	Linking word	Subject	Verb	By whom/what
			Dependent clause	
A Areas	which	which*	have to be considered	by companies
B Hospitality businesses have known for a long time	that	success	is increased	by improved marketing.
C Companies should use a marketing system	in which	all these aspects	are checked.	
D It is clear	that	this question	is now being addressed	by the majority of hospitality operators.

*note that in A the relative pronoun is the subject of the dependent clause. In C it is not the subject – instead, the subject is *all these aspects*.

3 A Areas which companies have to consider include customer service and staffing.

B Hospitality businesses have known for a long time that good marketing increases their success.

C Companies should use a marketing system in which they check all these aspects.

D It is clear that the majority of hospitality providers are now addressing this question.

Exercise C

Tell students to look back at the essay questions in Lesson 2. You may also need to remind them of the topics which you decided were suitable for the essay.

Set all three questions for individual work and pairwork checking. Feed back with the whole class. Ask students to say what aspects of the plans and the extracts enabled them to be identified. Check that students can match the parts of the extracts with the corresponding parts of the essay plan.

Answers

Model answers:

1 Plan A = essay question C: *Explain why there are three distinctly different 'worlds' within the hospitality industry and why it is difficult in a hospitality career to cross over from one to the other.*

Plan B = essay question D: *What are the basic components that make up tourism and hospitality products or services? Describe one or two products or services that you know which show evidence of these.*

2 Extract 1 = plan B

Extract 2 = plan A

3 Extract 1 = Plan B, point 2

Extract 2 = Plan A, point 5a

Exercise D

Remind students about writing topic sentences. Set for pairwork. Students who chose these two questions in Lesson 2 can refer to their notes. Students who did not make notes on these two questions in Lesson 2 can refer back to the reading text for information. In all cases, students should write using their own words, i.e., paraphrase the ideas in the text, if they use these.

If you wish, you could ask some students – perhaps those who finish early – to write their paragraphs on an OHT or other visual medium for all the class to look at. Comment on the extent to which students have managed to paraphrase, whether they have successfully covered the point in the plan, and whether their topic sentence is supported well by the sentences that follow.

Closure

Ask students to finish the following sentences as quickly as possible.

The basic objective of marketing is …

If you decide to build up your trade …

There are two effective ways to boost your income: …

To attract more customers …

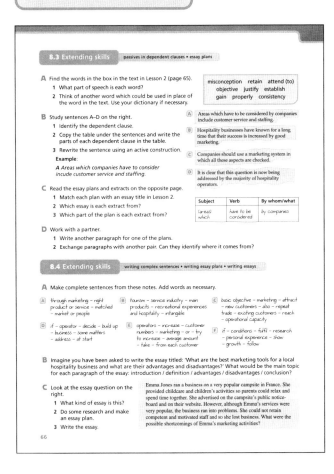

8.4 Extending skills

Lesson aims

- expand notes into complex sentences
- make an essay plan
- write an essay

Further practice in:

- writing topic sentences
- expanding a topic sentence into a paragraph
- writing complex sentences with passives
- identifying required essay type

Introduction

Remind students about complex and compound sentences – that is, sentences with more than one clause. Remind students that academic texts typically consist of sentences with several clauses. Give the following simple sentences (or make your own) and ask students to add some more clauses to them:

Good marketing results in increased profits.

Companies must look at their customers' needs.

The majority of business owners have to take the initiative themselves.

Exercise A

Set for individual work and pairwork checking. Remind students that they should try to make sentences in a good 'academic' style. Also remind them to use passives where necessary/possible, and to look out for ways of making dependent clauses, such as relative pronouns, linking words, etc. They will also need to pay attention to making correct verb tenses.

Feed back with the whole class.

Answers

Possible answers:

A Through marketing, the right product or service is matched with the right market or people.

B As tourism is a service industry, its main products, such as recreational experiences and hospitality, are intangible.

C One of the basic objectives of marketing is not only to attract new customers but also to attract repeat trade from existing customers in order to reach operational capacity.

D If an operator decides to build up its business, there are some matters which should be addressed at the very start.

E Operators can either increase customer numbers by marketing, or they can try to increase the average amount they take from each customer.

F If those conditions are fulfilled, research as well as personal experience have shown that growth will follow.

Exercise B

Remind students of the four essays in Lesson 2 and establish that this is essay A. Elicit the essay type (comparison).

Set for individual work. Point out how this comparison essay is organized by discussing all the advantages first and then all the disadvantages. (See *Skills bank* for an alternative approach to comparison.) If you wish, you could ask students to write the topic sentences and then orally suggest ideas that could follow each topic sentence. For this they will need to refer to ideas in the reading text.

Feed back with the whole class.

Answers

Model answers:

The main topics would be:

Introduction	short description of the industry setting
Definition	description of internal and external marketing tools
Advantages	comparison of advantages of both tools
Disadvantages	comparison of disadvantages of both tools
Conclusion	conclusion about the optimal tools

Possible topic sentences/paragraph content:

Introduction	**The hospitality industry deals in intangible experiences.** Customers may experience and enjoy a nice meal, a pleasant stay, a beneficial health treatment, a smoothly organized conference, or punctuality of staff. Hospitality makes the customer feel welcome.
Definition	**To be successful, operators need to practise both internal and external marketing.** Effective tools are those that either show potential customers what the experience will be like, or those that actually give them the experience. The owner of a restaurant, for instance, could advertise. At the same time, he should make sure that his organization runs smoothly and staff are trained.
Advantages	**Both advertising and training can be very effective in a local setting.** The advantage of advertising is that it builds the name of the establishment in the community, provided enough people see the advertisement often enough. If this is supported by staff who are friendly, helpful, patient and happy to provide a service, then the combination of the two tools will work well.
Disadvantages	**The disadvantages of both training and advertising are that they can be costly.** If not enough people see the advertisement, or not often enough, advertising will have only limited effect. At the same time, training may not necessarily make personnel stay. It can be expensive and retaining staff in the hospitality sector, where wages are traditionally low, is hard.
Conclusion	**Marketing may be most successful if various internal and external tools are combined.** Despite the financial disadvantages of both advertising and training, it seems to be beneficial to restauranteurs to invest in both, as they increase positive exposure in the community. They should complement this with other tools such as special promotions both for customers and staff.

Exercise C

Discuss with the class what kind of essay this is. Set the research and planning for group work and the writing for individual work (which could be done at home). Students can do Web searches.

Answers

1 Model answer:

This essay is largely analytical since it requires (possible) reasons why something happened.

2 Possible essay plan:

- Introduction: aims of essay
- Definition and description of the business and business environment
- Aspects of the business which can cause problems, e.g.,
  - needs very good organization and administration
  - needs reliable staff
  - difficult to cope with sudden increase in demand
  - customers may go elsewhere if supervision is not available
- Conclusion: HR problems → lack of internal marketing

Closure

Ask students if they can remember words from the unit:

	Example(s)
beginning with *c*	consistency
beginning with *i*	initiative, insufficient
ending with *y*	entirely, consistency
ending with *s*	misconceptions, opportunities
with two syllables	attract, retain, decline
with three syllables	justify, objective, distinction
with four syllables	disposable, insufficient
a verb	achieve, boost
a countable noun	perception, objective
an adverb	entirely, properly
a word which is difficult to pronounce	substantial (students' answers will vary)

Extra activities

1 Work through the *Vocabulary bank* and *Skills bank* if you have not already done so, or as a revision of previous study.

2 Use the *Activity bank* (Teacher's Book additional resources section, Resource 8A).

   A Set the wordsearch for individual work (including homework) or pairwork.

   Answers

   B Set the spelling exercise for individual work and pairwork checking.

   Answers

Jumbled word	Correct spelling
ceptionrep	perception
tcider amil	direct mail
cistyencons	consistency
dwro fo tmhuo	word of mouth
uyporionptt	opportunity
yasergtt	strategy
dgbtue	budget
stco-fetfeeicv	cost-effective

3 Check word stress by writing the following words on the board *without* stress markings. Students have to mark the stress and pronounce the words correctly.

   al'ternative

   dis'tinction

   e'ffective (but 'cost effective)

   en'tirely

   e'quipped

   ex'pense

   i'nitiative

   ob'jective

   oppor'tunity

   per'ception

   pro'motion

   'strategy

   'turnover

4 Remind students of how to give definitions (see Lesson 2). Give definitions and ask students to guess the word; once they get the idea, students can come up with items, questions and definitions themselves. Other forms for definitions can include:

   This is a place where …

   This is a company which …

   If you want to … , you need to go to …

An alternative is the Weakest Link TV quiz show format, e.g., What 'A' is a well-known brand of computer? (Apple)

9 TOURISM AND CULTURE

This unit examines the impact that the development of a tourism industry can have on the culture of a host country. The impact can be positive (wealth and job creation), but also negative (damage to the physical environment by overdevelopment; use of scarce natural resources; weakening of the local culture and traditions/'Westernization').

Skills focus

🎧 Listening
- using the Cornell note-taking system
- recognizing digressions in lectures

Speaking
- making effective contributions to a seminar
- referring to other people's ideas in a seminar

Vocabulary focus
- fixed phrases from tourism and hospitality
- fixed phrases from academic English

Key vocabulary

See also the list of fixed phrases from academic English in the *Vocabulary bank* (Course Book page 76).

agent of change	environment	mainstream tourism
belief	exploit (v)	policy
budget travel	genuine	preserve (v)
commercialization	heritage	protection
community	host country	resources
culture clash	impact (n)	sustainable
custom	inaccessible	tradition
destination planning	indigenous	unique
developing country	influx	values
diversity	infrastructure	

9.1 Vocabulary

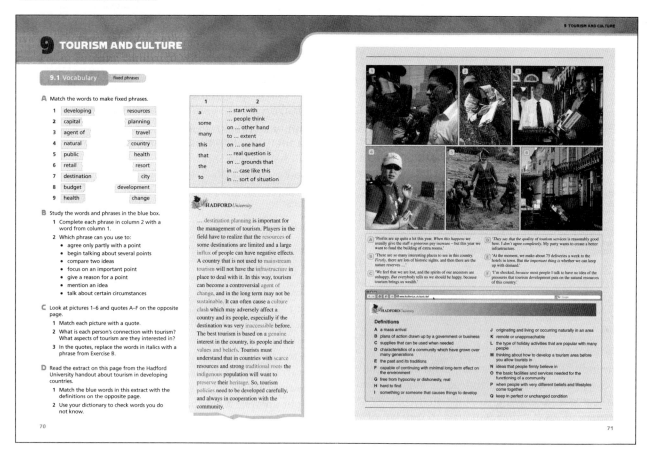

General note

Read the *Vocabulary bank* at the end of the Course Book unit. Decide when, if at all, to refer your students to it. The best time is probably at the very end of the lesson or the beginning of the next lesson, as a summary/revision.

Lesson aims

- understand and use some fixed phrases/compound nouns from tourism and hospitality studies
- understand and use some fixed phrases from academic English

Introduction

Introduce the topic for the next two units. Ask students to say what 'culture' is and arrive at a definition on the board, such as: 'the behaviour, attitudes and products of a particular society, social group or organization'.

Exercise A

This gives revision of some compound noun phrases (noun + noun, adjective + noun) connected with tourism.

Set for individual work or pairwork. Check that students remember the meanings and that they can pronounce the compounds with the main stress on the correct word. Accept any reasonable alternatives which apply to the topic of tourism and hospitality.

Check students realize what the words mean: a good test for this is to ask them to use the phrase in a meaningful sentence.

Answers

Model answers:

1	developing	'country
2	capital	'city
3	agent of	'change
4	natural	re'sources*
5	public	'health
6	'retail	development
7	desti'nation	planning
8	'budget	travel
9	'health	resort

*AmE normally '*resources*

Exercise B

Set for individual work and pairwork checking. Point out that there is more than one phrase for some of the functions (question 2). Feed back with the whole class.

Answers

Model answers:

to start with	to begin talking about several points
many/some people think	to mention an idea
on the other hand	to compare two ideas
to some extent	to agree only partly with a point
on the one hand	to compare two ideas
the real question is	to focus on an important point
on the grounds that	to give a reason for a point
in a case like this	to talk about certain circumstances
in this/that sort of situation	to talk about certain circumstances

Exercise C

1/2 Set for pairwork discussion. Feed back.

3 Set for individual work. Tell students that in some cases it will be necessary to change the word order of the sentence. You can also point out that for one of the quotations (C) they will need to use two of the phrases from Exercise B, although only one word is in italic. Check with the whole class, asking students to read out the quotation with the alternative phrase in place of the original words in italics.

Answers

Model answers:

1/2 1 D a politician or government official (planning, regulation)

2 F an environmentalist (protection of resources)

3 A a hotel operator (growth of hotel business)

4 B a tourist (places to visit)

5 C indigenous people (preservation of culture, tourism income)

6 E a supplier to a hotel (small-business interest)

3

A *When this happens*	*In this sort of situation* we usually give the staff a generous pay increase …
B *Firstly, …*	*To start with*, there are lots of historic sights …
C *But*	*On the one hand*, we feel that we are lost, … *On the other hand*, everybody tells us we should be happy, …
D *They say that …* *don't … completely*	*Many/Some people think* that the quality of tourism services is reasonably good here. I agree *to some extent*.
E *the important thing is*	But *the real question is* whether we can …
F *because*	I'm shocked, *on the grounds that* most people …

Exercise D

This exercise gives some key tourism terms. Tell students to read the handout extract first and ask them to discuss in pairs which of the blue words they know and which are new for them. Feed back with the whole class, to establish how much is known. Where students give correct explanations tell them they are right, and where they are wrong also tell them, but do not give the right answer at this point.

Set the exercise for individual work and pairwork checking. Feed back with the whole class, checking the meaning of other possibly unknown words. The words will be used throughout the unit. However, for extra practice at this point if you wish, set students to work in pairs. One student should shut the book. The other student should say one of the words for Student B to explain. Then change over.

Answers

Model answers:

See table on next page.

destination planning	M	thinking about how to develop a tourism area before you allow tourists in
resources	C	supplies that can be used when needed
influx	A	a mass arrival
mainstream tourism	L	the type of holiday activities that are popular with many people
infrastructure	O	the basic facilities and services needed for the functioning of a community
agent of change	I	something or someone that causes things to develop
sustainable	F	capable of continuing with minimal long-term effect on the environment
culture clash	P	when people with very different beliefs and lifestyles come together
inaccessible	K	remote or unapproachable
genuine	G	free from hypocrisy or dishonesty, real
values and beliefs	N	ideas that people firmly believe in
scarce	H	hard to find
traditional roots	D	characteristics of a community which have grown over many generations
indigenous	J	originating and living or occurring naturally in an area
preserve	Q	keep in perfect or unchanged condition
heritage	E	the past and its traditions
policies	B	plans of action drawn up by a government or business

Closure

On the board write some terms from the lesson and ask students to give a definition; choose items from Exercises A and D. Or read out a definition and ask students to tell you the appropriate word or phrase. Check the pronunciation. This exercise can also be done as a dictation.

Alternatively, write the words and definitions on different cards and give a card to each student. The student then reads out the word or the definition and the rest of the class must produce the correct answer.

Introduction

1 Review key vocabulary from this unit by writing a selection of words from Lesson 1 on the board and asking students to put the words in groups, giving reasons for their decisions.

2 Revise note-taking symbols and abbreviations by using extra activity 3 at the end of this unit.

3 Introduce the elements of the Cornell note-taking system. Try to elicit some of the R words. Ask students to try to think of five words beginning with *re-* with six or seven letters that are good strategies to use when studying and taking notes. Write the words as follows on the board:

RE _ _ _ _	= *record*
RE _ _ _ _	= *reduce*
RE _ _ _ _	= *recite*
RE _ _ _ _ _	= *reflect*
RE _ _ _ _	= *review*

Discuss with the class what each word might mean when taking notes. Try to elicit the following, helping where needed.

record	Take notes during the lecture.
reduce	After the lecture, turn the notes into one- or two-word questions or 'cues' which help you remember the key information.
recite	Say the questions and answers aloud.
reflect	Decide on the best way to summarize the key information in the lecture.
review	Look again at the key words and the summary (and do this regularly).

Tell students that in this lesson they will be introduced to this system of note-taking – which can be used both for lectures, and also for reading and for revision for exams later. Do not say much more at this point; they will see how the system works as the lesson progresses.

Subject note

The Cornell system was developed by Walter Pauk at Cornell University, USA. (Pauk, W. and Owens, R. (2004). *How to study in college* (8th ed.). Boston: Houghton Mifflin). Pauk advised students to use a large, loose-leaf notebook, with holes punched for filing. This is better than a bound notebook, because you can organize the notes in a file binder. You can also take out notes and rewrite them. Pauk's method, which is now called the Cornell system, is based on a specific page layout.

General note

Read the *Skills bank – Using the Cornell note-taking system* at the end of the Course Book unit. Decide when, if at all, to refer students to it. The best time is probably at the very end of the lesson or the beginning of the next lesson, as a summary/revision.

Lesson aims

● use the Cornell note-taking system

Further practice in:

● listening for an established purpose

● recognition of fixed phrases and what type of information comes next

● using abbreviations and symbols in note-taking

Pauk told students to divide up the page into three areas. The first area is a column 5 cm wide on the left side of the page. This is the cue area. The main part of the page is the note-taking area. At the bottom of the page, there is a row 8 cm high, which is the summary area. This basic grid, with information on what each section should contain, is reproduced in the additional resources section (Resource 9B).

The note-taking and learning process involves the *Five Rs* in the order listed in the introduction to this lesson (and in the *Skills bank*). There are many references on the Internet for this system. Two useful ones at the time of writing are:

www.yorku.ca/cdc/lsp/notesonline/note4.htm

www.clt.cornell.edu/campus/learn/LSC%20 Resources/cornellsystem.pdf

Exercise A

Set for pairwork discussion. Refer students to the lecture slide. Tell them to look at the title and bullet points, and for each bullet point to make questions which they expect the lecturer to answer. Do not explain any words from the slide or allow students to check in their dictionaries at this point, as the meanings of these words will be dealt with in the lecture. Feed back with the whole class, asking several students to read out their questions. Write some of the questions on the board if you wish.

🎧 Exercise B

1/2 Refer students to the notes at the bottom of the page. Tell them that this student has used the Cornell system to take notes but has not managed to complete everything and so has left some gaps. (Note that this is quite a normal occurrence in note-taking – details may need to be filled in later, for example by checking with other people.)

Allow students time to read the gapped notes. Also make sure they read question 4 and are ready to listen out for a story.

Play Part 1, pausing after each major point if you wish.

Tell students to work in pairs to compare their answers to question 1, and to complete the summary in 2. Feed back with the whole class, using an OHT or other visual display of the answers if you wish. The completed notes are reproduced in the additional resources section – Resource 9C – to facilitate this.

3 Now focus on the *recite* element of the Cornell system. Point out that here the student has completed the *Review* section. Cover up the *Notes* section of the answer and ask students if they can say anything about the first and second questions in the *Review* section. Then put students in pairs to test each other on the remaining notes.

4 Set for pairwork. Feed back with whole class.

Answers

Model answers:

1/2 See table below and Resource 9C.

Review	Notes
	Impact of tourism on *culture*
	The story = example of *mismanagement*/*chaos*
Main issue is … ?	Main issue: countries don't have basic *infrastructure*
2 types of impact are … ?	Two impacts: 1) tourism *industry* 2) on local *people*
Issues … ?	Issues
1) spending?	1) spending $ in wrong places: *attracting tourists* but not *improving* infrastructure
2) infrastructure?	2) infrastructure improvements, e.g., *modern concrete tourist accommodation* → spoil atmosphere
3) people?	3) influence on *local people*/*population*
Culture clash = ?	strengthening of local *culture* v. growth of *consumption*
Summary	
Tourism development impacts on culture. The main issues are: money is spent to attract tourists, without improving infrastructure; improvements are often no more than quick fixes; one group is concerned about profits, the other about loss of culture.	

4 The lecturer talks about an imaginary country which serves as an example for similar experiences all over the world.

Transcript 🎧 2.1

Part 1

Good morning, everyone. I'm going to talk to you this morning about the impact of tourism on culture. You will agree with me that each of the countries you are from has its own unique culture. Some of you may be from developing countries that are very keen to develop their natural and cultural resources. Others will be from countries that have a well-developed tourism sector already. Today, we will be looking at tourism in developing countries.

But before we begin I have a story to tell you. In this lecture, I'll talk about an imaginary country opening its doors to tourism for the first time and I will outline some of the major consequences of the influx of tourists. I'll also give you a summary of possible solutions at the end.

It's a story of mismanagement and chaos. Every year thousands of tourists visit the capital city of this small country, which in the past was closed off to mainstream tourism. Realistically, the country can only just support its own largely agricultural society. I'm sure you can imagine the large numbers of hotel operators trying to attract tourists as they greet them at the airport on arrival; you can see the noisy and polluting cars, trucks, taxis, motorized rickshaws and buses carrying them away along overcrowded roads, through streets littered with garbage, to badly built hotels where street vendors keep pestering them to buy things they don't need. Does this sound familiar to you? The seriousness of these problems cannot be exaggerated.

Of the many agents of change in society, tourism seems to be one of the strongest. It is also one of the most controversial. Of course, the point of the story is that it's really very dangerous for tourism operators *not* to pay attention to the culture of a country. I admit, there are not many undiscovered countries anymore, but there are still plenty of small and faraway places that are not prepared for discovery, and do not even have basic infrastructure.

OK, so how should we look at this? To start with we might make a distinction between two different types of impact on a new tourist destination. On the one hand, there is the impact of tourism as an industry. On the other, tourism and tourists themselves have an influence on the people living there. It's the first of these points that I'm going to focus on now, but it's worth pointing out that, in terms of effect, both are equally important.

So, to get back to the main part of my lecture … there are – as we will see – ways to help countries like these to manage and control their tourism growth. However, when you look at the tourism industry, you see that governments and foreign tourist operators often overlook a number of important issues.

Firstly – and let's continue, for a moment, to study our imaginary country – during the past few decades, there has been very little planning and investment in things like public health, electricity, drinking water, and last but not least, training local people for the tourism sector. But millions of dollars *have* been spent on publicity abroad to attract more tourists from richer countries. So, they are using scarce financial resources to promote tourism that is not sustainable at all. Which issues are playing a role here?

From the point of view of tourism management, there seems to be a 'use-and-discard' policy. You open up a region and, when tourists have left, you just open up a new one. As a result, a country eats into its own resources. As we will see, people are often neither educated about the needs and tastes of tourists nor about tourism-related problems.

So just to recap for a moment: as we have seen, countries opening up for tourism often make fundamental mistakes in their drive to boost their national or regional economies. Investment focuses on attracting tourists, but not on building a tourist destination. It's true to say that this is not unique and happens all over the world.

Secondly, and this always happens when an area is already overflowing with tourists, considerable energy and resources are spent on so-called 'improvements'. These are 'quick-fix' changes to the environment that actually spoil the atmosphere of a place. We see modern, ugly, concrete tourist accommodation among beautiful traditional local houses. These probably cost twice as much to build as it would take to build a local house in local style with locally available materials. The tourism operator fails to realize that what he builds is a poor copy of cheap, tasteless accommodation which, in the countries where the tourists come from, is generally used by poorer people.

Thirdly, there is the influence tourists have on the local population. The difficulty is that different players in the market may have different aims. Some are worried about the visible impact of tourism (housing, traffic, retail development, and so on) while operators who are trying to build a business only see the profits ahead. What they often don't realize is that there are two things at stake and they can clash. One is about strengthening local culture, and the other is about the growth of consumption. In many cases, these two turn the country into an uneasy mix of traditional culture and (let's admit it) Westernized business models. Globalization has a lot to answer for …

🎧 Exercise C

1 Tell students to divide up a page of their notebooks into the three sections of the Cornell system. They should complete the *Notes* section as they listen. Warn them that they may not be able to complete their notes while writing so they should leave spaces which they can fill in later.

Play Part 2 straight through. Then put students in pairs to complete any gaps in their notes. Feed back with the whole class. Build up a set of notes on the board.

2/3 Tell students to work in pairs to complete the review questions and the summary. Feed back with the whole class.

4 Discuss with the class the extent to which their pre-questions in Exercise A have been answered.

Answers

Model answers:

Review	Notes
	History of tourism development
When tourism began?	Opened up in 1970s
Why tourists came?	• interest in culture, people, religion (inaccessible ∴ genuine interest only)
	• timing: 1970s = Western disillusion with environmental problems, etc.
Benefits to destination …?	Benefits to destination:
	• self-confidence of local population
	• at first, strengthens local culture
Downsides … ?	Downsides:
	• greed → commercialization of culture
	• damage to traditional beliefs

Summary
The first tourists were genuinely interested in the country and culture. At first these tourists benefited the indigenous populations, but after a while commercialization overturned the benefits.

Transcript 🎧 2.2

Part 2

Let's now turn to our imaginary country again. As we shall see, tourism development had a profound impact on it. It was opened to tourism in the 1970s, in the sense that it allowed international exposure. In terms of cultural change, it started to understand global developments beyond its own borders. There are aspects of tourism that had a positive effect on the country when it first opened up to tourists. But first, let's take a look at what attracted the tourists to the country in the first place.

Like many of the undiscovered places on our planet, our imaginary country was a difficult and inaccessible place, and therefore only those with a genuine interest in its people, culture and religion visited it. Hmm, this is interesting. I've just remembered a Tibetan proverb that says, ... let me think: 'If a valley is reached by high passes, only the best of friends and the worst of enemies are its visitors.' There's certainly some truth in that, because that is what it was like at first. Only those who were really interested came to visit.

If we move on now to the second factor, we realize that *timing* was very important. It could be argued that in the seventies, many people in the West had become disillusioned with the price of economic growth. Environmental disasters, pollution and fears about nuclear power and weapons were having their effect on people. So when the first travellers came to our country, they were impressed by its natural and pollution-free condition. They were impressed by the lifestyle of its people. Research has shown that they were also impressed by the way people with limited resources were able to support their lives and their culture without damaging the environment.

And you know what else? It did the local population's self-confidence and cultural pride a lot of good. They realized that their way of life was meaningful to other people – people they had always been looking up to. So from the point of view of tourism development we need to remember that it was through tourism that they learnt about the environmental, social and emotional problems that were part of the Western consumerist lifestyle.

An important point about the relationship between tourism and culture is that in countries that are developing tourism, there is often a strong indigenous culture that has not yet been washed away by the tsunami of modernization. For a while tourism actually makes this culture stronger. Increasingly, however, we find that this development is overturned as time goes by. People become hungry for money, and use a cheap, two-flights-a-day tourism strategy. This encourages people to come in their thousands and make the destination little more than a theme park.

It's not surprising there is a real fear among people that this will affect the old culture. Tourism can have a negative effect on their way of life. Large numbers of tourists can undermine traditional beliefs, values and customs. In fact, there is a real risk of commercializing the very culture that they find so interesting. And where tourists are not sensitive to local traditions their behaviour can cause great offence. To quote Professor Neil Leiper in his book *Tourism Management* (one of your core texts), 'relationships between tourists and locals are often shaped and damaged by stereotyped images that each part holds'.

It's true to say that the physical pollution of our environment can be prevented, but when the minds and the culture of a people are polluted, the effects can be long-lasting. So it should be clear that sensitivity to the cultural landscape is extremely important in the development of tourism.

So, what exactly have we looked at this morning so far? Well, to sum up, we have seen that in countries opening up to tourism, tourists are usually impressed with the lifestyle that the indigenous people lead. At the same time, the native population, often led by government policy or simply by greed, develops tourism activities without much care for the environment and the cultural heritage. If developments are positive to start with, these are often overturned and become negative.

Finally, and this is an interesting way of looking at the problem, we sometimes find that people focus on the wrong things. In fact, as Macleod points out in his article 'Cultural commodification and tourism: A very special relationship', in volume 6 of *Tourism, Culture and Communication*, published in 2006, it may be that policymakers and others are missing aspects of culture that could give advantage to certain regions and their local population.

Now I think that's all I'm going to say for the moment on the basics of tourism, culture and destination planning. Are there any questions so far? ... No? Good.

Oh, one last thing, perhaps ... to quote Mark Mann, from the *Community tourism guide*: 'Next time you go on holiday, ask yourself who owns your hotel or the airline or the tour agency who booked your holiday, or who supplied the drink with your dinner. Who is making money from your holiday? Much of what we spend on holiday – even in the developing world – ends up back in Western countries.'

🎧 Exercise D

Allow students time to read the phrases and the types of information, making sure that they understand any difficult words. Note that they are being asked not for the words that the speaker uses but what *type* of information the words represent. Note also that the information types may be needed more than once. Play the sentences one at a time allowing time for students to identify the type of information which follows. Check answers after each sentence, making sure that students understand what the information actually is that follows.

Answers

Model answers:

Fixed phrase	Type of information which follows	Actual words/information
1 As we shall see, …	information about a point the speaker will make later	tourism development had a profound impact on it.
2 In terms of …	an aspect of a topic the speaker wants to focus on	cultural change, it started to understand global developments beyond its own borders.
3 It could be argued that …	an idea the speaker may or may not agree with	in the seventies, many people in the West had become disillusioned …
4 Research has shown that …	a statement the speaker agrees with	they were also impressed by the way people … were able to support their lives …
5 Increasingly, we find that …	a developing trend	this development is overturned as time goes by.
6 It's true to say that …	a statement the speaker agrees with	the physical pollution of our environment can be prevented, but …
7 So it should be clear that …	a conclusion	sensitivity to the cultural landscape is extremely important …

Transcript 🎧 2.3

1 As we shall see, tourism development had a profound impact on it.

2 In terms of cultural change, it started to understand global developments beyond its own borders.

3 It could be argued that in the seventies, many people in the West had become disillusioned with the price of economic growth.

4 Research has shown that they were also impressed by the way people with limited resources were able to support their lives and their culture without damaging the environment.

5 Increasingly, however, we find that this development is overturned as time goes by.

6 It's true to say that the physical pollution of our environment can be prevented, but when the minds and the culture of a people are polluted, the effects can be long-lasting.

7 So it should be clear that sensitivity to the cultural landscape is extremely important in the development of tourism.

Closure

Play short sections from Part 2 of the lecture again. Stop the recording just before a word or phrase you want the students to produce and ask them what comes next in the lecture. For example:

For a while tourism actually makes this culture stronger. Increasingly, however, we find that [STOP]

Large numbers of tourists can undermine [STOP]

Alternatively, you can do this exercise by reading out parts of the transcript.

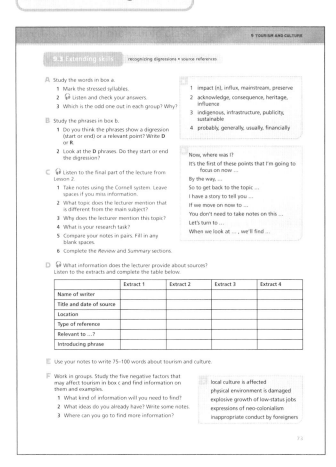

Lesson aims

- recognize digressions: start and end
- understand reference to other people's ideas: source, quotes, relevance

Further practice in:

- stress within words
- leaving space in notes for missing information – especially digressions

Introduction

Revise the lecture in Lesson 2 by asking students to use their Cornell notes. They should cover up the *Notes* section and use the *Review* and *Summary* sections to help recall the contents of the lecture. They could work in pairs to do this.

🎧 Exercise A

1 Set for individual work and pairwork checking. Students can underline the stressed syllables.

2 Play the recording for students to check their answers.

3 Set for individual work and pairwork checking. Tell students they need to identify the odd one out in terms of stress (not the meaning of the words).

Feed back with the whole class, checking students' pronunciation, and eliciting the odd ones out.

Answers

Model answers:

1/3 (odd one out in italics)

1 'impact (n), 'influx, 'mainstream, *pre'serve*

2 *ack'nowledge*, 'consequence, 'heritage, 'influence

3 in'digenous, *'infrastructure*, pub'licity, sus'tainable

4 'probably, 'generally, 'usually, *fi'nancially*

Transcript 🎧 2.4

1 impact, influx, mainstream, preserve

2 acknowledge, consequence, heritage, influence

3 indigenous, infrastructure, publicity, sustainable

4 probably, generally, usually, financially

Exercise B

Point out that the phrases in the box are likely to introduce either a digression or a relevant point. Students' task is to identify which is more probable.

Set for individual work and pairwork checking. Feed back with the whole class. Note that some of these phrases occurred in the lecture in Lesson 2. Some have occurred in previous units and one or two are new. Note also that the end of a digression is actually a transition back to the main point.

Answers

Model answers:

1/2 Now, where was I …? D (end)

It's the first of these points that I'm going to focus on now … R

By the way, … D (start)

So to get back to the topic … D (end)

I have a story to tell you … D (start)

If we move on now to … R

You don't need to take notes on this … D (start)

Let's turn to … R

When we look at … , we'll find … R

🎧 Exercise C

Refer students to the lecture slide in Lesson 2. Ask them what they know already. What else would they like to know? Tell them to prepare a page to take notes using the Cornell system. Remind them that they may not get all the information. If they miss something, they should leave a space. They can fill it in after the lecture. Let them read the questions through and tell them to listen out for the answers to questions 2, 3 and 4.

1 Play Part 3 straight through. Students should complete the *Notes* section.

2–4 Set for pairwork. Feed back with the whole class. Ask for suggestions for phrases to use to find out about the importance of digressions, e.g., *Why did she start talking about ...? I didn't understand the bit about ... Is it important?* and so on (see *Skills bank*).

5/6 Set for pairwork. Students compare their notes, complete any blank spaces and then write the *Review* and *Summary* sections. Feed back with the whole class, building a set of notes on the board.

Answers

Possible answers:

1 See notes below.

2 The Cornell note-taking system.

3 It's important to know how to take good notes.

4 To find out about a tourism destination and the impact the development of the area has had, or is having, on the culture of the place.

5/6 See notes below.

Transcript 🎧 2.5

Part 3

OK, let's turn to possible solutions to the challenge of dealing with culture in tourism. Now, it's important to remember here that globalization is happening all around us and the challenge of the preservation of cultural communities around the world is becoming harder. So what do countries need to do to stop the negative effects? ...Well, let me give you a hint. Do the words *destination planning* mean anything to you now? Destination planning should be a national, regional or local community effort to plan tourism activities. It can make sure that the negative effects on a community or country are minimized.

By the way, I saw last week that some of you are using the Cornell note-taking system. That's very good. Do you all know about this? No? Right, well, if you want to know more about it, I suggest you look at *How to Study in College* by Walter Pauk, P-A-U-K, the 8th edition, published in 2004. It's very good, and it should be in the University Library. I'm sure that you all know the importance of taking good notes – and this system is particularly useful.

So, to get back to the topic: destination planning. Let's look at this idea in a bit more detail. Trying to make economic progress in traditional communities is essential but it's also very difficult. The problem is that people are using culture as the main tourist attraction. So they must create sustainable development to prevent the destruction of the community's identity. After all, not everybody is charmed by six-lane highways, global fast-food restaurants, high-rise hotels and coffee bars on every street corner.

But what exactly *is* culture then? Is it the beliefs of people in an area? Is it architecture? Is it nature? Is

Review	Notes
	Possible solutions
Main solution is ...?	Main solution = destination planning • = national/regional/community effort to plan tourism • must prevent destruction of community's identity • must take into account diversity of culture
Quality of tourism depends on ...?	Cultural environment of present not past e.g., infrastructure, laws, means of transport
What does this mean for tourism operators ... ?	Develop policies in cooperation with local communities, e.g., • protection of natural resources • numbers of tourists monitored
Summary	Main solution is destination planning. Must use present-day tools to protect culture (in widest sense): e.g., infrastructure, laws. Policies must be in cooperation with local communities.

it the activities organized for tourists? Is it the regional or national cuisine? Is it a political system? Is it all of these? It's important that a destination planner takes into account the diversity of culture just because the term is very subjective. Even though the development of tourism is often about satisfying tourists' interests such as landscapes, seascapes, art, nature, traditions and ways of life, there is much more to a culture than meets the eye. One definition of culture given by thefreedictionary.com on the Web is: 'The totality of socially transmitted behaviour patterns, arts, beliefs, institutions, and all other products of human work and thought.'

What I'm going to say next may sound strange. When we look at tourism and culture, I believe that the quality of tourism depends on the cultural environment of the present, not on the cultural heritage of the past. What do I mean by that? I mean to say that tourism is developed and practised by people here and now, with present-day infrastructure, under present-day laws, with present-day means of transport, and so on. Therefore, I believe that to make sure that tourism operators develop responsible activities, policies need to be developed in cooperation with the community. There should, for instance, be strict regulation on the protection of the natural resources in a community.

Tourism operators and government should ensure that resources are conserved, and not abused. For example, tours to primitive communities in a certain area cannot be run by an endless number of operators, because the pressure on the environment and the community would become too large. Numbers of tourists in an area should be closely monitored, because if numbers are too high they put pressure on infrastructure such as roads, and on the natural environment.

OK, now, when I see you in tutorials, we'll look in more detail at all these issues. In the meantime, I'm going to set you a research task. Right, now listen carefully ... your task is to find out about a particular tourism destination and the impact the development of the area has had, or is having, on the culture of the place. I'd like you to work in groups of four. Each group should report back on its findings.

🎧 Exercise D

Tell students that lecturers will often give references while they talk and it is important to note these down. The kinds of information may differ – they may just be names of books or articles, they may be an exact quotation (a 'direct quote') or they may be a paraphrase (sometimes called an 'indirect quotation'). Refer students to the table and check that they know what each row represents.

Play each extract and allow students time to complete the sections of the table. Check with the whole class.

Answers

Model answers:

	Extract 1	Extract 2	Extract 3	Extract 4
Name of writer	Neil Leiper	Macleod	Walter Pauk	Not applicable
Title and date of source	*Tourism Management* (no date given)	'Cultural Commodification and Tourism: A very special relationship', in volume 6 of *Tourism, Culture and Communication*, published 2006	*How to Study in College* 8th edition 2004	thefreedictionary.com (no date)
Location	core text	not mentioned	university library	Web
Type of reference	direct quotation	indirect quotation/ paraphrase	name of book	direct quotation
Relevant to ... ?	relationships between tourists and locals	negatives of tourism development	Cornell note-taking	culture
Introducing phrase	To quote Professor Neil Leiper ...	... as Macleod points out in ...	I suggest you look at ...	One definition of ... given by ...

Transcript 🎧 2.6

Extract 1

Tourism can have a negative effect on their way of life. Large numbers of tourists can undermine traditional beliefs, values and customs. In fact there is a real risk of commercializing the very culture that they find so interesting. And where tourists are not sensitive to local traditions their behaviour can cause great offence. To quote Professor Neil Leiper in his book *Tourism Management* (one of your core texts), 'relationships between tourists and locals are often shaped and damaged by stereotyped images that each part holds'.

Extract 2

In fact, as Macleod points out in his article 'Cultural Commodification and Tourism: A very special relationship', in volume 6 of *Tourism, Culture and Communication*, published in 2006, it may be that policymakers and others are missing aspects of culture that could give advantage to certain regions and their local population.

Extract 3

By the way, I saw last week that some of you are using the Cornell note-taking system. That's very good. Do you all know about this? No? Right, well, if you want to know more about it, I suggest you look at *How to Study in College* by Walter Pauk, P-A-U-K, the 8th edition, published in 2004. It's very good, and it should be in the University Library.

Extract 4

Even though the development of tourism is often about satisfying tourists' interests such as landscapes, seascapes, art, nature, traditions and ways of life, there is much more to a culture than meets the eye. One definition of culture given by thefreedictionary.com on the Web is: 'The totality of socially transmitted behaviour patterns, arts, beliefs, institutions, and all other products of human work and thought.'

Exercise E

Set for individual work – possibly homework – or else a pair/small group writing task. If the latter, tell students to put their writing on an OHT or other visual medium so that the whole class can see and comment on what has been written. You can correct language errors on the OHT.

Exercise F

Set students to work in groups of three or four. Either give each group a topic or allow them to choose one or more topics from the box. Make sure that each topic is covered by at least one and preferably two groups.

Feed back on questions 1–3 with the whole class. Tell students that each student should now carry out research into the group's topic. They should each look at a different source and so will need to decide who is going to look at which one. You will also need to arrange the date for the feedback and discussion of the information – this forms part of Exercise E in Lesson 4. Tell students that in Lesson 4 they will take part in a seminar during which they can use the information they have found.

Answers

Possible answers:

1 Students should look for examples of tourism in the developing world: what is the impact on local culture? What is the effect on the physical environment? What sorts of jobs are created in the local economy? What is the relationship with former colonial powers? Is foreigners' conduct appropriate to the culture?

3 Use subject course books, the library and/or the Internet to look for newspaper/magazine articles, case studies, Internet articles, websites of example tourism projects.

Closure

Tell students to make a word web around any of the topics in Exercise F to 'release' some of their ideas and knowledge.

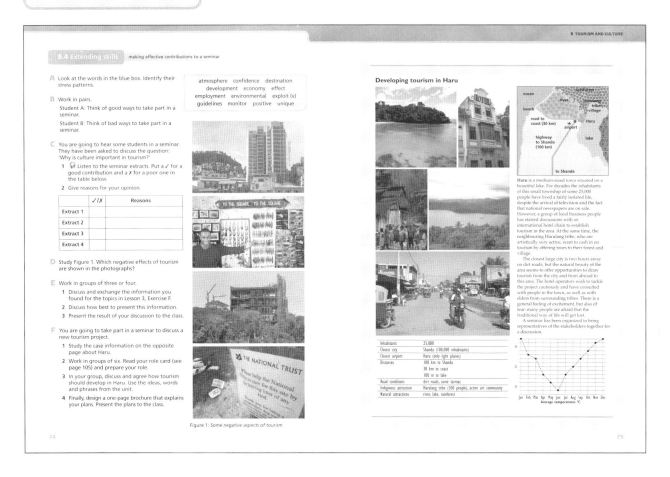

Lesson aims

- make effective contributions to a seminar through a role-play activity

Further practice in:

- stress within words

Introduction

Use a few of the review cues from the Cornell notes in Lesson 3 for students to try to recall the ideas on destination planning in the lecture. If students appear to be having difficulty remembering, ask them to look again at their own notes from Exercise C in Lesson 3.

Exercise A

Set for individual work and pairwork checking. Most have not been worked on in previous lessons. They have been selected to give students a few more tools (in combination with previously practised vocabulary and standard phrases) to carry out discussions during a seminar/role-play activity. Tell students to discuss and make notes on the type of word (verb, noun or adjective).

Answers

Model answers:

Oo	guidelines
oO	effect, exploit (v), unique
Ooo	atmosphere, confidence, monitor, positive
oOo	employment
oOoo	development, economy
ooOo	destination
oooOo	environmental

Exercise B

This is revision from Unit 5. Set for individual work and pairwork checking. Feed back with the whole class. Give a time limit and see which pair can think of the most Do's and Don'ts in the time. Refer to Unit 5 Lesson 4 for suggestions if you need to.

Answers

Possible answers:

See table on next page.

Do's	Don'ts
ask politely for information	demand information from other students
try to use correct language	
speak clearly	mumble, whisper or shout
say when you agree with someone	get angry if someone disagrees with you
contribute to the discussion	sit quietly and say nothing
link correctly with previous speakers	
answer the question	make points that aren't relevant
be constructive	be negative
explain your point clearly	
listen carefully to what others say	start a side conversation
bring in other speakers	dominate the discussion
give specific examples to help explain a point	
paraphrase to check understanding	
use clear visuals	
prepare the topic beforehand	

🎧 Exercise C

Check that students understand the topic for the seminar discussion. Ask them what they might expect to hear. Work through these extracts one at a time. Complete both questions for each extract before moving on to the next.

1 Ask students to copy the grid. Set for individual work.

2 First check that students have understood the extract as well as possible. Then ask for opinions from the whole class on the contribution.

Answers

Model answers:

	✔/✘	Reasons
Extract 1	✔	speaks clearly explains the point clearly answers the question uses good fixed phrases
Extract 2	✘	doesn't answer the question (is talking about low status jobs) poor use of visuals
Extract 3	✘	speaks clearly, but doesn't answer the question the points are not relevant to the question (is talking about consultants, not about culture)
Extract 4	✔	speaks clearly explains the point clearly answers the question uses good fixed phrases; has prepared well has a good visual

Transcript 🎧 2.7

Extract 1

It seems quite clear that culture is a very important aspect of tourism. Whether you are an operator, a government or a local community, a knowledge of the destination's culture will help you to manage its development better. Let's look at two basic advantages that come from understanding local culture: firstly, you will appreciate the type of people the destination might appeal to; secondly, you will understand how the development of tourism will affect local people and, therefore, who needs to be involved in planning and decision-making.

Extract 2

... erm, I think one big problem is the fact that tourism leads to jobs that have very low status. This is very important. It is possible, we can see how this is very important ... So let's look at the chart and ... oh sorry, that's the wrong chart, just a minute ... right, so here is some overview of the kinds of jobs in tourism ... er, you can see, I think, this difference ... do you have any questions about this chart?

Extract 3

We could ask the question: how much does it cost to hire a consultant? Usually, this is very expensive but it is necessary because if you use a consultant you can get a good idea of what is possible and then you can let the community know how good your ideas are. A good consultant is also very important for the public because they can explain to a community what you are planning to do. Here we must look also at organizing meetings with locals.

Extract 4

So this is the main thing – culture is all-important in tourism. Why? Any area where you develop tourism has a culture. It doesn't matter what your definition of culture is: in terms of identity, all cultures are different anyway, which is what makes developing tourism so challenging. From the point of view of the local community, their desire is to improve their standard of living. At the same time, it's true to say that they don't want to give up their unique lifestyle. And as we shall see, the majority of tourists would like to experience something of that unique culture and compare it with their own. If we look at the chart I've prepared, we can see the main reasons why tourists travel. We could link this to the reasons why people want to develop tourism. Bearing in mind that you cannot develop tourism without building a good infrastructure, …

Exercise D

This exercise links back to Exercise F of the previous lesson. Set for pairwork and whole class feedback/discussion.

Answers

Possible answers:

1 A high-rise modern city hotel flanked by local traditional buildings (local culture is affected).
2 A hospitality worker at a trinket stall trying to attract the attention of tourists (growth of low-status jobs).
3 A resort being built in a rainforest area (physical environment is damaged).
4 Rubbish generated by tourism (physical environment is damaged).

Exercise E

Students should work in the same groups as their research groups from Lesson 3. Each student will need to bring the research they have done individually on the topic from Lesson 3, Exercise F to class.

Decide how you want students to present their information, e.g.,

● short talk with/without PowerPoint, OHT, or other visual medium
● to the whole class or to another group

Make sure that students understand the options for the presentation types.

1 Tell each group to discuss the information that they have found and agree on the relevance to the topic.
2 In discussing this question, students will need to decide who is going to speak when and say what. Encourage them to practise presenting to each other before talking to the whole class.

3 Allow each group a maximum of five minutes for the presentation. Then allow some time for questions. If more than one group have done the same topic, encourage disagreement and critical analysis. Remind the groups when discussing to use all the good techniques and phrases they have learnt.

Exercise F

This is a case study of a community in a developing country that wishes to build tourism in cooperation with local businesses and international interests.

1 To set the context, first refer students to the pictures on the opposite page, and refer back to the pictures in Exercise D. Read the instructions and the case information. When students have done this, ask them whether they have been to a place like Haru and what their experiences were as (presumably) a tourist.

2 Put students in groups of six and give them time to prepare their roles individually. Explain that the role cards contain three components: (1) what that person wants out of the seminar; (2) what that person needs from other people around the table; (3) what that person is willing to offer, if others offer them something they want.

   They can write notes. Everybody can use the information on the page, and should be stimulated to jot down words and phrases from the unit that they could use in their subsequent discussion. One student is assigned the role of chairperson: this person must ensure that the seminar runs smoothly, everybody gets to talk and some sort of decision is reached at the end.

3 Give students a set time (depending on your teaching situation) to reach some form of agreement. If you can record the discussions on video this would be useful for feedback.

4 Have students finalize the activity by making a one-page brochure outlining the plans. It's important for students to choose an audience for their brochure, as this will determine the style of presentation and writing.

An alternative approach is, after the discussion stage, to select each of the six roles, one from each group, and have one seminar acted out, rather than each group acting out their own. If you choose the latter option, you could then get students who are not participating in the seminar to observe their fellow students and feed back afterwards on what they thought was good and what they thought could be improved.

Closure

Use the *Vocabulary bank* to check that the group can remember the meaning, spelling and pronunciation of the tourism vocabulary.

Extra activities

1 Work through the *Vocabulary bank* and *Skills bank* if you have not already done so, or as revision of previous study.

2 Use the *Activity bank* (Teacher's Book additional resources section, Resource 9A).

A Set the crossword for individual work (including homework) or pairwork.

Answers

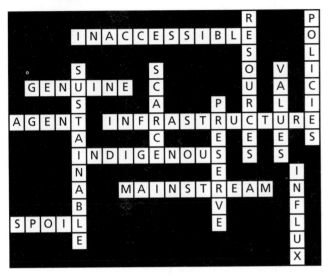

B Ask students to look at the nouns in the table: are plural forms of the nouns possible? Tell students to use an English–English dictionary or online definitions to help them find out the answers to the following questions. Tell students to add any information they find in dictionaries to the *Notes* part of the table.

1 Which forms are countable and which uncountable?

2 Do the countable and uncountable forms have different meanings?

Answers

Noun	C/U?	Notes
belief	C/U	*belief* (U) usually occurs in a set phrase such as *It is my belief that … .*
community	C/U	plural: *communities*
custom	C/U	refers to the traditions of a country or group of people *customs* can also refer to the department which collects tax on goods brought into the country *custom* can also mean 'habit': *As was their custom, they went out on Friday night.* Not used in plural in this meaning
diversity	U	
heritage	C	usually singular
influx	C	usually singular stress on first syllable
infrastructure	usually U	the word *structure* is often used in both singular and plural
issue	C/U	
policy	C/U	plural: *policies*
publicity	U	
resource	C/U	*natural resources* refers to things like oil, water, minerals, etc.

3 Revise note-taking symbols – see the list at the back of the Course Book. Check back to Unit 5 if necessary. Give the meanings and ask students to write down the symbol (or do it the other way round). Then ask students to think about and discuss which ones they actually use. Are there any other ones that they have come across that they think are useful?

Alternatively, write the meanings on a set of cards. Put students in groups of about six with two teams in each group. Give each group a pile of cards. A student from each team picks a card and, without showing the members of his/her team, draws the appropriate symbol. The members of his/her team must say what the symbol stands for. If the student writes the correct symbol and the team gets the meaning right, the team gets a point. If the student writes the wrong symbol and/or the team gets it wrong, the team loses a point. The teams take it in turns to pick a card.

10 MANAGING PEOPLE AND MONEY

This unit looks at how different types of tourism and hospitality businesses structure their operations. The first reading text contrasts top-down and bottom-up management styles. The last two lessons look at how capital can be raised to begin trading or to expand, and the different forms this funding may take: start-up loans, overdraft facilities, shares issues, etc.

Skills focus

Reading

- recognizing the writer's stance and level of confidence or tentativeness
- inferring implicit ideas

Writing

- writing situation–problem–solution–evaluation essays
- using direct quotations
- compiling a reference list

Vocabulary focus

- 'neutral' and 'marked' words
- fixed phrases from business management
- fixed phrases from academic English

Key vocabulary

adopt	expand	perform
advice	finance (n and v)	performance-driven
bottom-up	human resources	productivity
commitment	lease (n and v)	profit (n)
corporate	loan (n)	short-term
decentralize	long-term	start-up (n)
empower	management style	strategic
empowerment	managerial	tactical
enhance	medium-term	top-down
entrepreneur	operational	

10.1 Vocabulary

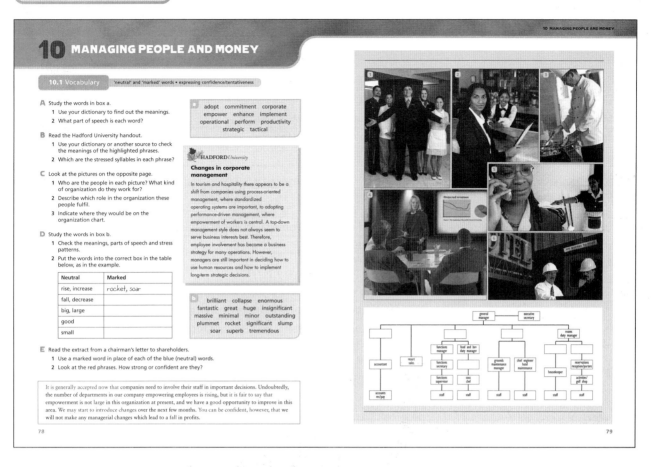

General note

Read the *Vocabulary bank* at the end of the Course Book unit. Decide when, if at all, to refer your students to it. The best time is probably at the very end of the lesson or the beginning of the next lesson, as a summary/revision.

Lesson aims

- understand when words are 'neutral' and when they are 'marked' (see *Vocabulary bank*)
- understand and use phrases expressing confidence/tentativeness (see *Vocabulary bank*)

Further practice in:

- fixed phrases/compound nouns from the discipline
- fixed phrases from academic English
- stress within words and phrases
- synonyms

Introduction

Revise the following phrases used in academic writing. Ask students what sort of information will follow these phrases.

on the other hand

in conclusion

to put it another way

as Smith (2002) pointed out

research has shown that

to start with

this can be defined as

as a result

finally

given what has been shown above

Exercise A

Set for individual work and pairwork checking. Feed back with the whole class.

Answers

Model answers:

Word	Part of speech	Meaning/synonym
adopt	v (T)	start using, take up
commitment	n (C)	an agreement, an obligation
corporate	adj	relating to a (large) company
empower	v (T)	give someone more control
enhance	v (T)	improve
implement	v (T), n (C)	(v) put into effect (n) tool
operational	adj	relating to the day-to-day management of a business or other organization
perform	v (I, T)	1. do something (well) 2. work or function 3. entertain people (e.g., in a play)
productivity	n (U)	efficiency in terms of how quickly goods are produced or services are provided
strategic	adj	relating to the long-term needs of an organization
tactical	adj	relating to the medium- or short-term needs of an organization

Exercise B

1 Set for individual work and pairwork checking. Other sources besides dictionaries could be business textbooks, other reference books, or the Internet.

2 Show students how they can draw the stress pattern for the whole word as well as just locating the stressed syllable. If they use the system of big and small circles shown in the Answers section, they can see the pattern for the whole phrase quite easily.

Answers

Model answers:

1

process-oriented	focused on processes, regulations, structures
operating systems	the systems (organizational structures, rules, etc.) a company works by
performance-driven	focused on people delivering results
top-down	decisions are taken by a management team and handed down to the workers
business interests	the interests of a company
employee involvement	the degree to which employees are involved in decision making
human resources	the employees of a company
long-term	focused on results over a longer period of time

2

process-oriented	Oo Oooo
operating systems	Oooo Oo
performance-driven	oOo Oo
top-down	oO
business interests	Oo Oo
employee involvement	oOo oOo
human resources	Oo oOo (BrE) Oo Oooo (AmE)
long-term	Oo

Exercise C

Set for pairwork or class discussion. Encourage students to speculate about who the people might be (job/role in the company) and what might be happening. In the case of pictures 1, 2, 5 and 6 they should focus on the staff in managerial roles.

Feed back with the whole class. Accept any reasonable answers.

Answers

Possible answers:

1/2 These people all work in/for a hotel.

    1 front office supervisor

    2 food and beverages manager

    3 executive chef

    4 financial controller

    5 executive housekeeper

    6 maintenance manager

3

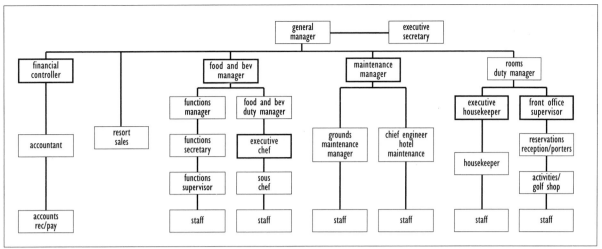

Exercise D

Introduce the idea of 'neutral' and 'marked' vocabulary (see *Language note* and *Vocabulary bank*). Set for individual work and pairwork checking.

Feed back, discussing any differences of opinion about whether the words are marked, and in what sense they are marked. (Some students may argue that *minimal, significant* and *insignificant* are not marked, for example. Others may argue that they are marked, because they suggest not just that something is big/small, but that it is important/unimportant. Compare *There is a small problem with the program* and *There is an insignificant problem with the program*.)

Answers

Model answers:

Neutral	Marked
rise, increase	'rocket, soar (v)
fall, decrease	co'llapse (v and n), 'plummet (v), slump (v and n)
big, large	e'normous, huge, 'massive, sig'nificant, tre'mendous* (adj)
good	'brilliant, fan'tastic, great, out'standing, su'perb, tre'mendous*(adj)
small	insig'nificant, 'minimal, 'minor (adj)

* *tremendous* can mean both very large and very good, so students may place this word in either category

Language note

One way of looking at vocabulary is to think about 'neutral' and 'marked' items. Many words in English are neutral, i.e., they are very common and they do not imply any particular view on the part of the writer or speaker. However, there are often apparent synonyms which are 'marked' for stance or opinion. Neutral words are usually thought of as basic vocabulary (the adjectives often have opposites, e.g., *big/small*; *light/dark*). Marked words tend to be less frequent and are therefore learnt later.

The marked words in Exercise D are not totally synonymous. Their appropriate use and interpretation will be dependent on the context and also on collocation constraints. For example, one can say that a building is 'massive' but not (in the same sense) 'significant'.

Exercise E

1 Set for individual work and pairwork checking. Make sure that students understand any words they are not sure of. Feed back with the whole class by asking individual students to read out a sentence. Make sure that the pronunciation and stress patterns of the marked words are correct.

2 Put the table from the Answers section on the board. Make sure that students understand *confident* and *tentative*. Elicit answers from the whole class and complete the table, discussing any differences of opinion. Point out that these phrases are usually found in conversation or in informal writing such as this. Academic writing also requires writers to show degrees of confidence and tentativeness.
The mechanisms for this will be covered in the next lesson.

Answers

Model answers:

1 It is generally accepted now that companies need to involve their staff in important decisions. Undoubtedly, the number of departments in our company empowering employees is (*rising*) soaring/rocketing, but it is fair to say that empowerment is not (*large*) enormous/huge/massive in this organization at present, and we have a (*good*) fantastic/superb/tremendous opportunity to improve in this area. We may start to introduce changes over the next few months. You can be confident, however, that we will not make any managerial changes which lead to a (*fall*) collapse/slump in profits.

2

	Very confident	Fairly confident	Tentative (= not confident)
It is generally accepted now that		✓	
It is fair to say that		✓	
We may start to introduce changes			✓
You can be confident, however, that	✓		

Closure

1 For further practice of neutral and marked vocabulary, ask students to write down some basic words, e.g., four verbs, four nouns and four adjectives. Put a list of these on the board and ask students if they are neutral or marked. See if you can find any opposites. Use the students and dictionaries to find some synonyms for neutral words. A synonyms dictionary or Microsoft Word thesaurus can be useful here as well.

2 Ask pairs or groups to define as accurately as they can three of the fixed phrases from the *Vocabulary bank*. Give them a few minutes to think of their definitions, then feed back and discuss as a class.

10.2 Reading

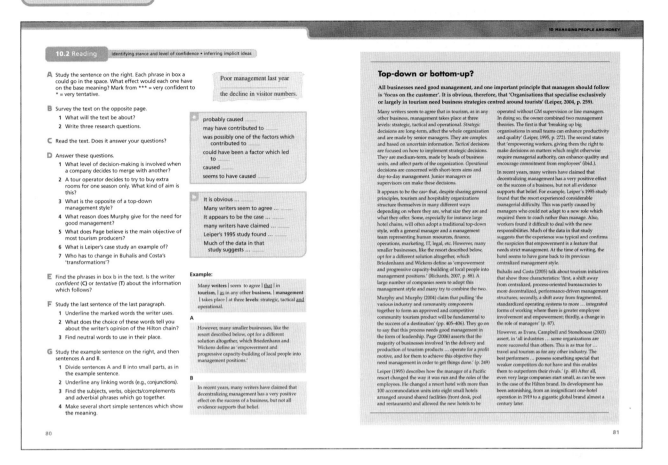

General note

Read the *Skills bank – Identifying the parts of a long sentence* at the end of the Course Book unit. Decide when, if at all, to refer students to it. The best time is probably at the very end of the lesson or the beginning of the next lesson, as a summary/revision.

Lesson aims

- identify the writer's stance on information from the use of marked words
- identify the writer's level of confidence in the research or information
- infer implicit ideas

Further practice in:

- finding the main information in a sentence

Introduction

Introduce the idea of degree of confidence in information, which is usually shown in academic writing. More often that not, writers will avoid very categorical statements such as 'X was the cause of Y' and will demonstrate the extent to which they are sure about something through various different linguistic devices such as modals and hedging words and phrases. Put this table on the board to help explain the idea:

100% *** definitely true. The writer is very confident	X caused Y
75% ** probably true. The writer is a little tentative	X probably/is likely to have caused Y
50% * possibly true. The writer is very tentative	X may/might/could have/ possibly caused Y

Exercise A

Set the exercise for pairwork. Students should refer to the table on the board to explain the rating system. Feed back with the whole class, pointing out the aspects of the language that contribute to the degree of confidence.

Answers

Model answers:

Word/phrase	Rating	Words which show less than 100% confidence
probably caused	**	probably
may have contributed to	*	may contributed (i.e., there were other reasons)
was possibly one of the factors which contributed to	*	possibly one of the factors (i.e., there were several factors) contributed
could have been a factor which led to	*	could a factor (i.e., there were other factors)
caused	***	–
seems to have caused	**	seems

Exercise B

Remind students that surveying the text means skim-reading to get an approximate idea of the text contents. They should:

- look at the title
- look at the first few lines and the final few lines of the text
- look at the first sentence of each paragraph

Note that this is in order to get a very approximate idea of the contents of the text. This will enable students to formulate questions about the text for which they might try to find answers. Students should be discouraged from reading deeply at this point, as they will be able to do this later.

Set for individual work and pairwork discussion. Each pair should agree three questions. Feed back with the whole class. Write some research questions on the board.

Exercise C

Set for individual work followed by pairwork discussion. Feed back with the whole class. Ask whether the questions you have put on the board have been answered in the text.

Exercise D

These questions require students to 'infer' information – that is, understand what is not directly stated and interpret information asserted in quotes from external sources.

Set for individual work and pairwork checking. Feed back with the whole class, making sure that students understand the answers and discussing any differences in interpretation.

Answers

Model answers:

1 Strategic.
2 Medium-term/tactical.
3 Bottom-up.
4 To ensure that any tourism product is both accepted by the community and profitable/competitive.
5 Profit.
6 Empowerment management strategy.
7 Everyone (workers and managers).

Exercise E

Set for individual work and pairwork checking. Feed back with the whole class. Point out that these phrases are very important in academic writing and will help to determine whether something is a fact or an opinion – an important aspect of reading comprehension. They are also used by writers in developing their arguments for or against a particular point of view.

Answers

Model answers:

It is obvious, therefore, that 'Organisations that specialise exclusively or largely in tourism need business strategies centred around tourists …'	C
Many writers seem to agree that in tourism, as in any other business, management takes place at three levels: strategic, tactical and operational.	T
It appears to be the case that, despite sharing general principles, tourism and hospitality organizations structure themselves in many different ways depending on where they are, what size they are and what they offer.	T
many writers have claimed that decentralizing management has a very positive effect on the success of a business …	T
Leiper's 1995 study found that the resort experienced considerable managerial difficulty.	C
Much of the data in that study suggests that the experience was typical …	T

Exercise F

Set for pairwork. Feed back with whole class. Discuss any differences in students' answers, and whether neutral equivalents are hard to find for some of the words.

Answers

Possible answers:

1 Its development has been <u>astonishing</u>, from an <u>insignificant</u> one-hotel operation in 1919 to a <u>gigantic</u> global brand almost a century later.

2 The choice of words emphasizes the dramatic development of Hilton and gives the impression that the writer is impressed by it.

3

Marked word	Neutral alternative
astonishing	successful, rapid
insignificant	small
gigantic	large

Exercise G

Draw the table from the Answers section on the board. Ask students to look at the example sentence and say which box each part of the sentence should go in. Complete the table for the example sentence as shown. Point out how each of the noun phrases is made up of several words. In each case, elicit which words are the core of the noun phrases (shown in bold in the table below). Do the same with the verb phrases. Ask students to suggest how the sentence can be rewritten in several short, very simple sentences in which noun phrases and verb phrases are reduced to the core meaning as far as possible. Demonstrate with these examples if necessary:

Many writers agree on a point.
In tourism, management takes place at three levels.
These levels are strategic, tactical and operational.
Tourism is like any other business in this way.

Set questions 1–4 (relating to sentences A and B) for individual work and pairwork checking. Feed back with the whole class.

Note that in sentence A the word *and* in *Briedenhann and Wickens* is not underlined, as Briedenhann and Wickens is a single entity in this context.

Answers

Model answers:

1/2 A <u>However</u>, | many smaller businesses, | <u>like</u> the resort described below, | opt for a different solution altogether, | <u>which</u> Briedenhann and Wickens define as | 'empowerment and progressive capacity-building | of local people into management positions.'

  B In recent years, | many writers have claimed | <u>that</u> decentralizing management has a very positive effect | on the success of a business, | <u>but</u> not all evidence supports that belief.

3 See table below.

	Subject noun phrases	Verb phrases	Object/ complement noun phrases	Adverbial phrases	Notes
Example	Many **writers**	seem to **agree**	that	as in any other business, in tourism	*that* is a linking word here
	management	takes place at	three **levels:** strategic, tactical and operational		
A	many smaller **businesses**	**opt** for	a different **solution**	altogether, like the resort described below	*however* is a linking word
	Briedenhann and Wickens	**define** as	**empowerment** and progressive **capacity-building** of local people into management positions		*which* is a linking word (relative pronoun) referring back to the 'different solution'
B	many **writers**	**have claimed**	that	In recent years,	*that* is a linking word here
	decentralizing management	**has**	a very positive **effect** on the success of a business		
	not all **evidence**	supports	that **belief**		*but* is a linking word

4 Possible sentences:

A Smaller businesses opt for a different solution.

Briedenhann and Wickens define the solution.

The solution is/involves empowerment and capacity building.

Local people are trained to be managers.

The resort is a small business.

The resort(s) opt(s) for a different solution.

B Decentralizing management has a positive effect.

Decentralized management makes businesses successful.

Decentralizing management is very positive.

(In recent years) Many writers have claimed this.

Not all evidence supports this.

Language note

1 Subjects and objects will always be nouns, with or without modifying adjectives. Complements can be:

- nouns: *He is a doctor.*
- adjectives: *He is French.*

2 There are several types of conjunction in English.

Coordinating conjunctions such as *and, or, but* link elements of equal grammatical status.

Correlative conjunctions have two items: *either ... or ...*; *both ... and ....*

Subordinating conjunctions relate clauses to each other using single words (e.g., *that* with verbs of saying, thinking, etc., *after, as, before, if, although, while*) or phrases (e.g., *as soon as, in order to, provided that ...*).

See a good grammar reference book for full explanations.

3 *Adverbial phrases* add information about the actions or processes described by the verb phrase.

Closure

Here is some advertising language from the website of a company that sells package tours to a tropical island. Ask students to identify any marked vocabulary items in each sentence and to suggest more neutral words. Feed back, comparing answers and discussing any differences of opinion.

Brilliant opportunity for a fun holiday with friends!

Stylish accommodation to make your holiday a dream!

Innovative ideas for children's activities!

Fabulous experiences for everyone!

Do you need some inspiration? We have some great ways for you to relax!

Possible changes:

(*Brilliant opportunity*) <u>Good ideas </u>for a (*fun*) <u>pleasant</u>/<u>enjoyable</u> holiday with friends!

(*Stylish accommodation*) <u>Fashionable accommodation</u> to make your holiday (*a dream*) <u>nice</u>/<u>pleasant</u>!

(*Innovative*) <u>New</u> ideas for children's activities!

(*Fabulous*) <u>Good</u>/<u>Enjoyable</u> experiences for everyone!

Do you need some (*inspiration*) <u>ideas</u>? We have some (*great*) <u>good</u> ways for you to relax!

10.3 Extending skills

10.3 Extending skills recognizing essay types • situation–problem–solution–evaluation essays

A Read the four essay questions. What types of essays are they?

B Look at text A on the opposite page. Copy and complete Table 1 below.

C Look at text B on the opposite page. Copy and complete Table 2.

D Read the title of essay 4 again.
1 Make a plan for this essay.
2 Write a topic sentence for each paragraph in the body of the essay.
3 Write a concluding paragraph.

1 Compare decisions a company might take to achieve a short-term goal, and that it might take to achieve a long-term goal.

2 Explain from a managerial viewpoint how some of a company's main resources might help it to achieve its goals.

3 Outline some of the ways in which a company can raise finance for its operations.

4 Describe, with some examples, the financial problems faced by small tourism or hospitality business start-ups. Consider how small businesses can best solve these difficulties.

Table 1

Situation	
Problem	
Solutions	

Table 2

Solution	
Argument for	
Argument against	

10.4 Extending skills writing complex sentences • references • quotations

A Expand these simple sentences. Add extra information. Use the ideas you discussed in Lessons 2 and 3.
1 High street banks do not always give loans to new small businesses.
2 Small entrepreneurs cannot issue shares to the public.
3 Not all evidence shows that decentralizing management is positive.
4 Allowing employees to take strategic decisions is risky.

B Look at the reference list (C) on the opposite page. Copy and complete Tables 1–3.

C Look at the pages from a book (D) on the opposite page.
1 Complete a further row of Table 1.
2 How could you write this as a reference?

D What do the abbreviations in the blue box mean?

E Look back at the text on page 81 (Lesson 2).
1 Find all the research sources (e.g., Leiper, 2004, page 259).
2 Add the page numbers to the correct reference in the list on the opposite page.
3 What punctuation is used to introduce each direct quote?
4 What words are used to introduce each direct quote? Why does the writer choose each word?

Table 1: *Referencing books*

Author(s)	Date	Place	Publisher

Table 2: *Referencing journals*

Name of journal	Volume	Pages

Table 3: *Referencing websites*

Retrieval date	URL

&	©	cf.	edn.	ed(s).	et al.
ibid.	n.d.	op. cit.	p.	pp.	vol.

82

Case Study 1: Financing a tourism business

In 2006, Alison Cole left her nine-to-five job and set up a company called Moreton's Myth Horse Treks which organized horse-riding adventures for tourists. She operated from her five-acre country property. Her high street bank refused her a loan but agreed to an overdraft of £4,000. With this and a government Small Business Start-up loan of £5,000, Alison was able to lease a stall in a market in her local town and also set up a website through which she could sell her treks. When, in 2007, she wanted to expand her business to a small stables operating from the local park, her bank again refused her a loan, despite the fact that she was now beginning to make a profit. Eventually, Alison borrowed the money from her mother and brother.

(adapted from Venture, 2005)

Management of a small hospitality business involves dealing with money as much as with people. It is clear that small businesses cannot rely on banks for financial help. Another alternative which may be considered by small entrepreneurs is to raise finance through the sale of equity in the business to a venture capitalist (Brookes, 2003). Grange (2005) argues that this represents a 'sound option' (p. 34) since these investors are often experienced business people and the small business owner may benefit from their business advice. However, Grange (ibid.) also points out that, 'The disadvantage is that the small entrepreneur is no longer the sole owner, and more importantly perhaps, may well see their hard-earned profits go to someone else.'

References

Briedenhann, J. & Wickens, E. (2007). Developing cultural tourism in South Africa: potential and pitfalls. In Richards, G. (Ed.). *Cultural tourism: Global and local perspectives.* Binghamton, NY: The Haworth Press.

Buhalis, D., & Costa, C. (Eds.). (2005). *Tourism management dynamics: Trends, management and tools.* Oxford: Elsevier/Butterworth-Heinemann.

Evans, N., Campbell, D., & Stonehouse, S. (2003). *Strategic management for travel and tourism.* Oxford: Elsevier/Butterworth-Heinemann.

Hilton Hotels. (n.d.). *Hilton hotels.* Retrieved January 12, 2007, from http://en.wikipedia.org/wiki/Hilton_Hotels

Leiper, N. (1995). *Tourism management.* Melbourne: RMIT Publishing.

Leiper, N. (2004). *Tourism management* (3rd ed.). Frenchs Forest, NSW: Pearson Education Australia.

Murphy, P., & Murphy, A. (2004). *Strategic management for tourism communities: Bridging the gaps.* Clevedon: Channel View Publications.

Northcote, J., & Macbeth, J. (2006). Conceptualizing yield: Sustainable tourism management. *Annals of Tourism Research, 33*(1), 199–220.

Page, S. (2006). *Tourism management: Managing for change* (2nd ed.). Oxford: Elsevier/Butterworth-Heinemann.

Case Studies in Tourism and Hospitality Businesses

Miriam Whitmarsh

Wentworth & Bourne

First published in 2006
by Wentworth & Bourne Ltd.
11 Vine Lane, London EC4P 5EI
© 2006 Miriam Whitmarsh
Reprinted 2007

All rights reserved. No part of this publication may be reproduced, stored in a retrieval system, or transmitted in any form or by any means, electronic, mechanical, photocopying, recording or otherwise without the prior written permission of the Publishers.

British Library Cataloging-in-Publication Data
A catalogue record for this book is available from the British Library

Typeset by Glenda Graphics, Barnstaple, Devon, UK
Printed and bound by PW Enterprises, Bude, Cornwall, UK
ISBN 0-321-09487-4

83

Lesson aims

- understand situation–problem–solution–evaluation structure in essays
- understand the use of information in this type of essay structure to:

  describe

  give cause and effect

  compare

  evaluate

  argue for

Further practice in:

- identifying required essay types
- producing an outline
- writing key sentences – which can be expanded in the next lesson into longer sentences

Introduction

Revise the different types of essay that were examined in Unit 8. Say or write on the board some key words or phrases from essay titles such as the following:

State …

Outline …

Describe …

Compare …

Evaluate …

Discuss …

Why …?

How …?

To what extent …?

How far …?

Ask students to say

- what type of essay is required
- what type of organizational structure should be used

If students find this difficult, refer them to the *Skills bank* for Unit 8.

Exercise A

Set for individual work and pairwork checking.

Feed back with the whole class. Point out that in real life, essays given by lecturers often involve several types of writing in one essay. This is the case with essay 4 (see the following page for a possible structure). Tell students that this structure is commonly found in many types of writing (including newspapers and academic writing).

171

Possible structure for essay 4:

Situation: description of a state of affairs, often giving some reasons and background information	description
Problem(s): the problems which are caused by the state of affairs; plus the effects of these problems	description (cause and effect)
Solution(s): ways of dealing with the problems (i) which may have been tried in the past or are being tried now; (ii) which will, may or could be tried in the future; suggestions for further solutions	description (+ possibly suggestion)
Evaluation of solution(s): comparison of solutions; opinion on how successful the solutions are or could be + justification; an opinion on which is the best option + justification	argument

Tell students they will plan (and possibly write) this essay.

Answers

Model answers:

1 Comparison, plus some evaluation.
2 Analysis.
3 Description.
4 Description, then comparison and evaluation/argument/opinion, plus support (see table above).

Exercise B

Set for individual work and pairwork checking.
Feed back with the whole class.

Answers

Model answers:

Situation	Alison Cole started a small business in 2006; she needed finance, once at the start + again when she wanted to expand
Problem	her bank would not give her a loan (both when she started her business and when she wanted to expand)
Solutions	overdraft arrangement government start-up loan borrowing from family

Exercise C

Set for individual work and pairwork checking. Feed back with the whole class.

Answers

Model answers:

Solution	sell equity to a venture capitalist
Argument for	the investor may give useful advice
Argument against	the business owner will lose some of the profit

Exercise D

1 Set for pairwork discussion. Remind students about the basic structure of an essay (introduction – main body – conclusion).

If you wish, you can give students the first two columns of the table in the Answers section, with the third column empty for them to complete. The table is reproduced in the additional resources section (Resource 10B) for this purpose.

Feed back with the whole class. Build the plan on the board, using the ideas in the Answers section to help.

2 Ask students to write some topic sentences for the four body paragraphs, using the information in the plan. Remind students that topic sentences need to be very general. Set for individual work.

Feed back with the whole class, writing some examples on the board.

3 Set for pairwork, then discussion with the whole class. Or if you prefer, set for individual homework. The ideas should be those of the students. Remind them to introduce their ideas with suitable phrases.

Note: Students will need their essay plans again in Lesson 4.

Answers

1 Possible essay plan:

Introduction	Examples of ideas
introduce the topic area give the outline of the essay	small tourism/hospitality businesses → many difficulties when starting up … *In this essay, I will discuss financial difficulties …* *I will illustrate/describe … (examples)* *I will consider … (solutions)* *Finally, I will suggest … (best solution)*

Body	Para 1: situation/problems (general)	small businesses → financing problems ∵ 1. high street banks don't often give loans to new small businesses (evidence: a number of surveys) 2. large public share issues not possible for small entrepreneurs (not the case for large businesses)
	Para 2: problems (specific examples)	example of case: Alison Cole's Moreton's Myth Horse Treks
	Para 3: solutions	1. overdraft with bank 2. trade credit (suppliers) 3. government small business loan 4. family 5. private investor
	Para 4: evaluations of solutions	first 4 types of funds fairly easy to obtain but (i) short-term, (ii) small amounts of money, (iii) bank overdrafts = expensive family → certain risks (i.e., if business not successful → personal problems) private investor → will take some of the profits but = useful for advice
Conclusion		*In my view/As I see it, the best option is … because …* *Firstly …* *Secondly …* *Thirdly …*

2 Possible topic sentences:

Para 1	One of the most serious areas of difficulty which small businesses in tourism and hospitality face is how to raise enough money to begin the business.
Para 2	There are many example cases which illustrate the financial difficulties faced by business start-ups.
Para 3	There are a number of solutions available to small entrepreneurs.
Para 4	All of these solutions have disadvantages as well as advantages.

3 Students' own concluding paragraphs.

Language note

Although 'situation–problem–solution–evaluation of solution' is often said to be an organizing principle in writing, in practice it is sometimes difficult to distinguish between the situation and the problem: they may sometimes seem to be the same thing. The important thing is to be clear about the main *focus* of the essay – that is, the answer to the question 'What am I writing about?' – and to structure the essay around this.

Closure

Set up a 'Dragon's Den'-style role-play. Dragon's Den is a TV series in which entrepreneurs try to persuade a panel of investors to invest in their business. The investors are highly successful and experienced businessmen and women. The entrepreneurs are people who have a good idea for a business. The investors try to find out whether the entrepreneurs have really got a good idea, whether they have done the necessary preparation and planning for their business and whether their plans are financially sound.

Put students in groups of four. Within each group, students work in pairs. Each pair should think of a product or an idea for a business. They should prepare a short (one-minute) presentation on their idea, which should include why it is good idea, how they plan to put it into operation, how much money they will need and where they plan to get it. They should also decide how much to ask the investors for – bearing in mind that the investors will want a percentage (to be negotiated) of the profits. (If students need this, allow them to look back to the role-play in Unit 9, Lesson 4.)

When both pairs are ready, they should take in it turns to be the entrepreneurs and the investors. The entrepreneurs should try to persuade the investors to invest in their business for a reasonable return on their investment. The investors will need to be sure that the idea is a good one and that it is financially sound.

10.4 Extending skills

The following is a reproduction of pages 82–83 of the Course Book.

10.3 Extending skills — recognizing essay types • situation–problem–solution–evaluation essays

A Read the four essay questions. What types of essays are they?

B Look at text A on the opposite page. Copy and complete Table 1 below.

C Look at text B on the opposite page. Copy and complete Table 2.

D Read the title of essay 4 again.
1 Make a plan for this essay.
2 Write a topic sentence for each paragraph in the body of the essay.
3 Write a concluding paragraph.

1 Compare decisions a company might take to achieve a short-term goal, and those it might take to achieve a long-term goal.

2 Explain from a managerial viewpoint how some of a company's main resources might help it to achieve its goals.

3 Outline some of the ways in which a company can raise finance for its operations.

4 Describe, with some examples, the financial problems faced by small tourism or hospitality business start-ups. Consider how small businesses can best solve these difficulties.

Table 1

Situation	
Problem	
Solutions	

Table 2

Solution	
Argument for	
Argument against	

10.4 Extending skills — writing complex sentences • references • quotations

A Expand these simple sentences. Add extra information. Use the ideas you discussed in Lessons 2 and 3.
1 High street banks do not always give loans to new small businesses.
2 Small entrepreneurs cannot issue shares to the public.
3 Not all evidence shows that decentralizing management is positive.
4 Allowing employees to take strategic decisions is risky.

B Look at the reference list (C) on the opposite page. Copy and complete Tables 1–3.

C Look at the pages from a book (D) on the opposite page.
1 Complete a further row of Table 1.
2 How could you write this as a reference?

D What do the abbreviations in the blue box mean?

E Look back at the text on page 81 (Lesson 2).
1 Find all the research sources (e.g., Leiper, 2004, page 259).
2 Add the page numbers to the correct reference in the list on the opposite page.
3 What punctuation is used to introduce each direct quote?
4 What words are used to introduce each direct quote? Why does the writer choose each word?

Table 1: Referencing books

Author(s)	Date	Place	Publisher

Table 2: Referencing journals

Name of journal	Volume	Pages

Table 3: Referencing websites

Retrieval date	URL

&	©	cf.	edn.	ed(s).	et al.
ibid.	n.d.	op. cit.	p.	pp.	vol.

Case Study 1: Financing a tourism business

In 2006, Alison Cole left her nine-to-five job and set up a company called Moreton's Myth Horse Treks which organized horse-riding adventures for tourists. She operated from her five-acre country property. Her high street bank refused her a loan but agreed to an overdraft of £4,000. With this and a government Small Business Start-up loan of £5,000, Alison was able to lease a stall in a market in her local town and also set up a website through which she could sell her treks. When, in 2007, she wanted to expand her business to a small stables operating from the local park, her bank again refused her a loan, despite the fact that she was now beginning to make a profit. Eventually, Alison borrowed the money from her mother and brother.

(adapted from Venture, 2005)

Management of a small hospitality business involves dealing with money as much as with people. It is clear that small businesses cannot rely on banks for financial help. Another alternative which may be considered by small entrepreneurs is to raise finance through the sale of equity in the business to a venture capitalist (Brookes, 2003). Grange (2005) argues that this represents 'a sound option' (p. 34) since these investors are often experienced business people and the small business owner may benefit from their business advice. However, Grange (ibid.) also points out that, 'The disadvantage is that the small entrepreneur is no longer the sole owner, and more importantly perhaps, may well see their hard-earned profits go to someone else.'

References

Briedenham, J., & Wickens, E. (2007). Developing cultural tourism in South Africa: potential and pitfalls. In Richards, G. (Ed.). *Cultural tourism: Global and local perspectives*. Binghamton, NY: The Haworth Press.

Buhalis, D., & Costa, C. (Eds.). (2005). *Tourism management dynamics: Trends, management and tools*. Oxford: Elsevier/Butterworth-Heinemann.

Evans, N., Campbell, D., & Stonehouse, S. (2003). *Strategic management for travel and tourism*. Oxford: Elsevier/Butterworth-Heinemann.

Hilton Hotels. (n.d.). *Hilton hotels*. Retrieved January 12, 2007, from http://en.wikipedia.org/wiki/Hilton_Hotels

Leiper, N. (1995). *Tourism management*. Melbourne: RMIT Publishing.

Leiper, N. (2004). *Tourism management* (3rd ed.). Frenchs Forest, NSW: Pearson Education Australia.

Murphy, P., & Murphy, A. (2004). *Strategic management for tourism communities: Bridging the gaps*. Clevedon: Channel View Publications.

Northcote, J., & Macbeth, J. (2006). Conceptualizing yield: Sustainable tourism management. *Annals of Tourism Research*, 33(1), 199–220.

Page, S. (2006). *Tourism management: Managing for change* (2nd ed.). Oxford: Elsevier/Butterworth-Heinemann.

Case Studies in Tourism and Hospitality Businesses

Miriam Whitmarsh

Wentworth & Bourne

First published in 2006
by Wentworth & Bourne Ltd.
11 Vine Lane, London EC4P 5EI
© 2006 Miriam Whitmarsh
Reprinted 2007

All rights reserved. No part of this publication may be reproduced, stored in a retrieval system, or transmitted in any form or by any means, electronic, mechanical, photocopying, recording or otherwise without the prior written permission of the Publishers.

British Library Cataloguing-in-Publication Data
A catalogue record for this book is available from the British Library

Typeset by Glenda Graphics, Barnstaple, Devon, UK
Printed and bound by PW Enterprises, Bude, Cornwall, UK
ISBN 0-321-09487-4

82   83

General note

This lesson focuses on writing references for a bibliography according to the APA (American Psychological Society) system. Before the lesson, it would be useful to familiarize yourself with this system. See the *Skills bank*, and for more detailed information, websites such as http://owl.english.purdue.edu/owl/resource/560/10/ or www.westwords.com/guffey/apa.html (at the time of writing).

Lesson aims

- use quotations with appropriate punctuation and abbreviations such as *ibid*.
- write a reference list (APA system)

Further practice in:

- the reverse activity to Lesson 2, i.e., putting extra information into simple sentences in an appropriate way

Introduction

Introduce the idea of using sources in writing. Look back at the text in Lesson 2 and ask students to find all the places where a reference to a source is mentioned. Ask them to find a quotation and a paraphrase. What are the main differences?

In this text, students will probably find it easier to identify a direct quotation (of which there are several) than a paraphrase. They may identify the following as a paraphrase of Murphy and Murphy:

They go on to say that this process needs good management in the form of leadership.

They may also suggest the following:

Leiper (1995) describes how the manager of a Pacific resort changed the way it was run and the roles of the employees.

Discuss how this differs from the following extract, which students may argue is a summary rather than a paraphrase:

Leiper's 1995 study found that the resort experienced considerable managerial difficulty. This was partly caused by managers who could not adapt to a new role which required them to coach rather than manage.

Exercise A

Remind students of the essay plan in Lesson 3. Do the first sentence with the whole class as an example on the board. Students should feel free to add words as appropriate to make a coherent sentence; they can also paraphrase (e.g., *don't always give* ➔ *are often reluctant to give*). Set the remaining sentences for individual work.

Answers

Possible answers:

1 A number of surveys have shown that high street banks are often reluctant to give loans to small businesses in the initial start-up phase.

2 Unlike large businesses, small entrepreneurs cannot raise substantial sums of money through large-scale issues of shares to the public.

3 Although some evidence shows that decentralizing management has a beneficial effect on businesses, it is certainly not the case in every situation, as it depends very much on where the business is, what it does, and how big it is.

4 Allowing employees to take strategic decisions carries certain risks, because they are not always able to take the whole picture into account.

Exercise B

Tell students that this is a list of references from the text in Lesson 2. Note that it is called 'References' because it lists all the references actually given (it is not a list of all the references the author might have consulted but not referred to – that is a **bibliography**).

Set for individual work and pairwork checking. Note that these tables are intended to help students identify some key information. For a full set of categories to include in a reference list, see the *Skills bank*. Tell students that when writing a reference list they will need to pay close attention to the detail of the layout which is in the APA style (the American Psychological Association). See the *Skills bank* for relevant websites which (at the time of writing) give further details. In particular, students should note and will need to practise:

● putting the names of writers and multiple writers in the correct alphabetical order according to family name, with the right spacing and punctuation

● writing all numbers correctly, including dates and page references

● using punctuation including the role and placing of full stops, commas and colons

● laying out the references in the correct style with the correct positions (e.g., of indents and tabs)

● using standard APA style features such as italic and brackets

Finally, ask students if they can spot the entries in the reference list that are not referred to in the article (and therefore should have been omitted from the list, although they might be included in a bibliography):

Hilton Hotels. (n.d.). *Hilton hotels*. Retrieved January 12, 2007, from http://en.wikipedia.org/wiki/Hilton_Hotels

Northcote, J., & Macbeth, J. (2006). Conceptualizing yield: Sustainable tourism management. *Annals of Tourism Research*, *33*(1), 199–220.

Answers

Table 1:

Author(s)	Date of publication	Place of publication	Publisher
Briedenhann, J. Wickens, E.	2007	Binghamton, NY	The Haworth Press
Buhalis, D. Costa, C. (Eds.)	2005	Oxford	Elsevier/Butterworth-Heinemann
Evans, N. Campbell, D. Stonehouse, S.	2003	Oxford	Elsevier/Butterworth-Heinemann
Leiper, N.	1995	Melbourne	RMIT Publishing
Leiper, N.	2004	Frenchs Forest, NSW	Pearson Education Australia
Murphy, P. Murphy, A.	2004	Clevedon	Channel View Publications
Page, S.	2006	Oxford	Elsevier/Butterworth-Heinemann

Table 2:

Name of journal	Volume	Pages
Annals of Tourism Research	33	199–220

Table 3:

Retrieval date	URL
January 12, 2007	http://en.wikipedia.org/wiki/Hilton_Hotels

Language and subject note

In the case of journals, there is an increasing tendency to refer to the volume number only in reference lists, omitting the issue number. Thus, for example, *English for Specific Purposes*, *16*(1), 47–60 might become *English for Specific Purposes*, *16*, 47–60.

Exercise C

Set for individual work and pairwork checking.

Answers

1

Author(s)	Date of publication	Place of publication	Publisher
Whitmarsh, M.	2006	London	Wentworth & Bourne Ltd.

2 Whitmarsh, M. (2006). *Case studies in tourism and hospitality businesses*. London: Wentworth & Bourne.

> ### Language and subject note
>
> In the APA system, titles of books (but not articles or journal titles) are in italics, sentence case – that is, initial capital letter only, unless the title contains a proper noun. If the title contains a colon, the first word after the colon is also capitalized.
>
> Journal *titles* are in italics and 'headline' or 'title' style – that is, all key words are capitalized but not conjunctions and prepositions. For example: *Journal of Small Business Management*.
>
> Journal *articles* are sentence case, no italics.

Exercise D

Many of these were covered in Unit 5, so ask students to check back if they are not sure (they can refer to the list at the back of the Course Book); they can also check online at the APA site and/or the other sites given in the *Skills bank*.

Set for individual work and pairwork checking.

Answers

Model answers:

&	and
©	copyright
cf.	compare
edn.	edition
ed(s).	editor(s)
et al.	and other authors
ibid.	same place in a work already referred to
n.d.	no date (used in a reference list if there is no date – as is often the case with web articles)
op. cit.	the work already referred to
p.	page
pp.	pages
vol.	volume

Exercise E

Remind students (if you have not done so already) of the two main ways in which students can use sources (i.e., references to other writers' work) in their writing:

- by giving the exact words used by another writer
- by paraphrasing another writer's ideas, i.e., rewriting the ideas using their own, different words but retaining the meaning

The first method is referred to as quotation or direct quotation. Direct quotations are in quotation marks.

The second method is referred to as paraphrase, summary or indirect quotation. Note that for copyright reasons around 90% of the paraphrase should be new words.

1/2 Set for individual work. Tell students to look for all the direct quotations and to identify the research sources. They should then locate the source in the reference list on page 83 of the Course Book. Writing the page numbers on the reference list may seem a mechanical exercise, but it is useful for students to get into the habit of doing this. It will enable them to find an original source book, refer to the relevant part of the book, and read more about the subject.

3/4 Students should identify the introducing phrases used, plus the punctuation.

Feed back with the whole class. Make sure that students understand why the different introducing verbs were chosen.

Answers

Model answers:

Quote	Source	Punctuation around the quote	Introducing phrase + reason for choice
'Organisations that specialise exclusively or largely in tourism need business strategies centred around tourists'	page 259 of Leiper, N. (2004). *Tourism management* (3rd ed.). Frenchs Forest, NSW: Pearson Education Australia.	'Xxx'.	It is obvious, therefore, that reason: what follows is a conclusion or explanation
'empowerment and progressive capacity-building of local people into management positions.'	page 88 of Richards, G. (Ed.) *Cultural tourism: Global and local perspectives.* Binghamton, NY: The Haworth Press.	'xxx.'	which Briedenhann and Wickens define as reason: what follows is a definition
'the various industry and community components together to form an approved and competitive community tourism product will be fundamental to the success of a destination'	pages 405 and 406 of Murphy, P., & Murphy, A. (2004). *Strategic management for tourism communities: Bridging the gaps.* Clevedon: Channel View Publications.	'xxx'	Murphy and Murphy (2004) claim that pulling reason: what follows is an explanation of opinion
'in the delivery and production of tourism products … operate for a profit motive, and for them to achieve this objective they need management in order to get things done.'	page 249 of Page, S. (2006). *Tourism management: Managing for change* (2nd ed.). Oxford: Elsevier/Butterworth-Heinemann.	'xxx.'	Page (2006) asserts that the majority of businesses involved reason: this is Page's opinion and part of an argument
'breaking up big organisations in small teams can enhance productivity and quality'	page 272 of Leiper, N. (1995). *Tourism management.* Melbourne: RMIT Publishing.	'xxx'	The first is that reason: there are two points
'empowering workers, giving them the right to make decisions on matters which might otherwise require managerial authority, can enhance quality and encourage commitment from employees'	page 272 of Leiper, N. (1995). *Tourism management.* Melbourne: RMIT Publishing.	'xxx'	The second states that reason: there are two points
'first, a shift away from centralized, process-oriented bureaucracies to more decentralized, performance-driven management structures; secondly, a shift away from fragmented, standardized operating systems to more … integrated forms of working where there is greater employee involvement and empowerment; thirdly, a change in the role of managers'	page 87 of Buhalis, D., & Costa, C. (Eds.). (2005). *Tourism management dynamics: Trends, management and tools.* Oxford: Elsevier/Butterworth-Heinemann.	colon + 'xxx'	Buhalis & Costa (2005) talk about tourism initiatives that show three characteristics: reason: this introduces Buhalis and Costa's findings and indicates there are three points
'all industries … some organizations are more successful than others. This is as true for … travel and tourism as for any other industry. The best performers … possess something special that weaker competitors do not have and this enables them to outperform their rivals.'	page 48 of Evans, N., Campbell, D., & Stonehouse, S. (2003). *Strategic management for travel and tourism.* Oxford: Elsevier/ Butterworth-Heinemann.	'xxx.'	However, as Evans, Campbell and Stonehouse (2003) assert, in reason: 'assert' suggests this is the opinion of Evans et al. and part of an argument (use of 'as' implies agreement of the writer with the opinion)

Closure

Refer students to the *Skills bank* for a summary of writing references. Study how the following are used:

- names (order)
- punctuation (capital letters, full stops, commas, colons)
- layout (indentation, spacing)
- style features (italics, brackets)

For further practice, use Resource 10C from the additional resources section. Ask students to check the references on a library database or on the Internet (discuss which sources are likely to be the most accurate and give them all the information they need – often the best way to check bibliographical details is to use a university library catalogue, as information found on the Internet is frequently inaccurate or incomplete). They should also make any necessary changes to ensure the references fit the APA models used in this unit. If possible, they should use the online website references (see *Skills bank*) to help them. Remind students that they will also need to put the references in the right alphabetical order.

Correct versions are:

Arthur, C. (2004). Penguins in Antarctica. Dolphins in Scotland. Dingoes in Australia. They all face the same danger: ecotourism. Retrieved March 4, 2007, from *The Independent*, http://news.independent.co.uk/world/environment/story.jsp?story=497632

Becken, S. (2002). Analysing international tourist flows to estimate energy use associated with air travel. *Journal of Sustainable Tourism, 10*(2), 114–131.

Edgell, D. L. (2006). *Managing sustainable tourism: A legacy for the future*. Binghamton, NY: The Haworth Press.

Gossling, S. (2005). Tourism's contribution to global environmental change: Space, energy, disease, water. In C. M. Hall & J. Higham (Eds.), *Tourism, recreation and climate change* (pp. 286–300). Clevedon: Channel View Publications.

The World Commission on Environment and Development (1987). *Our common future*. Oxford: Oxford University Press.

Extra activities

1 Work through the *Skills bank* and *Vocabulary bank* if you have not already done so, or as revision of previous study.

2 Use the *Activity bank* (Teacher's Book additional resources section, Resource 10A).

A Set for individual work (including homework) or pairwork. Tell students to focus on the main meanings of the words in tourism and hospitality management. Feed back, eliciting example sentences.

Answers

Word	Part of speech	Noun – countable or uncountable?	Verb – transitive or intransitive?
commitment	n	C (in the sense of appointments), U (in the sense of loyalty and hard work)	
empowerment	n	U	
encourage	v		T
expand	v		T, I
implement	v, n	C	T
loan	n, v	C	T
managerial	adj		
performance	n	C, U (in tourism/ management generally U)	
recruitment	n	U	
resource	n	C	
shift	n, v	C	T, I
strategic	adj		

B Set for individual work (including homework) or pairwork. Accept all reasonable answers. Students should be able to explain the meaning.

Answers

Possible answers:

business	interests, unit, strategy, plan, development
hotel	manager, chain, occupancy rates
human	resources
long	-term
management	style, skills, position, team, structures, theories
medium	-term
operating	system
performance	-driven
process	-oriented
top	-down (management style)

3 Ask students to choose one of the other essays in Lesson 3 and make a plan. They can also write topic sentences for each paragraph in the essay.

11 EXTERNAL INFLUENCES

This unit looks at external factors which may affect tourism and hospitality businesses, with a focus on demographic, political, economic and especially environmental factors. In terms of environmental focus, the unit looks at sustainability of businesses and what they need to do to operate responsibly.

Skills focus

🎧 **Listening**
- recognizing the speaker's stance
- writing up notes in full

Speaking
- building an argument in a seminar
- agreeing/disagreeing

Vocabulary focus
- words/phrases used to link ideas (*moreover*, *as a result*, etc.)
- stress patterns in noun phrases and compounds
- fixed phrases from academic English
- words/phrases related to environmental issues

Key vocabulary

See also the list of fixed phrases from academic English in the *Vocabulary bank* (Course Book page 92).

campaign (n)	industrialization	**Environmental words**	fossil fuel
consultant	legal	carbon footprint	global warming
consumer (spending)	manufacturing	carbon offset(ting)	greenhouse gas
demographic	political	carbon trading	low-impact
diversify	population	climate change	pollution
economic	pressure group	conservation	recycling
education	social	emissions	renewable energy
immigrant	technological	environment	sustainable
		environmental	waste (n and v)
		environmentally friendly	

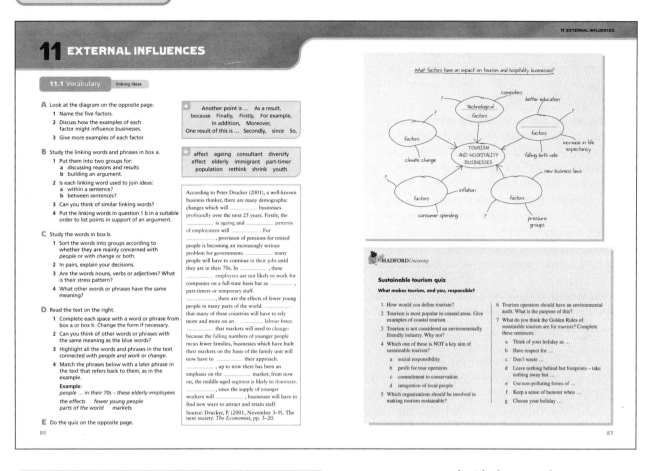

General note

Read the *Vocabulary bank* at the end of the Course Book unit. Decide when, if at all, to refer your students to it. The best time is probably at the very end of the lesson or the beginning of the next lesson, as a summary/revision.

Lesson aims

- use rhetorical markers: to add points in an argument; to signal cause and effect (between- and within-sentence linking)
- further understand lexical cohesion: the use of superordinates/synonyms to refer back to something already mentioned; building lexical chains

Further practice in:

- synonyms, antonyms and word sets from the discipline

Introduction

1 Revise some vocabulary from previous units. Give students some key words from previous units (examples in italic below) and ask them to think of terms connected with these words.

strategic (decision, aim)

top-down (management style)

management (team, style)

advertising (budget, campaign)

marketing (budget, manager, department)

2 Introduce the topic: before asking students to open their books, ask them what kinds of things businesses in the tourism and hospitality sector (or any sector for that matter) need to pay attention to outside their own organizations. Accept any reasonable suggestions.

Exercise A

Ask students to open their books and look at the diagram on the right-hand page. Check the meaning of the words in the diagram. If necessary, give some examples of pressure groups such as anti-globalization groups, Greenpeace, etc.

1 Set for pairwork. Feed back with the class. Ask students if they are familiar with the acronym PEST. It is often used in business for analysis and strategy decision purposes. The acronym stands for the Political, Economic, Social and Technological

181

issues that could affect the strategic development of a business. Identifying PEST influences is a useful way of summarizing the external environment in which a business operates. However, it should be followed by consideration of how a business could respond to such influences, which is what is done in the rest of this unit. Identify the additional factor here – *Environment* – sometimes added to the PEST acronym as EV (PEST EV).

2/3 With the whole class, discuss the technology part of the diagram. Ask students to explain how exactly computers could affect businesses (in terms of tourism you could think of booking systems, for instance, but also the Internet in general as a source of information). Discuss with the class other possible future technological developments and how they might affect businesses: for example, what effect might the development of efficient and cheap non-carbon fuels have on airline businesses? Answer: changing the way their machinery is powered would initially be a major expense, but might save money ultimately.

Next look at the social factors. Discuss with the class the likely effects of changing age structure and improved education (note that the topic of the changing age structure is considered further in the text in this lesson; it was also looked at in Unit 6 in the context of events management). Ask the class to suggest more social factors that might affect tourism and hospitality businesses. Accept any reasonable suggestions.

Set the remaining factors (environmental, political and economic) and their effects on business for pairwork discussion. It might be a good idea to ask each pair to think about a different factor. Ask a few pairs to feed back to the class. Accept any reasonable suggestions.

Answers

Possible answers:

1 See diagram below.

2 Answers depend on the students.

3 For the question marks, some more examples of factors are:

Technological factors

new communications technology (social networking communities, for instance, or personalized booking systems)

new industrial materials (bigger planes)

Social factors

new fashions such as in entertainment, food, clothes, sports, etc.

changes in attitudes to, for example, group travel or adventure travel

Political factors

the impact of government

deregulation

privatization

change in government

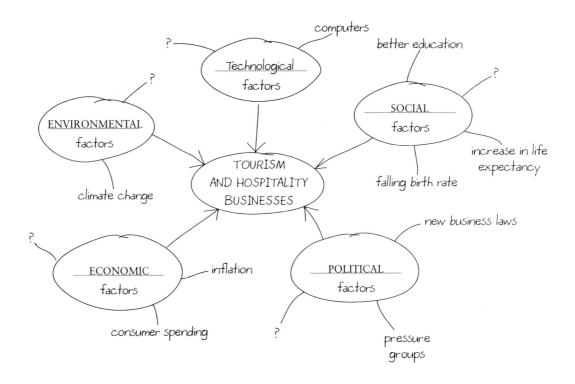

What factors have an impact on tourism and hospitality businesses?

trading standards

(for big companies) monopoly and competition control by governments

employment laws

local trading organizations

global organizations such as WTO (World Tourism Organization), World Bank, G8, United Nations

international conventions and agreements such as Kyoto

Economic factors

developing wealth

depression

taxes

growth of new economically powerful countries (China, India, etc.)

development of new or changing markets

changes in the fortunes of the large economies (e.g., the US)

Environmental factors

global warming

pollution

industrialization

development

green issues

areas of special interest or beauty

waste disposal

new laws on emissions

planning permission

Add some of these to the diagram, as appropriate and as students suggest them. It would be a good idea to make a large poster-sized copy of the diagram or put it on an OHT or other visual medium to which you can add more examples as the unit progresses. See whether students can come up with concrete examples of applications of the more general factors – later in the unit they will need to do this.

Exercise B

1 Set for individual work and pairwork checking. Feed back with the whole class, building the table in the Answers section.

2 Explain what is meant by 'within' and 'between' sentences: 'within-sentence' linking words and phrases join clauses in a sentence; 'between-sentence' linking words and phrases connect two sentences. Demonstrate with the following:

Within-sentence linking words:

The workforce has become highly skilled in many countries <u>because</u> education standards have improved.

Make sure students can see that the within-sentence linking words precede dependent clauses.

Between-sentence linking words:

Many countries have improved education standards.
<u>As a result</u>, the workforce has become highly skilled.

Point out that between-sentence linking words usually have a comma before the rest of the sentence.

Ask students to say which of the other words in box a are 'between' and which are 'within'.

3 Ask for suggestions for synonyms and add to the table.

4 First make sure that students understand the basic principle of an argument, which is:

> | Statement |
> | --- |

+

> | one or more support(s) for statement (= more facts, reasons, results, examples, evidence, etc.) |
> | --- |

Constructing a complex argument will usually entail a statement plus several supports.

With the whole class, elicit suggestions for how to use the linkers when constructing an argument. Build the table in the Answers section on the board.

Answers

Possible answers:

See table on next page.

Linking words/phrases	Use for	Within- or between-sentence linker	Other similar words/phrases
Another point is …	building an argument	between	And another thing:
As a result,	reasons and results	between	Consequently,
because …	reasons and results	within	as …
Finally,	building an argument	between	Lastly,
Firstly,	building an argument	between	To begin with/To start with, For one thing,
For example,	building an argument	between	For instance,
In addition,	building an argument	between	Also,
Moreover,	building an argument	between	Furthermore,
One result of this is …	reasons and results	between	One consequence of this is … Because of this,
Secondly,	building an argument	between	Next, Then,
since …	reasons and results	within	as …
So,	reasons and results	between	Therefore, Thus, Hence,

4 A typical argument is constructed like this:

Firstly,	making the major support point
For example,	supporting the point with a specific example
In addition,	adding another related point in support
Secondly,	making the second major support point
Another point is …	adding another related point in support
Moreover,	adding more information to the point above
Finally,	making the last point

Language note

1 Note that within-sentence linking words or phrases may be placed at the beginning of the sentence with a comma after the first clause, as in:

Because many countries have improved education standards, the workforce has become highly skilled.

2 Although between-sentence linking words or phrases are described above as joining two sentences, they can of course link two independent clauses joined by coordinating linking words *and* or *but*, as in:

Many countries have improved education standards and, as a result, the workforce has become highly skilled.

Exercise C

1 Set for individual work. Note that students should try to put each word into one of the two categories, even if it is not immediately clear how it could be relevant. If they are not sure which category to use, they should try to think of a phrase containing the word and imagine how it could be relevant to one of the categories.

2 Ask students to compare their answers and to justify their choices. Feed back with the whole class, discussing the words for which students feel the category is not obvious. If no decision can be reached, say you will come back to the words a little later.

3/4 Set for pairwork. Feed back with the whole class if you wish.

Answers

Possible answers:

Word/stress	Suggested categories	Part of speech	Other words/phrases
a'ffect	change	v (T)	influence
'ageing	people/change	v (I), adj	getting/becoming older
con'sultant	people	n (C)	(visiting) expert
di'versify	change	v (I)	change, become more varied
e'ffect	change	n (C)	consequence, outcome, result
'elderly	people	adj	old, older
'immigrant	people	n (C), adj	migrant
part-'timer	people	n (C)	employee who works part of the normal working week; not full time
popu'lation	people	n (C, U)	people
re'think	change	v (T)	reassess
shrink	change	v (I, T)	(I) become smaller/fewer (T) make something smaller
youth	people	n (U, C)	young people

Exercise D

Note: Students may need to use dictionaries in question 2.

Students should first read through the text to get an idea of the topic. Ask students which of the external factors the text relates to.

1/2 Set for individual work and pairwork checking. Make sure students understand that they can use the words and phrases from box a both within- and between-sentence (e.g., *So* can begin a sentence, but students can also use it lower case within a sentence – see *Language note* on previous page).

Feed back with the whole class. Point out that having done these questions, it should now be possible to say whether the words in box b can be put into a 'change' or a 'people' group. (In the case of *ageing*, a case can be made for both groups.) The point here is that the context will make clear what the meaning of a word should be. This is important when it comes to making a guess at the meaning of a word you are not sure of initially.

3 This text illustrates the influence of demographic changes. Since the text is about people in the context of work, ask students to identify all the words first about *people and work*, and then about *change*. (They can copy in a separate table or highlight with a marker.)

Set for individual work and pairwork checking. Feed back with the whole class, if you wish using an OHT and two coloured pens, or other visual medium. Point out how the two themes of *change* and *people and work* run through the text.

Tell students that a particular topic will have groups of words which are connected to or associated with it – known as 'lexical chains'. These lexical chains show us the themes that run through the text and which help 'glue' the ideas together to make a coherent piece of text. It is a good idea, therefore, to learn vocabulary according to topic areas.

4 It is also common to use synonymous words and phrases to refer back to something already mentioned. Ideally, use an OHT or other visual medium of the text (Resource 11B in the additional resources section), and with a coloured pen draw a line to show how *people … in their 70s* is referred to later in the text *as these elderly employees*.

Set for individual work and pairwork checking. Feed back with the class (linking the phrases with coloured pens if using Resource 11B).

Answers

Model answers:

1 According to Peter Drucker (2001), a well-known business thinker, there are many demographic changes which will <u>affect</u> businesses profoundly over the next 25 years. Firstly, the <u>population</u> is ageing and <u>so/as a result</u>, patterns of employment will <u>diversify</u>. For <u>example</u>, provision of pensions for retired people is becoming an increasingly serious problem for governments. <u>As a result/So</u>, many people will have to continue in their jobs until they are in their 70s. In <u>addition</u>, these <u>elderly</u> employees are not likely to work for companies on a full-time basis but as <u>consultants</u>, part-timers or temporary staff.

<u>Secondly</u>, there are the effects of fewer young people in many parts of the world. <u>One result of this is</u> that many countries will have to rely more and more on an <u>immigrant</u> labour force. <u>Another point is</u> that markets will need to change: because the falling numbers of young people mean fewer families, businesses which have built their markets on the basis of the family unit will now have to <u>rethink</u> their approach. <u>Moreover</u>, up to now there has been an emphasis on the <u>youth</u> market; from now on, the middle-aged segment is likely to dominate. <u>Finally</u>, since the supply of younger workers will <u>shrink</u>, businesses will have to find new ways to attract and retain staff.

2

Word	Synonym
profoundly	deeply/greatly/significantly
ageing	getting older
patterns of employment	ways of working
in their jobs	working
employees	workers
labour	work
change	alter
falling	decreasing, declining
mean	will result in
segment	(part of the) market
dominate	take over, be larger/more important

3

People and work	Change
demographic	changes
businesses	affect
population	ageing
ageing	profoundly
patterns of employment	diversify
pensions	is becoming
retired people	result
people	effects
in their jobs	fewer
in their 70s	result
elderly	increasingly
employees	change
to work for	falling numbers
on a full-time basis	fewer
consultants, part-timers or temporary	rethink
staff	up to now
young people	from now on
immigrant labour force	is likely to
younger people	will shrink
families	new
family unit	
youth	
middle-aged	
supply	
younger workers	
attract and retain staff	

4

First phrase	Second phrase
people … in their 70s	these elderly employees
the effects	one result of this
fewer young people	the falling numbers of younger people
parts of the world	these countries
markets	the youth market; the middle-aged segment

Exercise E

This general knowledge quiz focuses on environmental facts, linking the more general outlook of Lesson 1 with the more specific outlook of Lessons 2, 3 and 4. Time it if you wish. Alternatively, set it for homework for students to research the answers. Make sure students understand that they need not give expert and detailed answers: the purpose of the quiz is to lead them into the major topic of the unit, which is the influence of environmental issues on tourism, and to generate discussion.

Feed back with the whole class, using Resource 11C from the additional resources section if you wish. (These are model answers; students' own answers may be slightly different but equally valid.)

An interesting source of information on this topic (at the time of writing) is:

www.globaleducation.edna.edu.au/globaled/go/pid/2534

Answers

Model answers:

1 Movement of people out of their communities for leisure or business.

2 Hotels, resorts, marinas, restaurants, holiday homes, second homes, camp-sites, retail businesses, fishing shops, dive shops, fishing piers, recreational fishing facilities, beaches, ecotourism, cruises, swimming, snorkelling, diving, sailing, etc.

3 It puts a strain on water, energy, transport infrastructure and natural areas.

4 b: even though this is important for the operators, it is not the first priority when the aim is to build sustainable tourism.

5 Environment protection organizations (e.g., WWF, Greenpeace or similar national, regional or local organizations); local (council) and national government; transport companies (both public and private); tourism service providers (e.g., hotels, restaurants, events organizers); community representatives (e.g., local tribes, residents).

6 To check whether the operator sticks to the law; to see whether there are any problems and advise what the operator can do about them.

7 a … an opportunity to learn.

b … local culture/the environment.

c … resources.

d … photos/memories.

e … transport.

f … things go wrong.

g … carefully.

Closure

Ask students to review the lesson and list ten of the factors mentioned which affect tourism and hospitality businesses. Then divide the class into groups and tell the groups to discuss the factors and try to rank them in order of importance. They will need to think of specific countries if possible and the effects the factors may have on these countries in the context of their tourist industries. They should give reasons for their ranking.

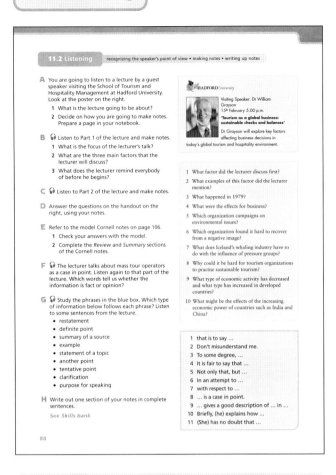

General note

Read the *Skills bank – Writing out notes in full* at the end of the Course Book unit. Decide when, if at all, to refer your students to it. The best time, as before, is probably at the very end of the lesson or the beginning of the next lesson, as a summary/revision.

Lesson aims

- recognize and understand phrases that identify the speaker's point of view
- convert notes into full sentences and paragraphs

Further practice in:

- making notes (use of heading systems and abbreviations)
- referring to sources
- general academic words and phrases

Introduction

1 Review phrases indicating a speaker's view of the truth value of a statement. Write a sentence such as the following on the board (i.e., a 'fact' about which there may be differences of opinion):

Growth of tourism in developing countries such as India and China has had a beneficial effect on the generation of wealth.

Ask students to say whether they think this is true or not. Elicit phrases they can use before the sentence to show how certain they are about their opinion.

Dictate or write on the board the following phrases. Ask students to say what the effect of each phrase is when put before the sentence on the board. In each case, does it make the writer sound confident or tentative?

> *The research shows that …*
>
> *A survey found that …*
>
> *The evidence does not support the idea that …*
>
> *It appears to be the case that …*
>
> *The evidence suggests that …*
>
> *The evidence shows that …*
>
> *It is clear that …*
>
> *It is possible that …*

2 Revise the Cornell note-taking system. Elicit the R words. Ask students to describe how to divide up the page (refer to Unit 9). Revise the other ways to take notes (see Units 1 and 3).

3 Revise note-taking symbols and abbreviations for listening (see Units 5 and 9, and Unit 9 extra activity 3 on page 161).

Exercise A

Refer students to the Hadford University lecture announcement. Tell them to look at the title and the summary of the talk. Check that they know the meaning of 'checks and balances' (factors which may have a limiting or controlling effect on business practice).

Set the questions for pairwork discussion. Feed back with the whole class.

Answers

Possible answers:

1 Accept any reasonable suggestions.

2 The lecturer is clearly going to list causes and effects. This suggests that possibly a flowchart or spidergram might be a suitable form of notes (as in Unit 1), as well as the Cornell system (which is used here) or the more conventional numbered points system.

🎧 Exercise B

Play Part 1 once through *without* allowing students time to focus on the questions.

Put students in pairs to answer the questions by referring to their notes. Feed back with the whole class, building a set of notes on the board if you wish. Add the examples to your spidergram from Lesson 1 if you have not already done so.

Ask students which method they are going to use to make notes, now that they have listened to the introduction. They should make any adjustments necessary to the page they have prepared for their notes.

Answers

Model answers:

1 External influences on tourism and hospitality businesses.

2 Political, economic and environmental factors.

3 He reminds students of the definition of a 'tourism system'. The five elements which form the tourism system are (1) tourists; (2) TGRs (tourism generating regions); (3) transit routes; (4) TDRs (tourism destination regions); and (5) tourism industries.

Transcript 🎧 2.8

Part 1

Good morning. My name is Dr William Grayson and I'm a business consultant. It's a pleasure to be here today as your guest speaker. My speciality is tourism and hospitality. I'm going to try to explain some of the major factors which exert pressure on the sector from the outside, that is to say, I shall mainly be looking at some of the different types of *external* influences which affect the way businesses in tourism and hospitality operate.

Don't misunderstand me, I don't want to imply that there are no *internal* questions for a company – as we all know, operators have to think about how they manage their businesses and their finance and so on. But there are also matters at a national and an international level which greatly influence decisions, and they're becoming increasingly important. To some degree, individual companies will be affected differently, but it is fair to say that they will all have to keep an eye on which way inflation or interest rates are going, or demand and competition in a particular location. Not only that, but they also have to keep track of the government policies of the country or the countries where they operate and adapt and diversify wherever they need. In an attempt to try to keep the discussion of external pressures on business reasonably simple, though, I'm going to focus mainly on three areas:

politics, economics and, very importantly, the environment.

Just to review something you've probably talked about in previous lectures. It's good to be aware that the best way to talk about tourism is to discuss it as a *system*. That way you can get a clearer picture of how the elements interact with each other and the surrounding environment. Do you remember the components? The five elements which form the tourism system are, one, tourists; two, TGRs (that's tourism generating regions); three, transit routes; four, TDRs (tourism destination regions); and, five, tourism industries.

🎧 Exercise C

Play the whole of the rest of lecture through once without stopping. Students should make notes as they listen.

Answers

See *Notes* section of the table in the Answers section for Exercise E.

Transcript 🎧 2.9

Part 2

To start with, then: the political influences on tourism and hospitality. Whether it's taxation policies, election results or pressure groups, politics has a crucial role to play. Governments often try to protect their country's businesses by signing up to a regional trading group which imposes tariffs or quotas. In the case of tourism, though, most countries will try to open up as much as they can; although I'm sure that some countries would rather have their own hotel chains establish themselves than have foreign multinationals dominate the market. Governments often encourage foreign companies and visitors to come into the country and visit sites and attractions or set up new operations and tourist venues such as hotels, theme parks and food chains. These things demonstrate the political dimension of business.

But let's take as an example the influence of election results. Historically, the UK is a good example of how a new government can bring about a major change affecting the business world in general. Let me take you back a few years, probably to before you were born. When Margaret Thatcher's Conservative government came to power in 1979, it started to address some of the difficulties of state-owned industries in both manufacturing and service sectors. By the mid-1980s the process of privatization of state industries had begun to change the business landscape for ever. Many new business opportunities were created, particularly in the service sector, of which tourism is a major part. While manufacturing declined overall, it is clear that the business world in general, and tourism in particular, benefited greatly. These politically driven policies have since been copied all over the world.

Another area which we can include in the political domain is the effect of pressure groups. Governments and businesses have to deal with the political influence and public protests of these groups. No doubt you all know Greenpeace, who campaign on environmental issues: in 1995 their protests made Royal Dutch Shell seem so morally wrong that the company lost about 50% of their sales. Greenpeace are also well known for their protests and campaigns in the area of tourism. Do you remember their protests against Iceland's whaling industry (getting people to declare they wouldn't visit the country if Iceland didn't stop whaling), or against tourism in the Antarctic? Greenpeace is also part of a coalition campaigning to stop the expansion of London's Heathrow Airport. Greenpeace also works with scientists, public activists and authorities to develop parks and nature reserves with the aim of creating responsible, environmental tourism opportunities that don't do too much damage. We call this sustainable tourism. There are many other pressure groups which have been able to bring about major changes in public awareness of issues with either positive or negative consequences for business.

The funny thing is – well, I wouldn't want to call it funny, it's much more of a challenge – that at the centre of the whole debate about sustainable tourism are issues which the tourism industry finds hard or impossible to control. Why? Well, simply because they need to maximize profit. The hotel industry, for instance, is trying hard to encourage the responsible use of water and introduce waste and energy management through recycling, conservation and alternative energy. InterContinental Hotels was the first to start an environmental audit of its hotels, and in the end they produced an environmental manual for their hotels. Such guidelines have since been adopted into a broader programme which is supported by major hotel chains such as Forte, Hilton International, Holiday Inn Worldwide and Sheraton. There is a growing number of smaller and large tourism and hospitality businesses trying to do the right thing for the environment.

You need to wonder, though, whether these attitudes can have an effect on the mainstream. Mass tour operators are a case in point. Can we really convince these operators, who take the majority of tourists around the world, to prioritize environmental issues? The UN-led *Tour Operators'*

Initiative for Sustainable Tourism Development is a positive step. However, critics of tour operators argue that they are always going to put their own interests first. The evidence shows that this is especially true with respect to airline carriers. In my view it will be incredibly hard to move them in the right direction. The effect of their unstoppable growth has been very harmful, in my opinion, especially from an environmental point of view. Their bottom line is market share and filling planes, isn't it?

Now, let's turn to economic influences on the world of business, including tourism and hospitality. An important economic dimension is the changing importance of different business sectors over a period of time. Peter Drucker, who was a major business thinker, gives a good description of this in his article entitled 'The New Society' published in *The Economist* in 2001. By the way, if you don't know anything about Drucker, a good introduction to his work can be found on a website at the University of Pennsylvania – I'll give you the URL later. Briefly, in *The Economist* article, Drucker explains how at the beginning of the 20th century (in 1913) farm products accounted for 70% of world trade, but farming has now fallen to less than one-fifth of the world's economic activity. In many developed countries the contribution by agriculture to their GDP has reduced dramatically. More recently also, manufacturing has seen a substantial decline in many of the developed nations. Manufacturing as an economic activity in many developed countries has given way to a major increase in service industries such as tourism and hospitality, with a consequent rise in the importance of finance and the money markets. These changes in the nature of economic output are, of course, reflected in the types of business which we find in these countries.

At the same time, in the newly emerging boom economies such as China, governments are trying hard to reduce people's reliance on farming in favour of new manufacturing and also tourism. India is another example of this: it has seen a boom in both these areas.

A thought to finish with is the question of to what extent these booming economies will become the main drivers of the global economy. One writer in *Money Management* magazine has no doubt that, and I quote, 'China will continue to be a dominant player driving world growth, which will have flow-through to other economies.' This could mean that we may see the older economies such as the United States losing out increasingly to China and India. In terms of tourism, we are likely to see improving facilities for tourists travelling to these countries, but also significant numbers of tourists from these countries travelling both within their own countries and to overseas tourist destinations. Now, I'm going to stop at this point ...

Exercise D

Put students in pairs to answer the questions by referring to their notes. Feed back with the class to see how much they have been able to get from the lecture. If they can't answer something, do not supply the answer at this stage.

Answers

Model answers:

1 Political.

2 Taxation policies, election results, pressure groups, regional trading groups/protection through tariffs or quotas, encouragement for foreign companies.

3 Margaret Thatcher's Conservative government came to power in the UK.

4 The privatization process was in place by the mid-1980s; many new business opportunities were created with privatization, especially in service industries like tourism and hospitality; manufacturing declined.

5 Greenpeace.

6 (Royal Dutch) Shell.

7 Greenpeace campaigned against Iceland's whaling industry by making people declare they wouldn't visit the country.

8 At the end of the day, these businesses have to make a profit, which may conflict with the environmental aims.

9 Decreased: manufacturing and agriculture. Increased: services.

10 Their economies may become the main drivers of the global economy, in the same way the US economy has fulfilled that function in the late 20th and early 21st centuries; in terms of tourism, an increase in tourism within these countries, and an increase in tourists from these countries.

Exercise E

1 Set for individual work.

2 Set for individual work and pairwork checking. Feed back with the whole class.

Answers

Possible answers:

Review	Notes
Types of political influence are: ...?	1 Political factors: e.g., taxation policies, pressure groups, election results, protection thro' tariffs or quotas, foreign companies coming into country
Example of a **political** influence on business ...?	(a) election results, e.g., Margaret Thatcher's new government 1979 UK → mid-1980s privatization → new business opportunities esp. service sector incl. tourism → manufacturing declined → policy copied by other countries
Example of pressure group ...?	(b) pressure groups, e.g., Greenpeace (environment) → Shell 1995 lost 50% sales Other Greenpeace campaigns relating to tourism: → Iceland anti-whaling protest → expansion Heathrow → park development
Challenge ... ?	Tourism industry = maximize profit ←→ sustainable tourism: bottom-line = $$$!
Sustainable examples ... ?	InterContinental Hotels → environmental audit major hotels Forte, Hilton, Holiday Inn, Sheraton shared programme mass tour operators → working together in UN project, but ...???

Developed countries: growth in ...? decline in ...?
 	
'New' economies: 'increase in ...?
 	
In future ...?
	2 Economic factors: e.g., changing importance of different business sectors. Drucker ('The New Society' 2001):
	• 1913: farm products = 70% of world trade. Now < ⅕ of economic activity
	• developed countries:
	  ○ = big ↓ in contribution by agriculture to GDP
	  ○ also manufacturing decline →↑ in service industries
	• 'new' economies: reduce farming →↑ manufacturing AND services (e.g., India, China)
	  → competition with developed countries
	• ? will China/India, etc. → dominate world economy instead of US?

Summary

Political, economic and environmental factors have all influenced the tourism and hospitality industry, and continue to do so. In developed countries there is now an emphasis on service industries rather than manufacturing, while boom economies in developing countries are increasing their manufacturing output as well as their tourism industries. Sustainable tourism is a powerful environmental force. The question is, though, whether it is something that clashes with the business interests of large hotels, tour operators, airlines, etc. New economies may become more powerful economically than older developed economies such as the US.

Note

Source references for lecture:

Dowling, J. (2006). Fluctuating global fortunes. *Money Management*, 20(21), 12–15. Retrieved May 25, 2007, from www.moneymanagement.com.au

Drucker, P. (2001, November 3–9). The next society. *The Economist*, pp. 3–20. Retrieved January 2, 2005, from www.economist.com/surveys/displaystory.cfm?story_id=770819

Knowledge@Wharton. (2005). *Farewell, Peter Drucker: A tribute to an intellectual giant.* Retrieved May 25, 2007, from http://knowledge.wharton.upenn.edu/article.cfm?articleid=1326

Perkins, J. (2004). *Confessions of an economic hit man.* San Francisco: Berrett Koehler.

United Nations Environment Programme. (n.d.). *Tour operators' initiative for sustainable tourism development.* Retrieved August 4, 2007, from http://www.uneptie.org/pc/tourism/private_sector/toinitiative.htm

🎧 Exercise F

Discuss the question with the whole class. Ask them if they can remember any phrases that signal whether the comments are true or just opinion.

Play the extract. Ask students to tell you to stop the recording when they hear key phrases. Write the phrases on the board. Remind students that it is important to recognize when someone is giving only their opinion, which others might well disagree with.

Answers

Model answers:

The UN-led *Tour Operators' Initiative for Sustainable Tourism Development* **is a positive step.**	Whether something is 'positive', 'good', 'interesting', etc. is always a matter of opinion.
… **critics of tour operators argue that** they are always going to put their own interests first.	This phrase can be used to give both a speaker's own opinion as well as an opposing view.
The evidence shows that this is especially true with respect to airline carriers.	Sometimes, to put their case strongly, people will present opinions as facts, very strongly stated, with no tentativeness (but also without providing data or references).
In my view, it will be incredibly hard to move them in the right direction.	This is clearly the lecturer's opinion.
The effect of their unstoppable growth **has been very harmful, in my opinion** …	This is a continuation of 'in my view'.

Transcript 🎧 2.10

You need to wonder, though, whether these attitudes can have an effect on the mainstream. Mass tour operators are a case in point. Can we really convince these operators, who take the majority of tourists around the world, to prioritize environmental issues? The UN-led *Tour Operators' Initiative for Sustainable Tourism Development* is a positive step. However, critics of tour operators argue that they are always going to put their own interests first. The evidence shows that this is especially true with respect to airline carriers. In my view, it will be incredibly hard to move them in the right direction. The effect of their unstoppable growth has been very harmful, in my opinion, especially from an environmental point of view. Their bottom line is market share and filling planes, isn't it?

🎧 Exercise G

Allow students time to read the phrases and the types of information, making sure that they understand any difficult words. Remind students that 'type' of information tells you what the speaker *intends to do* with the words. The words themselves are something different.

Ask students to try to match the phrases and types of information as far as they can. Note that it is not always possible to say what the function of a phrase is outside its context, so they may not be able to match all the phrases and information types before hearing the sentences. Note that some types of information are needed more than once.

When they have done as much as they can, play the extracts one at a time, allowing time for students to identify the type of information which follows. Check answers after each sentence, making sure that students understand the information that actually follows the phrase. If possible, students should also give the actual words.

Answers

Model answers:

Fixed phrase	Type of information which follows the phrase
1 that is to say …	restatement
2 Don't misunderstand me.	clarification
3 To some degree, …	tentative point
4 It is fair to say that …	tentative point
5 Not only that, but …	another point
6 In an attempt to …	purpose for speaking
7 with respect to …	statement of a topic/ example
8 … is [are] a case in point.	example
9 … gives a good description of … in …	summary of a source
10 Briefly, [he] explains how…	summary of a source
11 [She] has no doubt that …	definite point

Transcript 🎧 2.11

1

I'm going to try to explain some of the major factors which exert pressure on the sector from the outside, that is to say, I shall mainly be looking at some of the different types of external influences which affect the way businesses in tourism and hospitality operate.

2

Don't misunderstand me, I don't want to imply that there are no internal questions for a company.

3

To some degree, individual companies will be affected differently.

4

… but it is fair to say that they will all have to keep an eye on which way inflation or interest rates are going, or demand and competition in a particular location.

5

Not only that, but they also have to keep track of the government policies of the country or the countries where they operate.

6

In an attempt to try to keep the discussion of external pressures on business reasonably simple, though, I'm going to focus mainly on three areas: politics, economics and, very importantly, the environment.

7

The evidence shows that this is especially true with respect to airline carriers.

8

Mass tour operators are a case in point.

9

Peter Drucker, who was a major business thinker, gives a good description of this in his article entitled 'The New Society' published in *The Economist* in 2001.

10

Briefly, in *The Economist* article, Drucker explains how at the beginning the 20th century (in 1913) farm products accounted for 70% of world trade.

11

One writer in *Money Management* magazine has no doubt that, and I quote, 'China will continue to be a dominant player driving world growth, which will have flow-through to other economies.'

Exercise H

Use this section from the Cornell notes to demonstrate what to do:

> **Notes**
>
> 1 <u>Political factors</u>: e.g., taxation policies, pressure groups, election results, protection thro' tariffs or quotas, foreign companies coming into country
>
> (a) election results, e.g., Margaret Thatcher's new government 1979 UK → mid-1980s privatization
>
> → new business opportunities esp. service sector incl. tourism
> → manufacturing declined
> → policy copied by other countries

Elicit from the students suggestions on how to write up the notes in complete sentences. Write the suggestions on the board. Ask students to say what they need to add in to the notes to make a good piece of writing. For example:

Grammar: relative pronouns, articles and determiners, prepositions, auxiliary verbs, linking words, 'there was/were' clauses (in italics below)

Vocabulary: some vocabulary may need to be added, particularly where symbols are used in the notes, or where extra words are needed to make sense of the information or give a good sense of flow in the writing (in bold below).

Note that this of course works the other way: when making notes, these elements can be excluded from the notes.

Possible rewrite of the notes:

Political factors *which* **affect business include,** for example, taxation policies, pressure groups, election results, protection through tariffs or quotas and foreign companies coming into the country.

One **example** *of the* **effect** *of* election results *on* **business can be seen** *when* Margaret Thatcher's new government **came to power** *in* 1979 *in the* UK. *By the* mid 1980s *the* **process** of privatization had **begun.** There were several results of this process. *Firstly, there were many* new opportunities *for* business, *especially in the* service sector, including tourism. *Secondly, the* manufacturing sector declined. *Also this* **new** policy *was* copied by other countries **around the world.**

Set another section for individual writing in class or for homework. Either ask students to refer to their own notes, or to the Cornell notes on page 106 of the Course Book.

Answers

Answers depend on the students.

Closure

1 Tell students to review and make a list of the main topics and arguments presented in this lesson. Then ask them to try to summarize the viewpoints, using some of the language they have practised.

2 They could also give a two- or three- sentence summary of anything that they themselves have read, e.g., *I read a useful article on X by Y. It said that …*

3 Ask students to do some research and to make a list of useful or interesting books/articles/websites on the topics in this lesson. They should draw up a list, including correct referencing, and share their sources with other students.

11.3 Extending skills

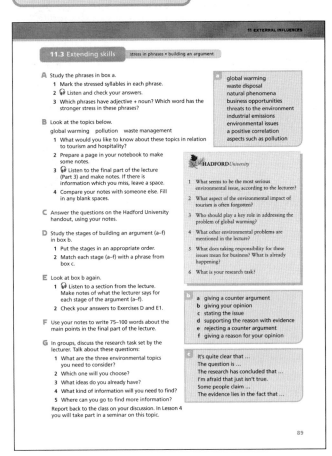

the speaker is certain or tentative?

There is no question that (= certain)

We have to accept the evidence (= certain)

Some people claim that (= tentative)

What seems obvious is that (= certain)

As everyone is aware (= certain)

To some degree (= tentative)

This means ultimately that (= certain)

It's quite clear that (= certain)

We could argue that (= tentative)

🎧 Exercise A

1/2 Set for individual work and pairwork checking. This is an exercise in perceiving rhythm. At this point there is no need to distinguish between different levels of stress. Students can underline all the stressed syllables. They will also need to count all the syllables. Feed back with the whole class, checking pronunciation of the phrases and meanings.

3 Discuss this with the class first. Demonstrate with ˌglobal ˈwarming, showing how if you say ˈglobal ˌwarming, it appears that a contrast is being made with another type of warming. Tell students that the usual pattern for the adjective + noun phrase is for a heavier stress to go on the noun. *Waste disposal* is, however, different: it is a compound made from a noun + noun, and the stress is: ˈwaste disˌposal – i.e., the heavier stress goes on the first noun. Set students to pick out the other adjective + noun patterns, writing each one on the board. Elicit the stress patterns and give students time to practise the phrases.

Answers

Model answers:

1/2 ˌglobal ˈwarming

  ˈwaste disˌposal

  ˌnatural pheˈnomena

  ˈbusiness opporˌtunities

  ˈthreats to the enˈvironment

  inˌdustrial eˈmissions

  enˌvironmental ˈissues

  a ˌpositive correˈlation

  ˈaspects such as polˈlution

3 Adjective + noun (second word has stronger stress): global warming, natural phenomena, industrial emissions, environmental issues, a positive correlation

Lesson aims

- recognize stress patterns in noun phrases
- understand how to develop an argument:

  stating the issue

  giving a counter argument

  rejecting a counter argument

  giving opinions

  supporting opinions

- understand more general academic words and phrases mainly used in speaking

Further practice in:

- expressing degrees of confidence/tentativeness
- reporting back

Introduction

1 Revise the lecture in Lesson 2. Ask students to use the model Cornell notes on page 106. They should cover up the *Notes* section and use the *Review* and *Summary* sections (which they completed in Lesson 2) to help recall the contents of the lecture. They could work in pairs to do this.

2 Revise phrases which express degrees of confidence in 'facts'. Dictate these phrases. Do they show that

Transcript 🎧 2.12

,global 'warming

'waste dis,posal

,natural phe'nomena

'business oppor,tunities

'threats to the en'vironment

in,dustrial e'missions

en,vironmental 'issues

a ,positive corre'lation

'aspects such as pol'lution

🎧 Exercise B

1 Look at the three topics. Discuss with the class what they already know about these topics and find out what opinions they may have. Put students in pairs and ask each pair to write down one question to which they would like an answer in the lecture.

2 Set for individual work.

3 Play Part 3 straight through; students make notes.

4 Put students in pairs to compare their notes and fill in any gaps they may have.

Transcript 🎧 2.13

Part 3

Turning now to the issue of the effect of environmental issues on tourism ... of course, a major concern is the problem of global warming. If it's as serious as some people claim, then it's likely to have a great many implications for tourism. Researchers like Braithwaite, Leiper and Witsel point out that not enough attention is paid to the transit route to tourism destinations. If destinations can be sustained, many people assume that tourism must be sustainable. But this assumption is rather misleading. We shouldn't forget the effect on transit routes – remember that component of the tourism system that I mentioned earlier – when deciding what impact tourism has on the environment.

So how serious a problem is global warming? First of all, there is no question that the Earth is heating up. We have to accept the evidence, such as the rise in temperatures, the melting of the polar ice-caps, the changing patterns in the habits of wildlife, and so on. But the real question is: is global warming the result of human activity? Some people claim, even some scientists have said, that it's nothing to do with humankind; it's the result of natural phenomena such as sunspots or volcano activity. But I'm afraid that just isn't true. It's quite clear that global warming is the direct result of human activity – especially business activity. Within that, travel and tourism has a lot to answer for.

Most of the research into global warming has concluded that the burning of fossil fuels is what is responsible. The evidence for this lies in the fact that there is a clear, positive correlation between the increase in the presence of CO_2 in the atmosphere and the rise in the Earth's temperature.

So if business is the cause, then business will have to be a part of the solution. Although some people may continue to claim that climate change is inevitable, what seems obvious is that business must play a key role trying to improve a dangerous situation – dangerous for the entire human race.

What's more, of course, we can see other threats to the environment from other aspects such as pollution, waste, and so on, many of which derive directly from the activities of tourism and hospitality. As everyone is aware, emissions from the airline industry or other forms of transport can damage both human and animal health as well as the environment generally. Waste disposal is becoming an ever more serious problem too. A lot of waste is generated by hotels, resorts, theme parks, festivals and so on. It's just not possible anymore to put all our garbage in a hole in the ground. Attitudes to waste – not just from industrial processes but also waste from the service industries – need to change radically.

When we look at environmental concerns such as these, the big question is how are we going to manage these problems? What strategies need to be put into place to help control CO_2 emissions, pollution and waste disposal? To some degree, as I've said, business must take responsibility for what is happening and must do something about it. This means ultimately that business and tourists must bear the costs of the changes that are necessary. Studies being carried out worldwide are looking at the 'footprint' we are leaving behind and what can be done to minimize it. In tourism and hospitality, for instance, a lot of research has been done into building environmentally friendly accommodation.

On the other hand, rather than being a threat, perhaps we should think about whether environmental issues actually offer business something positive too. Can tourism actually benefit from the steps which will be needed? We could argue that possible environmental solutions offer many opportunities. For example, environmental consultants can use their knowledge to advise operators; companies can develop environmental initiatives which appeal to consumers, ranging from environmentally friendly accommodation to restaurants serving only organic food. Other low-impact measures such as recycling may actually result in lower business costs.

Now I'm going to set you a task which will involve investigating some of the points I've raised. I want you to do some research into which areas of tourism and hospitality might actually be able to benefit from the changes which are going to be necessary for the environment. I want you to focus, firstly, on some of the new plans, methods and technologies for dealing with environmental problems, with respect to the environmental categories I've mentioned – global warming, pollution and waste – and in the context of tourism and hospitality. Secondly, I'd like you to think about whether these methods and plans to save the environment could actually benefit tourism businesses in the future or whether they will mainly affect them in a negative way.

Exercise C

Set for individual work and pairwork checking. Feed back with the class on question 6 to make sure that the research task is clear.

Answers

Model answers:

1 Global warming.
2 The impact of travel to and from the tourism destination (or, in more formal words, the transit route).
3 Business should play a key role.
4 Pollution/emissions and waste.
5 Bearing the costs; new initiatives such as building environmentally friendly accommodation.

6 Firstly, examine the new plans, methods and technologies which exist for dealing with global warming/pollution/waste in tourism and hospitality; and secondly, decide whether tourism businesses could benefit from these methods and plans or whether they will be negatively affected.

Exercise D

1 Set for pairwork discussion. Point out that there is no one 'correct' order; students should try to identify the most logical sequence for the argument. Explain that a 'counter argument' means an opinion which you do not agree with or think is wrong. 'Issue' means a question about which there is some debate.

2 Set for individual work and pairwork checking.

Do not feed back with the class at this point but move on to Exercise E where the answers will be given.

🎧 Exercise E

1 Play the extract. Tell students to stop you when they hear each item. Make sure students can say exactly what the words are in each case. Ask them also to paraphrase the words so that it is clear that they understand the meanings.

2 If necessary, play the extract again for students to check that they have the phrases and types of statement correct. Ask how many students had the stages of an argument (Exercise D question 1) in the same order as the recording/model answers below. Discuss any alternative possibilities (see *Language note* below).

Answers

Model answers:

Type of statement	Phrase	Lecturer's words
c stating the issue	The question is …	But the real question is: is global warming the result of human activity?
a giving a counter argument	Some people claim …	Some people claim … that it's nothing to do with humankind.
e rejecting a counter argument	I'm afraid that just isn't true.	But I'm afraid that just isn't true.
b giving your opinion	It's quite clear that …	It's quite clear that global warming is the direct result of human activity …
f giving a reason for your opinion	The research has concluded that …	Most of the research into global warming has concluded that the burning of fossil fuels is what is responsible.
d supporting the reason with evidence	The evidence lies in the fact that …	The evidence for this lies in the fact that there is a clear, positive correlation between the increase in the presence of CO_2 in the atmosphere and the rise in the Earth's temperature.

Language note

A common way in which an argument can be built is to give a counter argument, then reject the counter argument with reasons and evidence. There are, of course, other ways to build an argument. For example, the counter arguments may be given after the writer/speaker's own opinion. Or all the arguments against may be given followed by all the arguments for an issue (or vice versa), concluding with the speaker/writer's own opinion.

Transcript 🎧 2.14

But the real question is: is global warming the result of human activity? Some people claim, even some scientists have said, that it's nothing to do with humankind; it's the result of natural phenomena such as sunspots or volcano activity. But I'm afraid that just isn't true. It's quite clear that global warming is the direct result of human activity – especially business activity. Within that, travel and tourism has a lot to answer for. Most of the research into global warming has concluded that the burning of fossil fuels is what is responsible. The evidence for this lies in the fact that there is a clear, positive correlation between the increase in the presence of CO_2 in the atmosphere and the rise in the Earth's temperature.

Exercise F

In this exercise, students summarize the main points of the final part of the lecture, (i.e., Part 3, which they have studied in this lesson). Set for individual work – possibly homework – or else a pair/small group writing task. If the latter, tell students to put their writing on an OHT or other visual medium, so that the whole class can look and comment on what has been written. You can correct language errors on the OHT.

Exercise G

Set students to work in groups of three or four. Make sure they understand that they should choose to focus on one of the three topics: global warming, pollution or waste. Allow each group to choose their topic. Make sure that each topic is covered by at least one, preferably two groups. Ask one person from each group to present the results of the group's discussion.

Tell the class that they should carry out research into their group's topic. You will also need to arrange the date for the feedback and discussion of the information – this is the focus of Exercise G in Lesson 4.

Closure

Before you ask students to look at the statements below, tell them they should think about the methods seen above to build an argument. Then ask them to think about whether they agree with the statements below. They should prepare a brief summary of their viewpoints on the topics; they should also try to use some of the phrases used in this lesson.

1 Tourism contributes to a number of environmental problems – therefore the tourism industry should pay to solve them.

2 Tourism needs to be involved in all aspects of environmental strategy.

3 Global warming is inevitable and there is nothing anyone can do about it.

4 Space tourism is a waste of money which could be better spent on the environment.

5 Politics is not important in tourism.

6 All tourism businesses should use English because it is an international language.

11.4 Extending skills

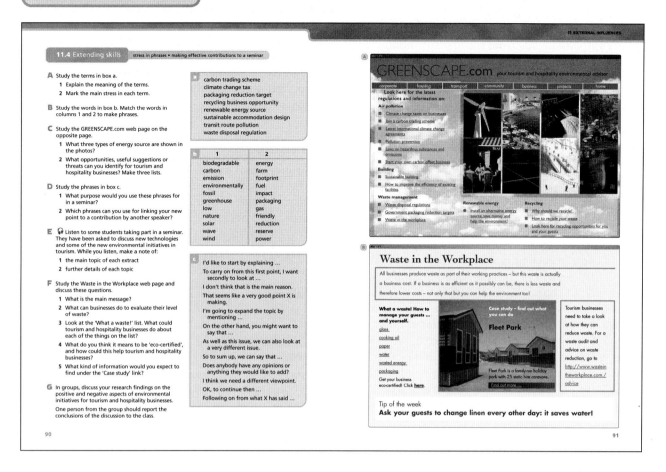

Lesson aims

- recognize stress in compound phrases
- link a contribution to previous contributions when speaking in a seminar
- understand vocabulary in the area of environmental issues

Further practice in:

- taking part in seminars:

  introducing, maintaining and concluding a contribution

  agreeing/disagreeing with other speakers

Introduction

1 Remind students that they are going to be presenting their research findings later in this lesson. Check that they can remember the main points from Lesson 3 lecture extracts. Key phrases from the lecture could be used as prompts, e.g.,

   So how serious a problem is it? (evidence of human and business activity)

   Business will have to be a part of the solution (i.e., play a key role in trying to improve a dangerous situation)

   Other threats to the environment (e.g., pollution, waste, emissions)

   The big question is … (how are we going to manage these problems?)

   But the real question is … (is global warming the result of human activity?)

2 The following activity is a good way to check that students are familiar with the terminology and vocabulary from Lesson 3. Ask students to write down 5–10 words or expressions from the previous lesson relating to the environment and the current problems. Then use two or three students as 'secretaries'. Ask the class to dictate the words so that the secretaries can write the vocabulary on the board. Use this as a brainstorming session.

Exercise A

These are more complex noun phrases than in Lesson 3, since they are made up of three words. In some cases the pattern is noun + noun + noun. In this case, there may be a compound made from the first two nouns, or the last two nouns. In other cases, the pattern is adjective + noun + noun, in which the second and third words make a compound. These patterns should become clear once the meaning is understood.

1 Discuss *climate change tax* with the class as an example. Elicit that it is a tax imposed to cover the cost of climate change. Set the remaining phrases for individual work and pairwork discussion. Feed back with the whole class, writing each phrase on the board and underlining the words which make a compound noun.

2 Tell students to try to identify where the main stress should come in each phrase. (Note that it will fall on the first element of the compound in each case. There will, of course, be secondary stresses on the other stressed syllables.) Demonstrate with *climate change tax: climate change* is a compound noun. Although it is acting in an adjectival role, the first noun will carry the main stress in the phrase: *'climate change tax*. Tell students only to identify the syllable on which the heaviest stress in the phrase falls.

Answers

Model answers:

'carbon trading scheme	a plan for trading carbon emissions
'climate change tax	a tax imposed on tourism businesses and tourists to combat the negative effects of climate change
'packaging reduction target	a target for packaging reduction, i.e., to reduce the amount of packaging used for goods
recycling 'business opportunity	a business opportunity in the field of recycling
renewable 'energy source	an energy source that is renewable
sustainable accommo'dation design	designing accommodation that is environmentally friendly or made with environmentally friendly materials
'transit route pollution	pollution of the route between two places, caused by use of transport
'waste disposal regulation	regulation (law) relating to the disposal of waste

Exercise B

Set for individual work and pairwork checking. Tell students that although in some cases it will be possible to make a phrase with more than one option, they must use each word once, and they must use all the words.

Feed back with the whole class. Check that the meaning of the phrases is understood. Check pronunciation.

Answers

Model answers:

biodegradable	packaging
carbon	footprint
emission	reduction
environmentally	friendly
fossil	fuel
greenhouse	gas
low	impact
nature	reserve
solar	energy
wave	power
wind	farm

Exercise C

Refer students to web page A on the opposite page. Set for pair or small group discussion.

1 Students should identify the three photos that show different types of energy source.

2 If you like, each pair or group could focus on one type of tourism or hospitality business: an airline, a restaurant, a travel agent, an events organizer, a resort, etc.

Students should identify which points can help companies reduce costs or may involve them in more costs.

Feed back, encouraging students to make their suggestions in the context of a particular type of business. For example:

If I was a restaurant owner, I'd be interested in recycling business waste and reducing waste in the workplace, making guests aware of recycling and perhaps starting a carbon offset programme. I'd want to know about the latest waste disposal regulations.

Answers

Possible answers:

1 solar, wind, hydro

2 **Opportunities**

(possibilities to make some money)

- selling product to people concerned about the environment, e.g.,

  restaurants: use locally sourced/organic food

  hotels: carbon-neutral

  transport: low-impact transport, e.g., train

Suggestions

(to help companies become more 'green')

- join a carbon trading scheme
- use renewable energy: solar, wind, hydro and biofuel energy sources
- recycle waste
- reduce waste

Threats

(likely to involve extra costs)

- climate change taxes on businesses
- latest international climate change agreements
- pollution prevention
- laws on hazardous substances and emissions
- waste disposal regulations
- government packaging reduction targets

Exercise D

This is mainly revision. Set for individual work or pairwork discussion. Feed back with the whole class.

Answers

Possible answers:

I'd like to start by explaining …	(= beginning)
To carry on from this first point, I want secondly to look at …	(= maintaining/ continuing a point)

I don't think that is the main reason.	(= disagreeing)
That seems like a very good point X is making.	(= confirming)
I'm going to expand the topic by mentioning …	(= adding a new point to someone else's previous contribution)
On the other hand, you might want to say that …	(= disagreeing)
As well as this issue, we can also look at a very different issue.	(= adding a new point to someone else's previous contribution)
So to sum up, we can say that …	(= summarizing/ concluding)
Does anybody have any opinions or anything they would like to add?	(= concluding)
I think we need a different viewpoint.	(= disagreeing)
OK, to continue then …	(= maintaining/continuing a point)
Following on from what X has said …	(= adding a new point to someone else's previous contribution)

🎧 Exercise E

Before students listen, tell them to look at the exercise and questions. Check that they understand the topic for the seminar discussion. Ask them what they might expect to hear. Then work through the extracts one at a time. Feed back after each one, checking the main topic and eliciting any further details.

Answers

Model answers:

	Main topic	Further details
Extract 1	new technologies	wind power, wave power, solar power, hydroelectric power, biofuels, application in resorts
Extract 2	carbon trading	carbon credits, carbon market – effect for tour operators and airlines
Extract 3	carbon offsetting	carbon offset credits, carbon footprint – programmes run by airlines
Extract 4	zero waste	get rid of 'Take, Make, Waste' instead adopt 'Waste = Resource' principle → responsible building, renewable energy, recycled materials

Transcript 🎧 2.15

Extract 1

MAJED: The lecturer we listened to last week introduced a number of interesting issues. In my part of the seminar, I would like to build on what he said and talk about a number of new technologies which have recently been introduced as alternatives to fossil fuels: these include wind, wave and solar power. It's obvious that these depend to some extent on the climate and on where a country is located, but there is a lot of scope for development, although some people dislike the impact on the countryside of things like wind-farms. Hydroelectric power is also an important source that has been around for quite a long time in countries such as Norway, where they have a lot of snow and heavy rainfall. And, of course, there's also the idea of biofuels, which is anything based on vegetable matter, such as wood, corn, etc., which we can use for heating and to replace petrol. Just think of all the tourism opportunities this offers – a health resort could run completely on hydroelectric power or solar power or biofuels and people would not have to feel guilty about leaving their footprint …

Extract 2

EVIE: OK, following on from what Majed has said, I'd like to mention some important environmental initiatives. You can see that as a result of global warming and because of worries about the environment, a new form of trading between companies has been created. This is usually called 'carbon trading'. Basically, what this means is that companies have an allowance for carbon emissions. If they create pollution beyond these emissions, that is, if they are heavy polluters, then they will have to buy 'carbon credits' from those companies who pollute less than their allowances. If they don't do this, they will face heavy penalties. This is what is known as the carbon 'trade'. So, what this means is that one company can be fined for creating pollution, while another may be rewarded if it reduces carbon emissions. The idea is to reduce overall production of greenhouse gases. Several trading systems already exist, the biggest of which is the one in the EU. The 'carbon market' is getting more popular in business circles as a way to manage climate change. You can imagine what this would do to global tour operators and airlines.

Extract 3

JACK: Right. Thank you, Evie. I'm going to expand on what Evie just said by mentioning another important initiative. What is usually called 'carbon offsetting' is similar in many ways to the concept of carbon trading. Carbon offsetting involves the calculation of your carbon footprint and then, depending on the result, the purchase of 'carbon offset credits'. Let me try and make this clearer with an example. For instance, if you travel a lot by plane then you might need to offset your carbon footprint (a concept developed by Wackernagel and Rees in 1995, by the way) by some more environmentally friendly green action such as reducing energy use in your house or not using your car so much. Several companies already exist to advise on this and to manage it: for example, carbonfootprint.com. So, in the context of tourism, airline companies, for instance, can be (and, in some countries, already are) forced to invest money in projects that undo (or try to undo) the damage they have caused. Operators will try to get some of this money back, of course, so if as a tourist you book a ticket online these days you will probably be asked whether you want to offset the distance you are flying by paying a little bit extra.

Extract 4

LEILA: As well as carbon issues we can also look at a very different sort of initiative. Here, I'm going to explain about the concept and philosophy of zero waste. Zero waste has been around for a while; basically, it is a strategy which looks for inefficiencies in the way materials are produced, packaged, used and disposed of. In terms of tourism you will agree with me that there is an endless array of materials out there – just think of brochures, packaging, food waste, etc., etc. As well as community, home and school programmes for waste reduction, there are business and industrial opportunities, for example in the design of products, maximization of energy use, and improved efficiency methods. The aim is to remove the 'Take, Make, Waste' principle which we have at present and to replace it with the 'Waste Equals Resource' approach. This would help to remove all waste from the environment. So basically what we're saying in terms of tourism and hospitality is, I suppose, that facilities must be designed in harmony with the local environment; that design must be sustainable; that people should avoid using non-renewable energy sources; that people should only use renewable or recycled materials.

Exercise F

Set for pairwork. Tell students to study the Waste in the Workplace web page (B).

Feed back with the whole class. For further information on these matters, see (at the time of writing):

www.green-tourism-awards.org.uk/index.html

www.rainforest-alliance.org/tourism/tourism_matters/0405_eng.html

Answers

Possible answers:

1 The main message is that waste is both an environmental problem and a business expense. Reducing waste will not only help the environment but will reduce business costs.

2 They can have an 'audit' done, i.e., an evaluation of the waste in their business; and they can get advice on how to deal with it.

3 glass: recycle

   cooking oil: recycle as fuel, if possible

   paper: recycle

   water: reduce use; mend leaks; turn down thermostat

   wasted energy: install insulation; turn down thermostat; turn off lights/computers when not in use

   packaging: reduce amount by buying in bulk or unpackaged where possible

4 Becoming eco-certified means that a business receives official recognition for 'doing the right thing' and producing/supplying environmentally friendly goods or services. It may enhance the image and, with that, popularity, of a business or brand.

5 An example of a company (in this case a holiday park) which has developed its business in environmentally positive ways.

Exercise G

Set for group work. Students should now present their research findings (from Lesson 3) to the rest of the group. Remind them that the task was to:

• investigate the new plans, methods and technologies which exist for dealing with global warming/pollution/waste

• decide whether tourism and hospitality businesses could benefit from these methods and plans, or whether they would be negatively affected

Encourage students to use the seminar language practised in this unit and earlier. In addition, students can, of course, make use of the information in Lesson 4. They should be looking at, or at least mentioning, some or all of the following:

• explaining the issues: climate change (global warming, CO_2 emissions, etc.), waste and pollution, and the rules and regulations that may (or have already) come into force

• saying what tourism and hospitality businesses need to think about (the aspects which currently cause problems): transport emissions, waste, destruction of the environment to build resorts, use of scarce local resources, etc.

• suggesting ways in which businesses might be able to benefit: for example, attracting customers by marketing their business as eco-friendly, organic, sustainable, low-impact, etc.

• suggesting ways in which businesses may be negatively affected: for example, limiting airport expansion and increasing taxes on air travel would affect airline businesses; tightening of planning controls/increase in designated conservation areas would affect resort development

As a group, students should try to come to an overall conclusion. This conclusion should be presented to the rest of the class, together with supporting evidence from students' own research.

Closure

Ask students to imagine that they are 10–15 years in the future. What differences do they think there will be in the environment and the way it is treated? How will the situation have changed? Ask them to think about the following:

crowded airports

polluted cities

traffic jams

rubbish

limits on air travel

carbon trading

nuclear power

wind farms

wave power

1 Work through the *Vocabulary bank* and *Skills bank* if you have not already done so, or as revision of previous study.

2 Use the *Activity bank* (Teacher's Book additional resources section, Resource 11A).

   A Set the wordsearch for individual work (including homework) or pairwork.

   Answers

   Possible two-word phrases are:

carbon footprint	climate change
environmental issues	fossil fuel
nature reserve	organic food
pressure group	solar power
sustainable tourism	zero waste

   B Set for individual work (including homework) or pairwork. Check students understand the meanings.

   Answers

carbon	dioxide
demographic	changes
environmentally	friendly
global	warming
greenhouse	gas
renewable	energy
tour	operator
tourism	destination
transit	route
waste	disposal

3 Tell students to add other words to each of the words below to make as many two-word phrases as possible. Elicit one or two examples, then set for individual work or pairwork.

   ● carbon

   ● environmental

   ● waste

   Possible phrases:

   carbon trading, carbon footprint, carbon offset(ting), carbon dioxide, carbon market

   environmental issues, environmental concerns, environmental pressure group, environmental action

   waste management, waste reduction, business waste, zero waste

4 Use an extended activity to allow students to practise some of the concepts they have studied in this unit. Tell students to work in groups. They are going to design a zero-waste process – the product is a three-course dinner for a group of 25 tourists at the restaurant of the hotel where they are staying. Divide the activities into stages as follows:

   a Identify the various stages involved in producing the meal from the beginning to the end, e.g., the ingredients, the production, the transportation, the marketing, the distribution, the retail selling.

   b The groups should make specific suggestions for:

   ● the ingredients and where they are going to come from

   ● the location of the restaurant

   ● aspects such as the workforce, cooking process, etc.

   ● waste systems (energy, waste disposal, recycling, etc.)

   ● how they will try to ensure zero-waste systems across the whole process (management strategies)

   c Draw up a flow plan showing the various stages of the product process – make sure that zero-waste factors are included at each stage. (Plans can be put onto A2 sheets, flipcharts or another visual medium and displayed for other groups to compare.)

12 INFORMATION, STRATEGY AND CHANGE

This unit provides an opportunity for revision of many of the concepts and vocabulary items used in the book. The unit takes students step by step through writing research reports. In activities spread across the lessons, students will build up the components of a report, based on a case study of a boutique resort hotel. Model reports are provided in Resources 12D and E in the additional resources section.

Skills focus

Reading

- understanding how ideas in a text are linked

Writing

- deciding whether to use direct quotation or paraphrase
- incorporating quotations
- writing research reports
- writing effective introductions/conclusions

Vocabulary focus

- verbs used to introduce ideas from other sources (*X contends/suggests/asserts that ...*)
- linking words/phrases conveying contrast (*whereas*), result (*consequently*), reasons (*due to*), etc.
- words for quantities (*a significant minority*)

Key vocabulary

back-of-house	front-of-house	strategic
blog (n)	hotelier	strategy
boutique hotel	infrastructure	survey (n)
core function	internal audit	SWOT analysis
customer base	interview (n and v)	touch-screen
customer loyalty	interviewee	value (n)
data	interviewer	value chain
distribution channel	Intranet	virtual community
diversification	investment	virtual tourism
external audit	joint venture	web publisher
Extranet	questionnaire	

12.1 Vocabulary

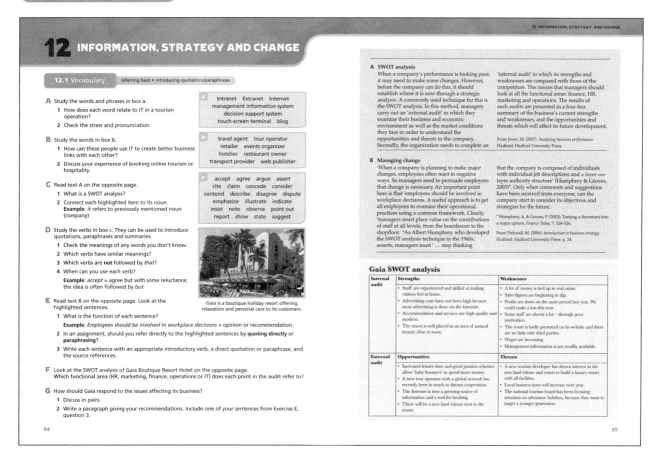

General note

Read the *Vocabulary bank* at the end of the Course Book unit. Decide when, if at all, to refer your students to it. The best time is probably at the very end of the lesson or the beginning of the next lesson, as a summary/revision.

Lesson aims

- understand deictic reference – pronouns and determiners
- refer to sources: the choice of introductory verb and stance of writer towards reference
- choose whether to quote or paraphrase

Further practice in:

- words and phrases from the discipline

Introduction

1 Revise the following words and phrases from the two previous units. Ask students to say which grammar class the words belong to and to provide definitions of them.

activists (n, C)

agriculture (n, U)

biofuel (n, C)

boom (n, C)

bottom line (n, C)

carbon (n, U) often used as adjective in combinations (e.g., *carbon footprint*)

imply (v)

in-depth (adj)

renewable (adj)

offset (n, U; e.g., *carbon offset*); (v, T; e.g., *offset carbon emissions*)

2 Introduce the topic of the unit: write the words *information*, *strategy* and *change* on the board. Ask students:

What do these signify for tourism and hospitality?

What factors do businesses need to take into consideration when they are thinking about strategy, change and information?

What processes will they need to go through in order to decide their plans for the future?

Have a class discussion on what businesses need to consider when they are thinking about future development. Accept any reasonable suggestions. Do not elaborate, but tell students that this will be the topic of this unit.

207

Exercise A

1 First of all, ask students what types of IT are used by tourism businesses. Let them brainstorm in pairs and come up with examples. Then ask students to look at box a and set the question for pairwork. Accept all reasonable suggestions and write them on the board. Feed back with the whole class, checking meanings.

2 Set for pairwork. Ask students to mark the most strongly stressed syllables in compounds.

Answers

Possible answers:

'Intranet (HR)

'Extranet (operations)

'Internet (marketing)

management infor'mation system (finance)

decision su'pport system (operations)

'touch-screen terminal (operations)

blog (marketing)

Exercise B

1 The idea is to get students to see (and perhaps their own experience will have told them this) that these players in the tourism market often have to work together. As the article in Lesson 2 will confirm, in terms of information strategy this is a necessity for businesses large and small.

  Set for individual work and pairwork checking. Feed back with the whole class. See the Answers section for a few example answers. Accept all reasonable suggestions.

2 Set for class discussion. If you haven't already done so, get students to talk about their own experiences with information technology in tourism and travel – let them mention anything that has anything to do with computers and tourism/hospitality, as these comments will no doubt highlight IT issues that tourism companies focus on.

Answers

Possible answers:

Hoteliers need to have online links with travel agents and tour operators.

They need a web publisher to publish information about their hotel.

They would benefit from online links with events organizers so they can arrange activities for their customers.

They could benefit from links with restaurant owners and transport providers in their immediate area.

Exercise C

Introduce the idea of textual cohesion, created by referring back to words or ideas already mentioned with pronouns such as *it* and *this* (pronouns and determiners). Say that this an important way in which the sentences in a text are 'held together'. In reading and understanding it is important to know what is being referred to by such words.

You can build up the answers to question 2 by copying Resource 12B in the additional resources section onto an OHT or other visual medium.

Set for individual work and pairwork checking. Feed back with the whole class. Establish why a writer might use a particular referring word (see table on next page).

Answers

Model answers:

1 A technique which enables à company to evaluate itself by analysing Strengths, Weaknesses, Opportunities and Threats.

2 When a company's performance is looking poor, it may need to make some changes. However, before the company can do this, it should establish where it is now through a strategic analysis. A commonly used technique for this is the SWOT analysis. In this method, managers carry out an 'external audit' in which they examine their business and economic environment as well as the market conditions they face in order to understand the opportunities and threats to the company. Secondly, the organization needs to complete an 'internal audit' in which its strengths and weaknesses are compared with those of the competitors. This means that managers should look at all the functional areas: finance, HR, marketing and operations. The results of such audits are presented in a four-box summary of the business's current strengths and weaknesses, and the opportunities and threats which will affect its future development.

Word	Refers to	Comments
the + noun	a previously mentioned noun	one of several ways in which choice of article is governed
it, they	a noun	generally refers to the nearest suitable noun previously mentioned or the subject of the previous sentence
its, their	a previously mentioned noun, indicating possession	other possessive pronouns used in text for reference: *his, her, hers, theirs,* etc.
this	an idea in a phrase or a sentence	• often found at the beginning of a sentence or a paragraph; a common mistake is to use 'it' for this purpose • also used with prepositions (e.g., *for this*)
this/these + noun	a previously mentioned noun/ noun phrase	also used with prepositions (e.g., *in this method*)
those	a previously mentioned noun/ noun phrase	• also used with prepositions • In this text 'those of the competitors' means 'the strengths and weaknesses of the competitors'; there is no need to repeat 'strengths and weaknesses'. *Those of* + noun is a useful construction to learn. • *Those* – not *these* – is used to show distance between the writer/speaker and the objects/concepts themselves.
such + plural noun	a previously mentioned noun	Meaning is: 'Xs like this'. Note that when referring to a singular noun, 'such a X' is used (e.g., *in such a situation*).

Language note

Clearly, in this text, there are also relative pronouns which refer back to previously mentioned nouns in relative clauses. However, the grammar of relative pronouns is not covered here.

This is a complex area of written language. The reference words here are commonly found and arguably students should be able to use them in their writing. There are, of course, various other ways to refer back to a word or idea, such as when comparing: *the former … the latter … ; some … others … .* For more information see a good grammar reference book.

Exercise D

1–3 Set for individual work or pairwork. Feed back. Discuss any differences of opinion in question 2 and allow alternative groupings, with reasonable justifications. Establish that not all the verbs have equivalents.

The verb *cite* is very similar to the verb *quote* in meaning. Both verbs introduce the ideas of others. But *quote* is normally followed by the actual words, whereas *cite* can also be followed by a paraphrase, e.g.,

> *Brown quotes Smith as saying, 'The reason for this problem is …'*
>
> *Brown cites Smith as agreeing with this idea.*

4 Discuss this with the whole class, building the table in the Answers section. Point out to students that the choice of introductory verb for a direct or indirect quote or a paraphrase or summary will reveal what they think about the sources. This is an important way in which, when writing essays, students can show a degree of criticality about their sources. Critically evaluating other writers' work is an important part of academic assignments, dissertations and theses.

Answers

Possible answers:

2 accept, agree, concede
argue, assert, claim, contend, insist
consider, note, observe, point out, state
disagree, dispute
describe, illustrate, indicate, show

3/4 See table on next page.

Verb	Followed by	Used when the writer ...
accept	*that*	reluctantly thinks this idea from someone else is true
agree	*that*	thinks this idea from someone else is true
argue	*that*	is giving an opinion that others may not agree with
assert	*that*	is giving an opinion that others may not agree with
cite	+ noun	is referring to someone else's ideas
claim	*that*	is giving an opinion that others may not agree with
concede	*that*	reluctantly thinks this idea from someone else is true
consider	*that*	is giving his/her opinion
contend	*that*	is giving an opinion that others may not agree with
describe	*how;* + noun	is giving a description
disagree	*that; with* + noun	thinks an idea is wrong
dispute	+ noun	thinks an idea is wrong
emphasize	*that*	is giving his/her opinion strongly
illustrate	*how;* + noun	is explaining, possibly with an example
indicate	*that*	is explaining, possibly with an example
insist	*that*	is giving an opinion that others may not agree with
note	*that*	is giving his/her opinion
observe	*that*	is giving his/her opinion
point out	*that*	is giving his/her opinion
report	*that*	is giving research findings
show	*that*	is explaining, possibly with an example
state	*that*	is giving his/her opinion
suggest	*that;* + gerund	is giving his/her opinion tentatively; *or* is giving his/her recommendation

Language note

Note that these are all verbs of saying and thinking. As such, they can be followed by a noun. Where *that* can be used, it indicates that the verbs are followed by a noun clause. The verbs may also be used with other kinds of construction. For more information on possible uses see a good dictionary.

Language note

When deciding between quoting directly and paraphrasing, students need to decide whether the writer's original words are special in any way. If they are, then a direct quote is better – for example, with a definition, or if the writer has chosen some slightly unusual words to express an idea. If the writer is giving factual information or description, a paraphrase is better. Opinions also tend to be paraphrased.

Exercise E

Discuss with the students when it is better to paraphrase and when to quote directly. Refer to the *Skills bank* if necessary.

1/2 Set for individual work and pairwork checking. Feed back with the whole class.

3 Set for individual work. Remind students that if they want to quote another source but to omit some words, they can use three dots (...) to show some words are missing.

Answers

Possible answers:

Original sentence	The writer is …	Direct quote or paraphrase?	Suggested sentence
1 When a company is planning to make major changes, employees often react in negative ways.	making a statement of fact	paraphrase	Pickwell (2006) points out that staff may be unhappy about possible changes in their company.
2 … employees should be involved in workplace decisions.	giving an opinion or recommendation	paraphrase	Pickwell (2006) argues that staff need to be consulted about any possible changes.
3 … managers must place value on the contributions of staff at all levels, from the boardroom to the shop floor.	giving a strong opinion	paraphrase with a direct quotation of the 'special' phrase	Pickwell (2006) emphasizes the need to take everyone's views seriously 'from the boardroom to the shop floor' (p. 24).
4 As Albert Humphrey … pointed out: managers must '… stop thinking that the company is composed of … a layer-on-layer authority structure'	quoting from another writer; the other writer is making a strong statement	direct quote	Pickwell (2006) cites Humphrey, who insists that managers should '… stop thinking that the company is composed of … a layer-on-layer authority structure' (Humphrey & Groves, 2003 pp. 124–126).

Exercise F

Talk about boutique hotels with students. These are luxury hotels, often small (although larger hotel chains have appropriated the term as well) that provide pampering for the wealthy.

Refer students to the picture and the SWOT analysis. Make sure they understand what Gaia is.

Set for pairwork discussion. Feed back with the whole class if necessary. Accept any reasonable suggestions.

Answers

Possible answers:

It is possible to indicate more than one functional area.

1 Internal audit:

Strengths	Functional area
Staff are experienced and skilled at making visitors feel at home.	HR
Advertising costs have not been high because most advertising is done via the Internet.	marketing, IT
Accommodation and services are high quality and modern.	marketing, operations
The resort is well placed in an area of natural beauty close to town.	marketing

Weaknesses	Functional area
A lot of money is tied up in real estate.	finance
Sales figures are beginning to dip.	finance, marketing
Profits are down on the same period last year. We could make a loss this year.	finance
Some staff are absent a lot – through poor motivation.	HR
The resort is badly presented on its website and there are no links with third parties.	marketing, IT
Wages are increasing.	finance, operations
Management information is not readily available.	IT

2 External audit:

Opportunities	Functional area
Increased leisure time and good pension schemes allow 'baby boomers' to spend more money.	finance, marketing
A new tour operator with a global network has recently been in touch to discuss cooperation.	operations, marketing
The Internet is now a growing source of information and a tool for booking.	IT, marketing
There will be a new land release next to the resort.	operations

Threats	Functional area
A new tourism developer has shown interest in the new land release and wants to build a luxury resort with all facilities.	finance, marketing
Local business taxes will increase next year.	finance
The national tourism board has been focusing attention on adventure holidays, because they want to target a younger generation.	marketing

Exercise G

1 Set for pairwork discussion, followed by class discussion.

2 Before setting the students to write, tell them they should refer to text B in their answer.

Answers

Possible answers:

1 Accept any reasonable suggestions.

2 It is clear that Gaia is heading for difficult times. This is partly caused by increased competition. But it is also clear that the staff need to have some training to increase their motivation. There are several possibilities that Gaia could consider, including acquiring new land for expansion, starting a new Internet operation, targeting new market segments (such as the younger, adventure market) alongside the market segment they are making the most profit out of, and forging links with tour operators and travel agents. However, Pickwell (2006) argues that staff need to be consulted about any possible changes. Therefore, I recommend that before any decisions are made, all the staff are asked for their views.

Closure

Ask students to think about tourism outlets that they have used in the past. They should do the following (the exercise can be done in groups or pairs):

- List their favourite outlets, the ones most used/visited, and so on; specify products, services, reasons for visiting, etc.
- Using this list, add what they like and don't like about the outlets, plus any problems they have noticed or encountered.
- Use the points they have listed above to create a SWOT framework – allocating each of the points in their list to the appropriate category in the SWOT framework.
- Finally, rank the outlets in some sort of order of excellence.

The object of the exercise is to look at SWOT from an informal, consumer viewpoint. It should also help to prime students for the questionnaires and the research reports in Lessons 3 and 4.

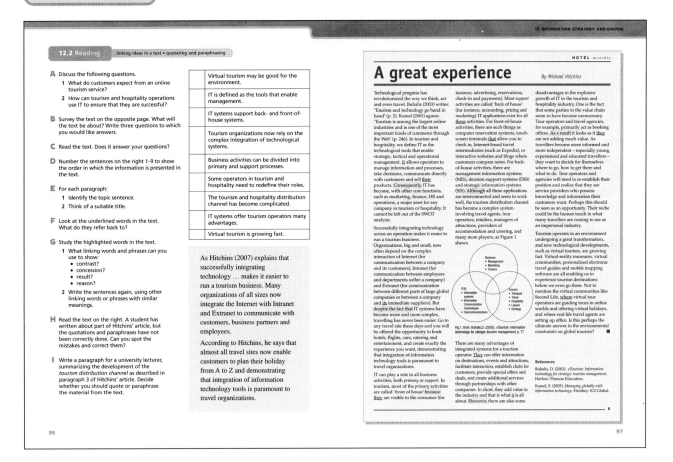

General note

Read the *Vocabulary bank* and *Skills bank* at the end of the Course Book unit. Decide when, if at all, to refer students to them. The best time is probably at the very end of the lesson or the beginning of the next lesson, as a summary/revision.

Lesson aims

- understand rhetorical markers in writing (*but* and *so* categories)
- use direct quotations from other writers:

  common mistakes

  missing words

  fitting to the grammar of the sentence

  adding emphasis to a quote

  continuing to quote from the same source

Further practice in:

- indirect quotations/paraphrases/summaries
- summarizing with a series of topic sentences
- rhetorical markers (adding points)
- deictic reference and relative pronouns

Introduction

Revise the main SWOT concepts from Lesson 1. What does each letter stand for?

To prepare students for the lesson's theme, ask them to think of a journey they have made recently and to describe the transport system, the route, and cost, value for money, the good things and the bad things about the destination and the services they were offered.

Exercise A

Set for pairwork or class discussion. Accept any reasonable suggestions.

Answers

Possible answers:

1. You might expect: value for money; ease of navigation; links with other travel sites; confirmation of choices; easy and secure payment.

2. Students may mention: management information systems to ensure the relevant staff members have fast access to up-to-date information; Internet-based marketing; booking of tickets/accommodation via a website, etc.

213

Exercise B

Remind students about surveying a text (skim-reading to get an approximate idea of the text contents by looking at the title, looking at the beginning few lines and the final few lines of the text, and by looking at the first sentence of each paragraph).

Set for individual work and pairwork discussion. Each pair should agree three questions. Feed back with the whole class. Write some questions on the board.

Exercise C

Set for individual work followed by pairwork discussion. Feed back with the whole class. Ask whether the questions you have put on the board have been answered in the text.

Exercise D

Set for individual work and pairwork checking. This activity could also be done using Resource 12C in the additional resources section. Photocopy and cut up the sentences and hand them out in a jumbled order. Ask students to put them in the correct order.

Answers

Model answers:

1	IT is defined as the tools that enable management.
2	Tourism organizations now rely on the complex integration of technological systems.
3	Business activities can be divided into primary and support processes.
4	IT systems support back- and front-of-house systems.
5	The tourism and hospitality distribution channel has become complicated.
6	IT systems offer tourism operators many advantages.
7	Some operators in tourism and hospitality need to redefine their roles.
8	Virtual tourism is growing fast.
9	Virtual tourism may be good for the environment.

Exercise E

1/2 Set for individual work and pairwork discussion.
The topic sentences should suggest a suitable title.

Answers

Possible answers:

	Topic sentence	Para title
Para 1	Technological progress has revolutionized the way we think, act and even travel.	The IT revolution
Para 2	Successfully integrating technology across an operation makes it easier to run a tourism business.	How tourism businesses can benefit from IT
Para 3	IT can play a role in all business activities, both *primary* or *support*.	IT in primary and support activities
Para 4	There are many advantages of integrated systems for a tourism operator.	Opportunities and threats
Para 5	Tourism operates in an environment undergoing a great transformation, and new technological developments, such as virtual tourism, are growing fast.	Virtual tourism

Exercise F

Set for individual work and pairwork checking.

Answers

Model answers:

Word	Para	Refers to
It	1	IT
their	1	operators
its	2	company
they	3	primary activities
these	3	primary activities and support activities
that	3	touch-screen terminals
They	4	integrated systems
it	4	the tourism industry
they	4	tour operators and travel agencies
where	5	virtual communities like Second Life

Exercise G

1 With the whole class, elicit from the students some linking words that can be used for:

- contrast and concession (i.e., words which have a *but* meaning)
- result and reason (i.e., words which have a *so* or *for* meaning)

Build the table in the Answers section on the board, reminding students of the difference between between- and within-sentence linking words or phrases (refer to Unit 11 *Skills bank*).

2 Set for individual work. Encourage students to rewrite the sentences using a different type of linking word from the original (i.e., swapping between- and within-sentence linkers).

Answers

Possible answers:

1

	Between-sentence linking words/phrases	Within-sentence linking words/phrases
Contrast (but) used when comparing	However, … In/By contrast, … On the other hand, …	… but … … whereas … … while …
Concession (but) used to concede/accept a point which simultaneously contrasts with the main point of a sentence or paragraph	However, … At the same time … Nevertheless, … Despite/In spite of (*this*/noun), … Yet …	… although … … despite/in spite of the fact that …
Result (so)	So, … As a result, … Consequently, … Therefore, …	… , so … … so that … … with the result that …
Reason (for)	Because of (*this*/noun), … Owing to (*this*/noun), … Due to (*this*/noun), …	… because … … since … … as … … due to/owing to the fact that …

2 *Because of this/As a result*, IT has become, with other core functions, such as marketing, finance, HR and operations, a major asset for any company in tourism or hospitality.

Although IT systems have become more and more complex, travelling has never been easier.

In tourism, most of the primary activities are called 'front of house', *as/since* they are visible to the consumer …

All these applications are interconnected and seem to work well. *Despite this/Nevertheless,* the tourism distribution channel has become a complex system …

On the other hand/At the same time, there are also some disadvantages in the explosive growth of IT in the tourism and hospitality industry.

Consequently/Therefore, it looks as if they are not adding much value.

Exercise H

Set for individual work and pairwork checking. Feed back with the whole class.

Answers

Possible answers:

The student has written about paragraph 2.

Corrected version	Comments
As Hitchins (2007) explains,	Note the grammar here: either *As Hitchins explains*, or *Hitchins explains that*, but not both. This is a common mistake.
'successfully integrating technology ... makes it easier to run a tourism business' (p. 6).	1. The words which are the same as the original need quotation marks. 2. Some words have been left out. Where this happens three dots are used to signify an omission. It is important that a quote is exactly the same as the original. Any changes (such as omitting words) need to be clearly shown.
Many organizations of all sizes now integrate the Internet with Intranet and Extranet to communicate with customers, business partners and employees.	This sentence is fine. Note that much of the information here has been paraphrased – which is the better option for information.
Hitchins (ibid.) further points out that almost all travel sites now enable customers to plan their holiday from A to Z, 'demonstrating that integration of information technology tools is paramount to travel organizations.'	1. When continuing to refer to a source you can use *further* or *also* or other similar words; *says* is not a good choice of introductory verb since it is too informal. You do not need *according to* as well as a verb of saying. 2. When referring to the same place in the same source, use *ibid.* instead of the full source reference. If it is the same publication (but not the same place in the text), use *op. cit.* 3. It is important to make a quotation fit the grammar of a sentence. Failing to do this properly is a common mistake. 4. The quotation marks must be added to the words which are the same as the source.

Exercise I

Set for individual work, possibly for homework. Alternatively, set for pair or small group work. Students can write the paragraph on an OHT or other visual medium, which you can display and give feedback on with the whole class.

Answers

Possible answers:

Students will not need to refer to the year again, as this was done in the previous exercise.

Hitchins explains that in tourism business activities are often referred to as 'back of house' and 'front of house'. He shows that there is a wide range of applications businesses can use. Hitchins (ibid.) further points out that, despite the fact that 'these processes are interconnected and seem to work well, the tourism distribution channel has become *a complex system*'. [italics added]

Closure

Ask students to discuss these questions.

1 Ask students to discuss Figure 1 in the reading text in groups and apply what they have learnt so far to the model. Get them to give examples.

2 Focus on one tourism or hospitality business you know. What other kinds of services or business activities can this company undertake if they want to expand or diversify?

3 Imagine you work for Gaia's marketing department and you want to find out what customers think about the company. What aspects of your service provision should you try to find out about?

Accept any reasonable suggestions.

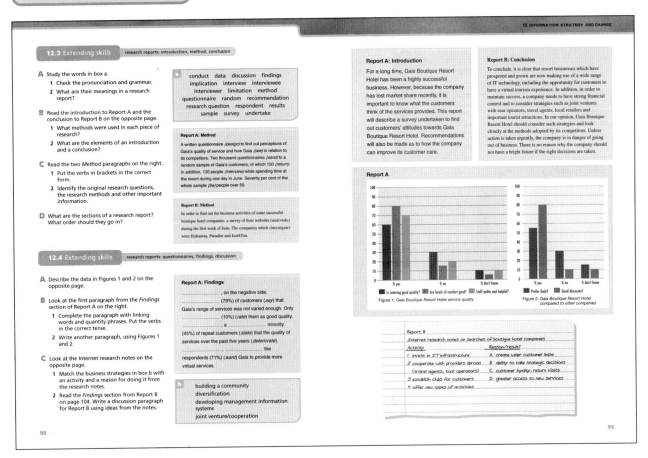

Lesson aims

- structure a research report:

  introduction

  method

  conclusion

Further practice in:

- essay structure
- research methods

Introduction

In preparation for looking at the structure of a research report, revise the sections for an essay: introduction, body, and conclusion. Ask students what should go in each section. Elicit ideas for introductions and conclusions. Do not correct at this point.

Remind students about the methods for doing research (see Unit 5). Ask students what kinds of research would be appropriate if you want to find out what customers think of a company's products or services. (Primary sources are best: survey, questionnaire, and interview, quantitative and qualitative methods.)

Ask students what kinds of research would be appropriate if you want to find out what business activities companies in a particular sector are involved in. (Secondary sources are the easiest: e.g., Internet research, company reports, and trade magazines.)

Tell students that the next two lessons will focus on writing up research in reports. Ask for suggestions for suitable sections of a research report. Do not correct at this point.

Language note

In the models presented here, the report is executed at a very simple level. For instance, in a real academic research report, there will be a literature review section before the methods section, and the research questions will be linked with this review. There are also different models for reports. For example, a business report (as opposed to an academic research report) may put conclusions and recommendations near the beginning and the findings as the final section.

Exercise A

Set for individual work and pairwork checking. Feed back with the whole class.

Answers

Model answers:

Word	Notes on pronunciation and grammar	Meaning in a research report
con'duct	v (noun is pronounced: 'conduct)	do (some research, a survey, an experiment)
'data	pl n	information; can be numerical (quantitative) or verbal (qualitative)
dis'cussion	n (U/C)	The title of the section in a research report which discusses the findings. Sometimes the discussion is included in the findings/ results section.
'findings	pl n	The title of the section in a research report which details what has been found out; each finding should be linked with a research question. The title *results* can also be used for this section.
impli'cation	n (C)	possible effect or result of the findings
'interview	n (C), v	noun: when someone is asked questions in a survey; verb: to ask someone questions in a survey
interview'ee	n (C)	the person being questioned
'interviewer	n (C)	the person asking the questions
limi'tation	n (C)	a problem with the research methods; an aspect which the research could not address
'method	n (C)	Title of the section in a research report which explains how the research was carried out. In the plural it refers to the research methods used.
questionn'aire	n (C)	a written set of questions
'random	adj	in no fixed order; with no organizing principle
recommen'dation	n (C)	suggestion for action as a result of the findings of the research
re'search ,question	n (C)	what the researcher wants to find out
res'pondent	n (C)	a person taking part in a questionnaire survey
re'sults	pl n	Same as *findings*. Used more or less interchangeably.
'sample	n (C), v	the group of people taking part in the research
'survey	n (C), v	a type of research in which the researcher sets out to describe a situation or set of ideas or behaviours, by reading a variety of documents or asking people questions
under'take	v	do (some research, a survey)

Exercise B

Explain to the students that these are examples of a typical introduction and conclusion. Set for pairwork discussion. Feed back with the whole class. Bring the class's attention to the tenses that are used here (present perfect, present simple, future) as well as the use of the passive.

Answers

Model answers:

1 Report A: Primary research. Probably questionnaire methods; perhaps interviews.

Report B: Probably secondary research, involving Internet searches or possibly company reports.

2 See table on next page.

2

Good introduction	Example sentence(s)
Introduce the topic. Give some background information.	For a long time, Gaia Boutique Resort Hotel has been a highly successful business.
Say why the topic is important.	However, because the company has lost market share recently, it is important to know what the customers think of the range of services provided.
Say what you will do in the report. Give a general statement of the purpose of the research.	This report will describe a survey undertaken to find out customers' attitudes towards Gaia Boutique Resort Hotel. Recommendations will also be made as to how the company can improve its customer care.

Good conclusion	Example sentence(s)
Give a general summary/restatement of findings.	To conclude, it is clear that resort businesses which have prospered and grown are now making use of a wide range of IT technology, including the opportunity for customers to have a virtual tourism experience. In addition, in order to maintain success, a company needs to have strong financial control and to consider strategies such as joint ventures with tour operators, travel agents, local retailers and important tourist attractions.
Say what your recommendations are.	In our opinion, Gaia Boutique Resort Hotel should consider such strategies and look closely at the methods adopted by its competitors.
Set out the implications of not taking action.	Unless action is taken urgently, the company is in danger of going out of business.
Comment on future possibilities if action *is* taken.	There is no reason why the company should not have a bright future if the right decisions are taken.

Language note

The impersonal use of the passive for research reports is not absolutely required. It is often possible to find students' work (assignments, dissertations) which contains the use of the first person singular. However, in more formal writing, such as in journal articles, the passive is usually used.

Exercise C

Explain to the students that these paragraphs are examples of the *Method* section of a research report.

1 Set for individual work. Feed back with the whole class, drawing students' attention to the use of the past tense when reporting methods of research, as well as the use of the passive.

2 Set for individual work and pairwork checking. Tell students that they should transform the research questions into real, direct questions. Feed back with the whole group, pointing out that the information given in the *Method* section should include these types of details.

Answers

Possible answers:

See table on next page.

	Research questions	Research method	Other important information
Method (A) A written questionnaire (*design*) <u>was designed</u> to find out perceptions of Gaia's quality of service and how Gaia (*see*) <u>was seen</u> in relation to its competitors. Two thousand questionnaires (*send*) <u>were sent</u> to a random sample of Gaia's customers, of which 150 (*return*) <u>were returned</u>. In addition, 130 people (*interview*) <u>were interviewed</u> while spending time at the resort during one day in June. Seventy per cent of the whole sample (*be*) <u>were</u> people over 50.	1. What are customers' perceptions of Gaia's quality of service? 2. How do customers see Gaia in relation to its competitors?	written questionnaire interview	2,000 questionnaires random sample of Gaia customers 150 returned 130 people interviewed in one day in June 70% of whole sample = over 50s
Method (B) In order to find out the business activities of some successful boutique hotel companies, a survey of their websites (*undertake*) <u>was undertaken</u> during the first week of June. The companies which (*investigate*) <u>were investigated</u> were Hideaway, Paradise and Just4You.	What business activities are successful boutique hotels engaged in?	Internet survey	done in first week of June 3 companies = Hideaway, Paradise and Just4You

Exercise D

Use this to confirm that students understand the organization of a research report. Elicit the answers from the whole class.

Answers

Model answers:

Section	Order in a research report
introduction	1
method	2
findings/results	3
discussion	4
conclusion	5

Closure

1 Refer students to the *Skills bank* to consolidate their understanding of the sections of a research report and their contents.

2 Ask students to choose a company into which they would like to carry out some customer research. They should think about aspects such as quality, service, reliability, customer perceptions, etc. What topics would they ask customers about in a questionnaire?

Language note

Different disciplines and reports for varying purposes may have different section names or organization. The model suggested here is a rather general one, and is a pattern commonly adopted in an academic context, though there are variations depending on the level of the writing (whether, for example, it is a Master's or PhD dissertation). If students are going to write about 500 words only, you may wish to include *discussion* with *findings/results* or with the *conclusion*.

12.4 Extending skills

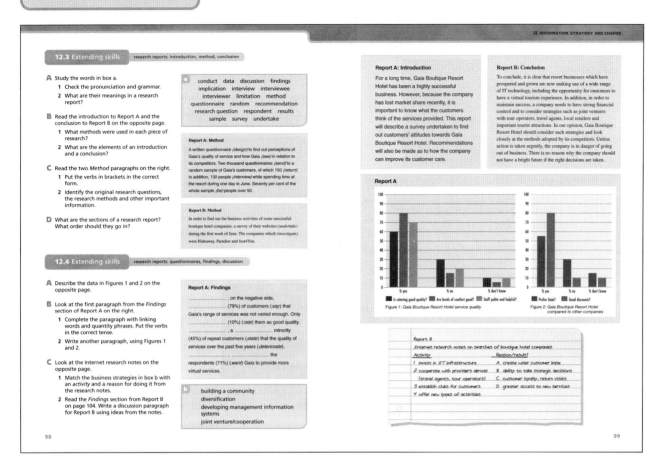

Lesson aims

- write part of a research report: findings and discussion
- analyse and use research data and information

Further practice in:

- using rhetorical markers for adding/listing points
- talking about numbers and quantities

Introduction

Write up the table below on the board. Give some example phrases and ask students to say approximately what percentage they represent, e.g., a large majority = 80% approximately?

	overwhelming large significant slight small insignificant tiny	majority	
A/An		minority	
		number	(of + noun)
Over		half a quarter a third	
More	than		
Less		x%	

Note that *of* is needed if the category for the numbers is given: *A slight minority of respondents said that …* but *A slight minority said that …*

Ask students: what is the difference between *many* and *most*?

Exercise A

Set students to work in pairs to talk about the key elements of the numbers shown in the charts. If you wish, ask students to write some sentences. Feed back with the whole class, writing some example sentences on the board. Ask the class what these results show about Gaia (some of its strengths).

Answers

Possible answers:

Figure 1

A majority (60%) of respondents said that Gaia's catering was good quality.

60% of respondents said the catering was good quality.

A significant minority (30%) said that catering was not good quality.

A small minority replied that they did not know if catering was good quality.

Figure 2

55% of respondents said they preferred Gaia to other companies.

An overwhelming majority of respondents (80%) said they thought Gaia provided good discounts compared to other companies.

A small minority (10%) disagreed that Gaia provided good discounts.

Exercise B

1 Set for individual work and pairwork checking. Remind students about linking words when giving a list of points. Tell students that each space may be for more than one word. They will also need to practise the expressions they used for quantity in Exercise A.

   Feed back with the whole class, pointing out the use of past tenses when reporting findings.

2 Set for individual work. Remind students to use linking words and to begin with a topic sentence. This paragraph continues the *Findings* section of Report A.

Answers

Possible answers:

Findings

1 <u>Firstly</u>, on the negative side, <u>a large majority</u> (79%) of customers (*say*) <u>said</u> that Gaia's range of services was not varied enough. <u>Only a small minority</u> (10%) (*rate*) <u>rated</u> them as good quality. <u>In addition</u>, a <u>significant</u> minority (45%) of repeat customers (*state*) <u>stated</u> that the quality of services over the past five years (*deteriorate*) <u>had deteriorated</u>. <u>Finally, most of</u> the respondents (71%) (*want*) <u>wanted</u> Gaia to provide more virtual services.

2 The survey also revealed some positive aspects. Firstly, a majority of the respondents (60%) said that the catering was good quality and that the staff were polite and helpful (70%). Moreover, although a small minority considered that the levels of comfort were not good enough, an overwhelming majority (80%) were satisfied with them. Secondly, in comparison with other companies, a very large majority thought that the discounts offered were good. Finally, a slight majority (55%) preferred Gaia to other companies.

Exercise C

1 Tell students to look at the notes on the right-hand page. These are the results of a student's Internet searches about the activities of some boutique hotel companies (as in Report B). They need to match the strategy word with the activities given, and also find why a company might do these things. Note that more than one answer might be possible. Set for pairwork discussion.

2 Refer students to page 104 of the Course Book, which gives the findings for Report B. Tell students that the discussion section of a report is where they can give their opinions on their findings. They should write a paragraph using the ideas they discussed in question 1. Set for individual work.

You may like to ask students to do some research of their own on the Internet. Some possible sites include:

www.boutiquehotelsandresorts.com/index.cfm?page=factsheet:

www.boutiquehotelsmagazine.com/content/view/49/14/

www.web-strategist.com/blog/2007/07/19/what-would-the-future-of-hotel-websites-look-like-think-social/

Answers

Possible answers:

Strategies	Activity	Reason/result?
building a community	3 establish clubs for customers	C customer loyalty, return visits
diversification	4 offer new types of activities	A create wider customer base
developing management information systems	1 invest in IT infrastructure	B ability to take strategic decisions
joint venture/ cooperation	2 cooperate with providers abroad	D greater access to new services

Discussion

From our research, it is clear that investment in IT infrastructure has enabled these organizations to take strategic decisions, using data collected from their customers and providers. Setting up joint ventures with other providers abroad has led to greater access to new services. Additionally, these organizations have set out to build a community by establishing clubs for their customers. These clubs inspire loyalty among customers and generate return business. Finally, by pursuing a strategy of diversification – offering new activities in addition to the core activities – these organizations have been able to create a wider customer base.

Closure

1 Ask students to work out the original questions used in the customer survey.

First, suggest some question types for questionnaires. Elicit the following:

- yes/no
- multiple choice
- open-ended

Tell students to concentrate on the *yes/no* or multiple choice types (open-ended questions will elicit qualitative information which is often hard to analyse) and to look at the data in Figures 1 and 2 and the sample *Findings* paragraph. They should try to formulate the actual questions given in the customer survey questionnaire.

Set for pairwork. Feed back with the whole class, writing examples of good questions up on the board. Refer to the model questionnaire in the additional resources section (Resource 12F).

2 Set a research report based on a questionnaire survey for homework. Students can use the ideas they have already discussed in this unit. They should write questionnaires, carry out the research amongst a suitable group of customers (20–40 respondents is fine) and then write up the report. Alternatively, students could choose to find out about the business activities of several global companies in the same sector.

1 Work through the *Vocabulary bank* and *Skills bank* if you have not already done so, or as revision of previous study.

2 Use the *Activity bank* (Teacher's Book additional resources section, Resource 12A).

A Set the crossword for individual work (including homework) or pairwork.

Answers

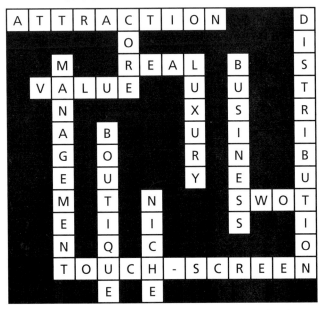

B Set for individual work and pairwork checking.

Answers

95%	the great majority
70%	a significant majority
53%	just over half
50%	half
48%	slightly less than half
10%	a small proportion
2%	a tiny minority

3 Ask students to practise making questionnaires for customer surveys. They could choose from the following topics (or other appropriate topics):

- booking holidays through the Internet
- virtual museums
- a travel TV channel
- computer check-in at airports

Activity bank

A Solve the crossword.

Across

   3 A type of holiday sold by a tour operator which includes transport, accommodation, etc.

   9 A stay of one night is an ... stay.

   10 The business of providing relaxing activities for tourists.

   11 ... travel began in the 19th century.

   12 The place you go when you travel.

   13 The state of being between two places.

Down

   1 One way of informing possible customers about travel products and services.

   2 A travel ... helps travellers plan their holidays.

   4 Someone who buys a product or service from a company.

   5 Another word for *drinks*.

   6 Another word for *make a reservation*.

   7 The noun from *relax*.

   8 The business of making tourists feel at home.

B Play noughts and crosses. Use the words in context or explain what they mean.

promotional	accommodation	information
intangible	dissatisfaction	reconfirm
stressful	overbook	multinational

Grand Tour	Professor Tribe	Professor Leiper
Virgin Galactic	World Tourism Organization	TDR
TGR	Thomas Cook	Phoenix

Activity bank

A Solve the crossword. All the words can go in front of the word *tourism*, except 6 across and 12 across, which contain the word *tourism*.

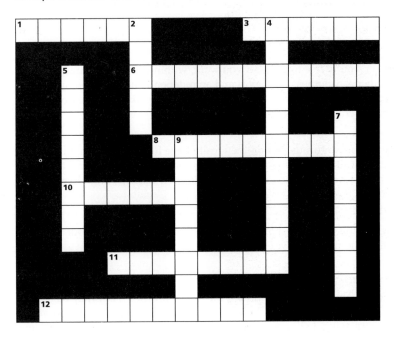

Across

1 Going on a skiing trip.
3 Going somewhere to improve your physical condition.
6 Supporting farmers in a community.
8 Doing a challenging activity like mountain climbing.
10 Travelling for a special occasion, e.g., a music festival.
11 Visiting museums and art galleries.
12 Enjoying nature and contributing to the local community.

Down

2 Tourist destination in the future?
4 Travelling to a special location to learn something.
5 Visiting conferences and trade fairs.
7 Visiting historic buildings and finding out about your country's history.
9 Travelling to see the scene of an earthquake.

B Play noughts and crosses. To get your symbol on a square, you must use the word correctly in a sentence related to tourism. The sentence must make the meaning of the word clear.

accommodation	boom	rough it
budget	itinerary	independent
backpacking	luxury	environment

Many students go backpacking in their gap year, that once-in-a-lifetime period between school and college, or college and work.	Have you considered going to a foreign country thousands of miles away, all on your own? Could you cope without plane tickets, car-hire vouchers and booked accommodation?
Backpacking is a great way to travel, they say.	As a backpacker, you're free to do what you want, within your shoestring budget, of course. You only need clothes, a passport and an independent spirit. You have no itinerary, except for some vague plans to 'do' Asia or 'go walking' in the Rockies. There's no tour operator to hold your hand.
Backpackers are proud that they 'rough it'.	They are free and adventurous. But do they really have fun, hitching on dusty roads, sleeping in uncomfortable lodging houses, eating poor-quality food and wandering aimlessly through towns with no interest for the tourist? Perhaps they should wait until they can be a flashpacker.
Flashpacking is the latest development in personal tourism.	As a flashpacker, you get the best of both worlds: the joy of real travel, but also luxury accommodation and transport when you want it.
Flashpackers are looking for adventure like backpackers, but there is one important difference.	They have money. They are usually in their thirties and forties. They may be on extended holidays or career breaks. They probably went backpacking in their youth and think they are doing it all over again. But unlike your average gap-year student, they will spend what it takes to get the experience they are after. That outback tour of Central Australia costs £5000? Where's the 4WD? Start the engine!
Travel companies are cashing in on this development.	They are selling round-the-world tickets like hot cakes. Greg Halpin, a 39-year-old marketing director, is a typical example: 'Flashpacking is a perfect word for what I've done. When I've changed jobs, I've used the break to go travelling. The last time, I went for six weeks, around Kenya and Tanzania. I put the trip together as I went along. I visited safari parks – some upmarket, some not. Then I went to Zanzibar, where I checked into a very flash hotel. It's always interesting doing that when you've been on the road. You turn up a bit grubby, with a dusty old backpack, and they look rather alarmed. They're very relieved an hour later, though, when you've cleaned up and walk back across the lobby looking decent. That's one essential tip for travelling this way: always keep a set of smart clothes in a plastic bag inside your pack.'
There are three countries where flashpacking works particularly well.	Each one can offer some of the most enjoyable aspects of budget travel – adventure, cultural insights, earthy simplicity – but with plenty of choice along the way.
First, there's Australia.	It's no surprise that Oz is well set up for budget travel, with a good network of cheap accommodation, silver beaches and the outback. Every Australian was a backpacker once. On the other hand, the Aussies have got a bit flash recently – cultural events, fancy cooking, etc. It adds up to perfect flashpacker territory.
Thailand is very cheap, relatively speaking.	The temptation is to be all flash and no pack. After all, when an upmarket Bangkok restaurant only charges £10 per head, why settle for anything less? But you should. If you use your money to spoil yourself all the time, you'll never touch the real character and excitement of Thailand. So stay in that £4 beach hut, eat that 50p street snack and only buy yourself luxury when you really need it.
Finally, Argentina is enjoying a boom from three types of traveller.	Gap-year kids have added the Andes to their list; holiday travellers are arriving in well-organized groups to trek around the countryside and now flashpackers have discovered that the continent has exactly their mix of wild adventures and home comforts.

Many students go backpacking in their gap year, that once-in-a-lifetime period between school and college, or college and work.

Backpacking is a great way to travel, they say.

Backpackers are proud that they 'rough it'.

Flashpacking is the latest development in personal tourism.

Flashpackers are looking for adventure like backpackers, but there is one important difference.

Travel companies are cashing in on this development.

There are three countries where flashpacking works particularly well.

First, there's Australia.

Thailand is very cheap, relatively speaking.

Finally, Argentina is enjoying a boom from three types of traveller.

Many students go backpacking in their gap year, that once-in-a-lifetime period between school and college, or college and work.

Backpacking is a great way to travel, they say.

Backpackers are proud that they 'rough it'.

Flashpacking is the latest development in personal tourism.

Flashpackers are looking for adventure like backpackers, but there is one important difference.

Travel companies are cashing in on this development.

There are three countries where flashpacking works particularly well.

First, there's Australia.

Thailand is very cheap, relatively speaking.

Finally, Argentina is enjoying a boom from three types of traveller.

More and more travellers realize that tourism has an effect on the environment.

Brazil is an example of a country which is developing ecotourism.

The environmental impact of travel is huge.

I try to be 'green' in my everyday life.

Praia do Forte calls itself Brazil's first 'eco-resort'.

The hotel certainly makes good use of the environment.

There are some features I do not like as much.

However, perhaps it is unfair to criticize Praia do Forte for the things it could do better.

More and more travellers realize that tourism has an effect on the environment.

Brazil is an example of a country which is developing ecotourism.

The environmental impact of travel is huge.

I try to be 'green' in my everyday life.

Praia do Forte calls itself Brazil's first 'eco-resort'.

The hotel certainly makes good use of the environment.

There are some features I do not like as much.

However, perhaps it is unfair to criticize Praia do Forte for the things it could do better.

More and more travellers realize that tourism has an effect on the environment.	Ecotourism is a result of this growing awareness. According to the International Ecotourism Society (TIES), ecotourism is 'responsible travel to natural areas that conserves the environment and improves the well-being of local people.' Ecotourists or organizers should make sure the impact on the environment is as small as possible. They should provide positive experiences for both visitors and hosts, and create financial benefits and a feeling of empowerment for local people.
Brazil is an example of a country which is developing ecotourism.	Praia do Forte claims to be Brazil's first eco-resort. We sent our reporter, Alison Marshall, to check out its green credentials.
The environmental impact of travel is huge.	Did you know that a return flight from London to Brazil releases 2,606 kg of carbon dioxide per passenger into the atmosphere? That's four times the annual carbon emissions of an average African. So just getting to the country damages the world environment. Then there's the long drive from the airport to the resort through the rainforest in a taxi on its last wheels. I'm beginning to wonder if this kind of tourism can be 'green' at all.
I try to be 'green' in my everyday life.	I recycle the Sunday papers, and all my light bulbs are those expensive ones that last for ages, but I also really enjoy driving around London, and can never quite remember to turn the tap off when I'm brushing my teeth. Was this trip part of the green me or the other one?
Praia do Forte calls itself Brazil's first 'eco-resort'.	The four-star, 247-bedroom hotel was opened by a Swiss–Brazilian industrialist who bought up 30,000 hectares of subtropical rainforest to the north of Salvador. The resort's motto is 'use without abuse'. It says it can cater for tourists without damaging the environment.
The hotel certainly makes good use of the environment.	There are forest hikes, river kayaking expeditions and moonlit walks to the silver beaches, where you can watch turtles lay their eggs. Biologists and guides accompany tourists on all these trips. They really try to show people the natural beauty of the area. They use local people as guides, and educate and train the local community.
There are some features I do not like as much.	For example, they have built a village for employees next door to the resort. They use the village as a toy town which the hotel maps refer to as 'the fishermen's village'. It has been nicely done, and it is a lively and pleasant place. No doubt it brings financial benefits to the local economy but the little sandy strip is for the holidaymaker. There are no fishermen in sight.
However, perhaps it is unfair to criticize Praia do Forte for the things it could do better.	It is a really lovely resort, and they are serious about the environment. Praia do Forte is not really green, in other words, but it is greener than many other resorts. If you are going to build something right in the middle of a natural paradise, then it is much better to build it like this. It is, after all, better to recycle the Sunday papers than to do nothing at all about the environment.

A Read the article on ecotourism (page 19) again. Decide on the meaning of these words. Check with your dictionary.

1 awareness _____

2 impact _____

3 release _____

4 abuse _____

5 cater for _____

6 accompany _____

7 features _____

B Use these words to complete the sentences. You will have to change the words using prefixes/suffixes. There is one word you don't need.

> aware   comfortable   environment
> expense   finance   nature   sustain

1 The _____ impact of tourism on poor countries is huge.

2 Ecotourism is the result of growing _____ that we have to be careful with the environment.

3 There are many _____ benefits for the local community.

4 Ecotourism activities have to be _____ and not damage the environment.

5 Tourists like to enjoy _____ beauty.

6 I feel _____ about flying to holiday destinations.

C First identify the part of speech. Then change the part of speech using prefixes or suffixes.
Example:

1 economy   This is a/an ____*noun*____ . The adjective is ____*economical*____ .

2 sustain   This is a/an _____ . The adjective is _____ .

3 environment   This is a/an _____ . The adjective is _____ .

4 important   This is a/an _____ . The noun is _____ .

5 develop   This is a/an _____ . The noun is _____ .

6 foreign   This is a/an _____ . The noun is _____ .

7 education   This is a/an _____ . The adjective is _____ .

8 poor   This is a/an _____ . The noun is _____ .

9 aware   This is a/an _____ . The noun is _____ .

10 expense   This is a/an _____ . The adjective is _____ .

Activity bank

A Solve the coded crossword.

- Each number represents a letter. So A = 15. Write A in all the number 15 squares.
- Write I in all the number 6 squares. Write T in all the number 10 squares.
- Look at the word at the top. You can see _ _ A _ TITATI _ _ . What word is this? Yes, *quantitative*.
- So 13 = Q. Write Q in the number 13 square on the right. Write Q in all the number 13 squares in the grid.
- Continue guessing the words.

B Play bingo.

- Think of words for each of the categories and write them on card 1.
- Each student says one of their words. Cross the squares on card 2 when you hear a word from that category.

1	hospitality word	research word	hospitality science word
	hospitality management word	hospitality studies word	systems theory word

2	hospitality word	research word	hospitality science word
	hospitality management word	hospitality studies word	hospitality theory word

---

Activity bank

A Find 20 verbs from this unit in the wordsearch.

- Copy the verbs into your notebook.
- Write a noun for each verb.

B	R	O	W	S	E	D	I	S	C	O	U	N	T	F	B
Q	T	O	P	E	R	A	T	E	P	T	P	Y	N	T	T
Q	U	Z	Q	L	Y	D	L	T	G	C	R	B	H	T	E
R	V	A	L	P	R	O	M	O	T	E	U	A	L	V	T
L	E	R	L	C	K	R	P	R	R	N	R	R	I	M	W
R	G	S	K	I	Y	L	O	F	K	E	G	E	A	N	V
K	E	M	E	O	F	P	Y	L	F	V	C	F	R	T	T
T	Q	S	L	A	S	Y	Q	E	N	R	Y	L	T	T	E
Z	L	P	E	N	R	L	R	G	E	R	C	N	V	V	R
K	M	P	A	R	L	C	K	P	Z	T	I	M	Y	E	N
E	L	R	R	K	V	B	H	U	R	O	Q	N	F	N	L
V	T	Z	B	R	J	E	Y	P	P	L	R	S	K	L	N
Z	P	T	P	L	A	N	R	P	L	D	N	H	R	G	D
Y	W	T	T	T	T	A	C	C	A	A	F	N	N	L
R	E	C	R	U	I	T	Q	L	R	K	H	T	I	V	F
A	T	T	R	A	C	T	P	T	X	D	M	F	E	G	K

B Play noughts and crosses. You must say the abbreviation or acronym and give the original words to place your symbol in a square.

DOO	HR	DOS
MD	T & T	COO
GM	CEO	CFO

ARR	B & B	BABA
WTTC	TIC	VAT
TIP	FIT	F & B

Most people, when they consider a career in tourism, hospitality or leisure, think of waiters and chefs, fitness instructors and travel agents.

Tourism-related employment is different from many other employment sectors.

This makes working with the TTH sector sound appealing, but it may not be suitable for everybody.

Not surprisingly, in such a varied world, there are many ways of entering the industry.

Most people, when they consider a career in tourism, hospitality or leisure, think of waiters and chefs, fitness instructors and travel agents.

Tourism-related employment is different from many other employment sectors.

This makes working with the TTH sector sound appealing, but it may not be suitable for everybody.

Not surprisingly, in such a varied world, there are many ways of entering the industry.

CEO	CFO	COO
DOO	GM	HRD
MD	AIT	APD
ARR	B&B	BABA
F&B	FIT	IT
QA	T&T	TIC
TIP	VAT	ACE
ANTOR	BATO	NAITA

Activity bank

A Solve the synonyms crossword. Find words with the same meaning as the clues.

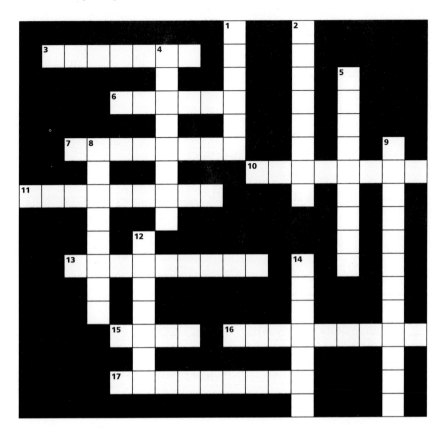

Down
- **1** finally
- **2** buy
- **4** usually
- **5** clearly
- **8** kids
- **9** needs
- **12** get better
- **14** old

Across
- **3** go down, worsen
- **6** aim
- **7** in fact
- **10** consumer
- **11** fundamentally
- **13** advertising
- **15** reserve
- **16** drinks
- **17** staff

B Play marketing bingo.
- Choose six marketing words from the box and write one word in each square of your bingo card.
- Somebody will call out some words. If you have the word on your bingo card, raise your hand. If you are first, you can say the definition or give an example sentence.
- The first person to cross out all the words on their card is the winner.

research strategy characteristics fail
ensure needs anticipate
requirements appeal mass accurate
data brand variety segment
categorize niche quantitative

Marketing of tourism is not ...

- ... the same as _____. This is only a small

  _____ of marketing.

- ... just about selling. There are many other related

  _____ which are involved.

So what is it?

There are four _____ aspects,

_____ the 'marketing mix' – also called

the 'Four Ps' – to which _____ must pay attention.

1   The **Product** – must _____ the

    _____ of the _____ .

2   **Promotion** – there are several _____ of

    promoting a product, including advertising, special offers, mailing

    and sponsorship.

3   The **Price** – this depends on the financial objectives as well as the

    _____ of consumer you _____ .

4   The **Place** – where do people _____ the

    products? This _____ both means of distribution

    and type of _____ .

Verbs	Nouns	Adverbs	Adjectives
rise		gradually	
increase		sharply	
grow		slightly	
improve		markedly	
fall		significantly	
decrease		rapidly	
drop		steeply	
decline		steadily	

Poor contributions	Student A	Student B	Student C
disagrees rudely			
doesn't explain how the point is relevant			
doesn't understand an idiom			
dominates the discussion			
gets angry when someone disagrees with them			
interrupts			
is negative			
mumbles or whispers			
says something irrelevant			
shouts			
sits quietly and says nothing			
starts a side conversation			
other:			

Good contributions	Student A	Student B	Student C
allows others to speak			
asks for clarification			
asks politely for information			
brings in another speaker			
builds on points made by other speakers			
contributes to the discussion			
explains the point clearly			
gives specific examples to help explain			
is constructive			
links correctly with previous speakers			
listens carefully to what others say			
makes clear how the point is relevant			
paraphrases to check understanding			
says when they agree with someone			
speaks clearly			
tries to use correct language			
other:			

Activity bank

A Find 20 words from this unit in the wordsearch.

L	C	O	N	V	E	N	T	I	O	N	V	A	L	U	E	R	R
X	O	L	C	K	R	D	H	F	V	D	W	P	R	G	L	Z	N
K	J	G	N	Z	V	C	L	H	E	E	I	W	N	M	D	H	N
D	P	R	I	Z	G	G	C	T	Q	H	N	T	X	T	J	F	L
P	Y	R	V	S	T	C	A	O	S	F	Y	T	N	W	L	V	G
M	V	B	E	N	T	C	E	R	R	L	E	E	U	L	T	E	H
L	K	I	E	G	I	I	O	L	A	P	M	S	N	R	T	Y	X
F	J	V	S	L	I	S	C	U	E	T	O	E	T	A	E	L	N
X	E	Y	P	I	N	O	T	S	S	B	C	R	P	I	C	Z	Q
D	B	M	B	O	B	R	N	E	R	N	R	I	A	R	V	D	K
K	O	R	P	B	I	I	V	A	A	W	C	A	G	T	T	A	G
C	K	S	H	V	V	N	L	D	L	I	K	C	T	K	E	B	L
H	R	N	K	R	I	P	N	I	T	P	T	T	M	I	V	M	Z
R	M	R	T	M	K	E	D	R	T	C	W	B	Y	B	O	N	M
K	R	Z	N	B	T	Z	A	G	W	Y	B	O	O	S	T	N	L
M	Y	J	H	T	J	P	E	X	H	I	B	I	T	I	O	N	L
H	T	M	A	L	E	I	S	U	R	E	G	V	K	V	F	L	W
K	R	N	L	T	P	R	O	F	E	S	S	I	O	N	A	L	M

B Imagine that you are part of an events management team or company.

- Decide on the type of event you are going to organize.
- Choose one of the roles in the diagram.
- Explain to others what your role is and how you are going to contribute to the event.

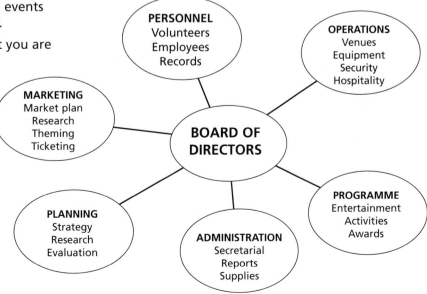

PERSONNEL
Volunteers
Employees
Records

OPERATIONS
Venues
Equipment
Security
Hospitality

MARKETING
Market plan
Research
Theming
Ticketing

BOARD OF DIRECTORS

PROGRAMME
Entertainment
Activities
Awards

PLANNING
Strategy
Research
Evaluation

ADMINISTRATION
Secretarial
Reports
Supplies

1 Cash flow is _____ during the development phase of an event.

2 In the _____ phase of an event, unit costs are high.

3 Cash flow becomes positive in the _____ phase.

4 _____ attendance means that costs per visitor are reduced.

5 Attendance is at its peak once the market has _____ .

6 Attendance may start to _____ when the market reaches saturation.

1 Cash flow is negative during the development phase of an event.

2 In the introduction phase of an event, costs are high.

3 Cash flow becomes positive in the maturity phase.

4 Increasing attendance means that costs per visitor are reduced.

5 Attendance is at its peak once the market has matured.

6 Attendance may start to fall when the market reaches saturation.

a It is not until the maturity phase is reached that cash flow is no longer negative.

b Peak attendance figures are achieved at the maturity phase.

c While the event is being designed and trialled, there are many expenses but no income.

d There may be a reduction in business if there are too many competitors.

e It costs a lot to produce each event early in the cycle.

f As ticket sales go up, each visitor will cost the events organizers less money.

Original sentence	Student A	Student B
Festivals are the most popular tourist events. They are huge, with hundreds if not thousands of people active and involved, complicated logistics, stressful management and considerable investment.	Festivals are major events which are attended by large groups of people; they are highly complex from an organizational point of view, and are expensive to put on.	Festivals are huge events, with many people involved, complicated logistics, management and considerable investment.
The tourism sector has seen a significant increase in the size, scope, length and visibility of these unique ventures, known as 'hallmark' or 'mega' events, creating the growing need for professional events managers.	The demand for professional events managers has increased as the number of big events has grown.	The tourism sector has seen a significant increase in these unique mega ventures, creating the need for professional events managers.
The rule of thumb seems to be that events can be as outrageous or complicated as money can buy. And nowadays, events can even be virtual …	There is no limit to what tourism events can look like, and they can be virtual as well as real.	The rule of thumb seems to be that events can be as complicated as people can afford. Events can be real or virtual.
There is one theory (Goldblatt, 2000) which claims that there is significantly more to celebrate as the Earth's population ages, and big events provide a forum for such celebrations.	One theory says that ageing contributes to the growth of events tourism.	Theories claim that big events provide a forum for such celebrations as people age.
We have already mentioned technology. Add to these increased income and more leisure time and you have a recipe for events tourism which increases the demand for events all around the world.	Apart from age and technology, income and increased leisure time contribute to this growth as well.	Added to ageing and technology, increased income and leisure time also form a recipe for growth in events tourism.

Festivals are the most popular tourist events.

If you are a young adult, the chances are that you belong to the large group of people who have visited a music festival at one point during their teen years.

The organization of events is big business and has a direct relationship with tourism.

Even though events organization is a professional skill, there do not seem to be hard and fast rules.

Quite a few theories have been put forward as to why events tourism is so popular.

So what really attracts people to events?

Festivals are the most popular tourist events.

If you are a young adult, the chances are that you belong to the large group of people who have visited a music festival at one point during their teen years.

The organization of events is big business and has a direct relationship with tourism.

Even though events organization is a professional skill, there do not seem to be hard and fast rules.

Quite a few theories have been put forward as to why events tourism is so popular.

So what really attracts people to events?

Activity bank

A Look at the synonyms and short definitions below. Study the two examples.
Find the other 15 words in the wordsearch.

```
T   I   N   G   R   E   D   I   E   N   T   R   H   B   M   X
P   T   L   V   Z   Y   M   N   B   X   E   Q   N   R   F   F
O   P   E   R   A   T   E   X   D   C   P   O   L   X   F   K
N   M   F   K   V   L   L   Z   N   E   I   O   L   T   E   R
T   V   F   K   T   T   K   A   W   T   S   S   S   R   R   D
H   K   D   E   M   A   N   D   C   C   T   I   U   U   M   M
C   R   L   F   A   E   X   U   L   N   T   T   G   N   R   M
M   E   J   S   T   S   R   R   E   H   A   N   M   N   R   E
F   R   L   N   I   T   I   M   Y   E   Y   L   P   P   B   W
N   N   I   E   S   M   P   B   F   X   I   F   K   T   W   D
R   A   V   N   B   I   U   L   I   A   P   P   E   A   L   D
M   I   O   C   U   R   X   L   T   L   B   M   W   R   E   W
Z   C   D   Q   T   T   I   E   A   X   I   L   K   M   Z   K
K   P   E   E   N   Y   R   T   W   T   D   T   E   L   M   Y
D   L   X   N   F   K   Q   L   Y   X   O   H   Y   K   T   N
N   Y   E   X   P   A   N   D   X   T   T   R   Z   R   N   W
```

Examples:

A characteristic of somebody or something. (noun, countable) – *feature*

The attractiveness of somebody or something. (noun, uncountable) – *appeal*

1 A well-known person, often in the public eye. (noun, countable)

2 The act of building something. (noun, uncountable)

3 The degree to which people want something. (noun, uncountable)

4 The visual and technical characteristics of a project. (noun, uncountable)

5 Machines and tools used for building. (noun, uncountable)

6 To make bigger something bigger. (verb)

7 Publicity through featuring in the media and through advertising. (noun, uncountable)

8 Whether something can be done or made, often financially. (noun, uncountable)

9 What goes into something. (noun, countable)

10 Keeping something in good condition. (noun, uncountable)

11 To run an organization. (verb, transitive)

12 Selling goods to the public. (noun, uncountable)

13 An attraction in a theme park, e.g., a rollercoaster. (noun, countable)

14 A machine that lets you experience something in a virtual way. (noun, countable)

15 Connected with a single idea, e.g., history or fantasy. (verb, past participle)

Activity bank

Student A

B Play 'battleships'.
Answer Student B's questions about this grid.

	A	B	C	D	E	F	G	H	I	J	K	L
1											M	
2		A	P	A	R	T	M	E	N	T	O	
3	M									T		
4	A		O		S	P	A	C	E		E	
5	X		R								L	
6	I		G									H
7	M		A		D	E	S	I	G	N		I
8	I		N									S
9	Z		I									T
10	E		Z									O
11			E									R
12				F	I	N	A	N	C	E		Y

Ask Student B questions to find the following words from this unit:

- two words for things you can find in theme parks
- two nouns ending in ~*ment*
- two verbs ending in ~*ate*
- two words which can be nouns or verbs

Ask: *Is there a letter in 1C?*
Use this grid to mark the letters/words you find. Mark empty squares with a cross.

	A	B	C	D	E	F	G	H	I	J	K	L
1												
2												
3												
4												
5												
6												
7												
8												
9												
10												
11												
12												

Activity bank

Student B

B Play 'battleships'.
Answer Student A's questions about this grid.

	A	B	C	D	E	F	G	H	I	J	K	L
1	R	E	S	T	A	U	R	A	N	T	S	
2			D									
3	E		E	G	E	N	E	R	A	T	E	I
4	X		V							B		N
5	P		E							E		V
6	E		L		R	I	D	E	S	N		E
7	R		O							E		S
8	I		P							F		T
9	E		M							I		M
10	N		E							T		E
11	C		N	E	V	A	L	U	A	T	E	N
12	E		T									T

Ask Student A questions to find the following words from this unit:

- two types of tourist accommodation
- two possible themes for theme parks
- two verbs ending in ~*ize*
- two words which can be nouns or verbs

Ask: *Is there a letter in 1C?*
Use this grid to mark the letters/words you find. Mark empty squares with a cross.

	A	B	C	D	E	F	G	H	I	J	K	L
1												
2												
3												
4												
5												
6												
7												
8												
9												
10												
11												
12												

Activity bank

	Fixed phrase	Followed by ...	Actual information (suggested answers)
1	What do I mean by ... ?	an explanation of a word or phrase	
2	As you can see, ...	a comment about something visual	
3	Looking at it another way, ...	a different way to think about the topic	
4	In financial terms, ...	a general idea put into a financial context	
5	Say ...	an imaginary example	
6	The point is ...	a key statement or idea	
7	In this way ...	a concluding comment giving a result	

Activity bank

A Find 14 verbs from this unit in the wordsearch.

- Copy the words into your notebook.
- Check the definition of any words you don't remember.

```
Z  W  I  N  C  R  E  A  S  E  K  G  T  D
C  T  X  L  A  D  V  E  R  T  I  S  E  C
N  M  G  F  A  T  T  R  A  C  T  K  K  E
K  J  V  M  Z  S  L  M  N  X  N  W  V  X
C  R  P  L  X  K  T  I  V  X  K  E  R  H
R  E  P  E  A  T  A  I  J  C  I  K  E  T
P  V  P  M  A  T  R  T  M  H  J  C  M  H
X  R  Y  E  N  S  V  C  U  R  C  C  G
R  Z  O  R  R  O  A  A  G  U  L  R  F  P
V  K  Z  M  O  C  X  L  O  A  A  A  M  C
R  X  K  B  O  T  E  S  Y  E  I  G  T  L
M  P  Z  M  P  T  T  I  S  S  B  N  W  E
Q  Y  X  J  D  U  E  E  V  G  E  K  K  T
C  K  K  X  O  H  R  V  N  E  R  F  C  Y
```

B Rearrange the letters to form correctly spelt words from this unit. The first letter of each word is underlined.

Jumbled word	Correct spelling
ceptionrep	
tcider amil	
cistyencons	
dwro fo tmhuo	
uyporionptt	
yasergtt	
dgbtue	
stco-fetfeeicv	

Activity bank

A Solve the crossword.

Across

3 Something which is … is remote or unapproachable.

7 A … person or action is free from hypocrisy or dishonesty.

9 An … of change is something or someone that causes things to develop.

10 … is the basic facilities and services needed for the functioning of a community.

11 … means originating and living or occurring naturally in an area.

13 The … represents the prevalent attitudes, values, and practices of a society or group.

14 To … something is to harm or ruin it.

Down

1 … are a supply that can be drawn on when needed.

2 … are plans of action or reaction drawn up by a government or business.

4 Something which is … is capable of being continued with minimal long-term effect on the environment.

5 Something which is … is hard to find.

6 … and beliefs are ideas that people believe in firmly.

8 … means to keep in perfect or unchanged condition.

12 … is a mass arrival, often of people.

B Are these nouns countable or uncountable? Use a dictionary to complete the table.

Noun	C/U?	Notes
belief		
community		
custom		
diversity		
heritage		
influx		
infrastructure		
issue		
policy		
publicity		
resource		

Review reduce + recite + review	**Notes** record
Here you write only important words and questions; this column is completed after the lecture. Later this column becomes your study or revision notes. You can use it by covering the right hand column and using the cue words and questions here to remember the contents on the right.	This column contains your notes. You should underline headings and indent main ideas. After the lecture or reading you need to identify the key points and write them in the review column as questions or cue words.

Summary
reflect + recite + review
After the class you can use this space to summarize the main points of the notes on this page.

Review	Notes
	Impact of tourism on _culture_
	The story = example of _mismanagement/chaos_
Main issue is … ?	Main issue: countries don't have basic _infrastructure_
2 types of impact are … ?	two impacts: 1) tourism _industry_ 2) on local _people_
Issues … ?	Issues
1) spending?	1) spending $ in wrong places: _attracting tourists_ but not _improving_ infrastructure
2) infrastructure?	2) infrastructure improvements, e.g. _modern concrete tourist accommodation_ ➜ spoil atmosphere
3) people?	3) influence on _local people/population_
Culture clash = ?	strengthening of _local culture_ v. growth of _consumption_

Summary

Tourism development impacts on culture. The main issues are: money is spent to attract tourists, without improving infrastructure; improvements are often no more than quick fixes; one group is concerned about profits, the other about loss of culture.

Activity bank

A Complete the table.
- Identify the part of speech: n, v (or both), adj.
- Say whether nouns are countable (C), uncountable (U) or both.
- Say whether verbs are transitive (T), intransitive (I) or both.

Word	Part of speech	Noun – countable or uncountable?	Verb – transitive or intransitive?
commitment			
empowerment			
encourage			
expand			
implement			
loan			
managerial			
performance			
recruitment			
resource			
shift			
strategic			

B Think of a word or words that can go after each of the words or phrases below to make a phrase. Explain the meaning.

Example: *hotel = hotel chain, hotel occupancy rates*

business _____

hotel _____

human _____

long _____

management _____

medium _____

operating _____

performance _____

process _____

top _____

Introduction		Examples of ideas
introduce the topic area give the outline of the essay		
Body	**Para 1:** situation/problems (general)	
	Para 2: problems (specific examples)	
	Para 3: solutions	
	Para 4: evaluations of solutions	
Conclusion		

arthur, C., (2004). Penguins in Antarctica. Dolphins in Scotland. Dingoes in Australia. They all face the same danger: ecotourism. The Independent, 4th March. http://news.independent.co.uk/world/environment/story.jsp?story=497632. Accessed 9 March 2007.

Becken, Susanne 2002. "Analysing International Tourist Flows to Estimate Energy Use Associated with Air Travel." *Journal of Sustainable Tourism* 10 (2): 114-131

Gossling, Stefan (2005). Tourism's Contribution to Global Environmental Change: Space, Energy, Disease, Water. In James E.S. Higham and C. Michael Hall (eds.) *Tourism, Recreation and Climate Change*, pp 286-300. Channel View Publications: Clevedon.

Edgell, David L. Managing sustainable tourism: a legacy for the future. Binghamton, NY: the Haworth Press (2006)

The World Commission on Environment and Development (1987). *Our Common Future* (Oxford: Oxford University press)

arthur, C., (2004). Penguins in Antarctica. Dolphins in Scotland. Dingoes in Australia. They all face the same danger: ecotourism. The Independent, 4th March. http://news.independent.co.uk/world/environment/story.jsp?story=497632. Accessed 9 March 2007.

Becken, Susanne 2002. "Analysing International Tourist Flows to Estimate Energy Use Associated with Air Travel." *Journal of Sustainable Tourism* 10 (2): 114-131

Gossling, Stefan (2005). Tourism's Contribution to Global Environmental Change: Space, Energy, Disease, Water. In James E.S. Higham and C. Michael Hall (eds.) *Tourism, Recreation and Climate Change*, pp 286-300. Channel View Publications: Clevedon.

Edgell, David L. Managing sustainable tourism: a legacy for the future. Binghamton, NY: the Haworth Press (2006)

The World Commission on Environment and Development (1987). *Our Common Future* (Oxford: Oxford University press)

Activity bank

A Find 20 words from this unit in the wordsearch.
- Copy the words into your notebook.
- Make 10 two-word phrases.
- Check the definition of any words/phrases you can't remember.

Q	N	T	B	L	W	M	F	L	H	K	P	P	W	R
Z	G	S	U	S	T	A	I	N	A	B	L	E	E	E
H	X	N	K	P	R	E	S	S	U	R	E	W	V	K
B	L	G	A	N	K	C	R	H	T	W	O	R	L	E
Z	F	O	O	T	P	R	I	N	T	P	E	I	G	N
K	E	G	C	E	U	W	K	P	L	S	S	N	O	K
K	I	R	T	L	S	R	N	Z	E	S	A	B	T	T
F	N	S	O	D	I	O	E	R	O	H	R	L	T	J
K	A	R	S	P	K	M	L	F	C	A	L	T	L	K
W	K	K	U	U	G	T	A	A	C	N	F	H	J	M
T	B	O	B	K	E	H	M	T	R	M	Z	O	H	J
P	R	Y	X	M	F	S	F	U	E	L	P	G	O	T
G	E	N	V	I	R	O	N	M	E	N	T	A	L	D
M	Q	C	D	R	V	Q	X	O	R	G	A	N	I	C
T	O	U	R	I	S	M	H	X	P	M	V	F	L	W

B Match a word in the first column with a word in the second column to make a two-word phrase. Make sure you know what they mean.

carbon	gas
demographic	route
environmentally	disposal
global	dioxide
greenhouse	changes
renewable	operator
tour	warming
tourism	destination
transit	friendly
waste	energy

According to Peter Drucker (2001), a well-known business thinker, there are many demographic changes which will affect businesses profoundly over the next 25 years. Firstly, the population is ageing and so/as a result, patterns of employment will diversify. For example, provision of pensions for retired people is becoming an increasingly serious problem for governments. As a result/So, many people will have to continue in their jobs until they are in their 70s. In addition, these elderly employees are not likely to work for companies on a full-time basis but as consultants, part-timers or temporary staff.

Secondly, there are the effects of fewer young people in many parts of the world. One result of this is that many countries will have to rely more and more on an immigrant labour force. Another point is that markets will need to change: because the falling numbers of young people mean fewer families, businesses which have built their markets on the basis of the family unit will now have to rethink their approach. Moreover, up to now there has been an emphasis on the youth market; from now on, the middle-aged segment is likely to dominate. Finally, since the supply of younger workers will shrink, businesses will have to find new ways to attract and retain staff.

Answers

1 Movement of people out of their communities for leisure or business.

2 Hotels, resorts, marinas, restaurants, holiday homes, second homes, camp-sites, retail businesses, fishing shops, dive shops, fishing piers, recreational fishing facilities, beaches, ecotourism, cruises, swimming, snorkelling, diving, sailing, etc.

3 It puts a strain on water, energy, transport infrastructure and natural areas.

4 b: even though this is important for the operators, it is not the first priority when the aim is to build sustainable tourism.

5 Environment protection organizations (e.g., WWF, Greenpeace or similar national, regional or local organizations); local (council) and national government; transport companies (both public and private); tourism service providers (e.g., hotels, restaurants, events organizers); community representatives (e.g., local tribes, residents).

6 To check whether the operator sticks to the law; to see whether there are any problems and advise what the operator can do about them.

7 a ... an opportunity to learn.

   b ... local culture/the environment.

   c ... resources.

   d ... photos/memories.

   e ... transport.

   f ... things go wrong.

   g ... carefully.

Activity bank

A Solve the crossword.

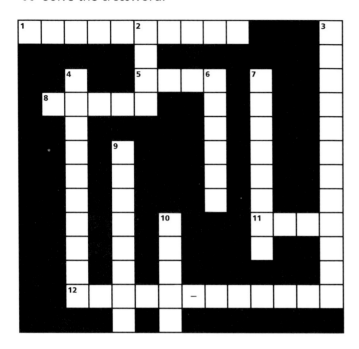

Down

2 ... functions are the main business activities that a company takes part in.

3 The ... channel is the way goods are transported to customers.

4 A ... system is a set of procedures designed to enable a company to run efficiently.

6 A ... resort is one with high-quality accommodation and leisure facilities.

7 ... tax is the special tax charged on companies rather than individuals.

9 A ... hotel is a small but expensive and fashionable hotel.

10 A ... market is a small but valuable part of a larger market.

Across

1 A tourist ... is a leisure facility which draws people to an area.

5 ... estate is buildings as opposed to land.

8 The ... chain is the set of activities required to design, procure, produce, market, distribute, and service a product or service.

11 A ... analysis looks at the internal strengths and weaknesses of an organization, and the external threats and opportunities.

12 A ... terminal is a useful way of presenting information to users.

B Match the percentages with a suitable phrase to describe numbers of respondents.

95%	a significant majority
70%	a small proportion
53%	half
50%	a tiny minority
48%	just over half
10%	slightly less than half
2%	the great majority

SWOT analysis

When a company's performance is looking poor, it may need to make some changes. However, before the company can do this, it should establish where it is now through a strategic analysis. A commonly used technique for this is the SWOT analysis. In this method, managers carry out an 'external audit' in which they examine their business and economic environment as well as the market conditions they face in order to understand the opportunities and threats to the company. Secondly, the organization needs to complete an 'internal audit' in which its strengths and weaknesses are compared with those of the competitors. This means that managers should look at all the functional areas: finance, HR, marketing and operations. The results of such audits are presented in a four-box summary of the business's current strengths and weaknesses, and the opportunities and threats which will affect its future development.

IT is defined as the tools that enable management.

Tourism organizations now rely on the complex integration of technological systems.

Business activities can be divided into primary and support processes.

IT systems support back- and front-of-house systems.

The tourism and hospitality distribution channel has become complicated.

IT systems offer tourism operators many advantages.

Some operators in tourism and hospitality need to redefine their roles.

Virtual tourism is growing fast.

Virtual tourism may be good for the environment.

Report A

Introduction

For a long time, Gaia Boutique Resort Hotel has been a highly successful business. However, because the company has lost market share recently, it is important to know what the customers think of the range of services provided. This report will describe a survey undertaken to find out customers' attitudes towards Gaia Boutique Resort Hotel. Recommendations will also be made as to how the company can improve its customer care.

Method

A written questionnaire was designed to find out perceptions of Gaia's quality of service and how Gaia was seen in relation to its competitors. Two thousand questionnaires were sent to a random sample of Gaia's customers, of which 150 were returned. In addition, 130 people were interviewed while spending time at the resort during one day in June. Seventy per cent of the whole sample were people over 50.

Findings

Firstly, on the negative side, a large majority (79%) of customers said that Gaia's range of services was not varied enough. Only a small minority (10%) rated them as good quality. In addition, a significant minority (45%) of repeat customers stated that the quality of services over the past five years had deteriorated. Finally, most of the respondents (71%) wanted Gaia to provide more virtual services.

The survey also revealed some positive aspects. Firstly, a majority of the respondents (60%) said that the catering was good quality and that the staff were polite and helpful (70%). Moreover, although a small minority considered that the levels of comfort were not good enough, an overwhelming majority (80%) were satisfied with them. Secondly, in comparison with other companies, a very large majority thought that the discounts offered were good. Finally, a slight majority (55%) preferred Gaia to other companies.

Discussion

It is clear from the results of this survey that Gaia is perceived by its customers in rather unfavourable ways. It seems that, on the whole, the range of services does not meet the needs of the customers. Even where the majority view was positive, there is still room for some improvement. A limitation of the research was that only 7.5% of the questionnaires were returned, which is a low return rate.

Conclusion

This survey has revealed some weaknesses, and to a more limited extent some strengths, in Gaia Boutique Resort Hotel. Meanwhile, it is clear that in order to improve services and to remain competitive, Gaia needs to invest in new IT infrastructure. In order to do this, financial backing will have to be found to enable a sufficient level of investment.

Report B

Introduction

For a long time, Gaia Boutique Resort Hotel has been a highly successful business. However, recently the company has lost market share to other bigger competitors. In order for Gaia to identify opportunities for developing and building its operation, it is useful for it to know what activities other successful similar companies are engaged in. This report will describe an investigation into three such companies. Strategies for the development and improvement of Gaia Boutique Resort Hotel will be suggested.

Method

In order to find out the business activities of some successful boutique hotel companies, a survey of their websites was undertaken during the first week of June. The companies which were investigated were Hideaway, Paradise and Just4You.

Findings

Key findings are as follows. Firstly, all three of the companies studied have several features in common: they are all luxury resort hotels in areas of natural beauty. They all emphasize that they use the latest technology, both for customer information systems and marketing. They have a strong focus on customer service.

Secondly, there are a few differences between the three companies. Hideaway has diversified into other areas such as on-site catering and events services. It has also gone into joint ventures with companies in Europe. Paradise has been active in the USA where it has recently bought up an IT company and has become involved in virtual tourism. Just4You is providing health services (a spa resort) and has created an online community for its customers.

Discussion

From our research, it is clear that investment in IT infrastructure has enabled these organizations to take strategic decisions, using data collected from their customers and providers. Setting up joint ventures with other providers abroad has led to greater access to new services. Additionally, these organizations have set out to build a community by establishing clubs for their customers. These clubs inspire loyalty among customers and generate return business. Finally, by pursuing a strategy of diversification – offering new activities in addition to the core activities – these organizations have been able to create a wider customer base.

Conclusion

To conclude, it is clear that resort businesses which have prospered and grown are now making use of a wide range of IT technology, including the opportunity for customers to have a virtual tourism experience. In addition, in order to maintain success, a company needs to have strong financial control and to consider strategies such as joint ventures with tour operators, travel agents, local retailers and important tourist attractions. In our opinion, Gaia Boutique Resort Hotel should consider such strategies and look closely at the methods adopted by its competitors. Unless action is taken urgently, the company is in danger of going out of business. There is no reason why the company should not have a bright future if the right decisions are taken.

Customer Survey

To all our customers:

Please help us to improve our services and our in-house operations by completing this questionnaire.

The first 10 questionnaires we receive will receive a 25% discount voucher on a weekend stay in our luxury boutique resort hotel.

Please indicate your answer by circling your choice.

1 What do you think of Gaia's catering? Is it?

A good quality   B not good quality   C don't know

2 How do you rate Gaia's levels of comfort?

A good   B poor   C don't know

3 Do you think Gaia's range of services is varied enough?

yes   no   don't know

4 Do you think staff are polite and helpful?

yes   no   don't know

5 What do you think of the quality of our services over the last five years? Have they:

A improved   B deteriorated   C neither

6 Do you prefer Gaia to other boutique resort hotels?

yes   no   don't know

7 Do you think Gaia offers good discounts?

yes   no   don't know

8 Would you like Gaia to provide more virtual services?

yes   no   don't know

9 Any other comments?

Thank you for your help!